CW00660794

The Way We Were

COLUMBIA PICTURES/ALBUM/ALAMY STOCK PHOTO

The Way We Were

The Making of a Romantic Classic

Tom Santopietro

Essex, Connecticut

An imprint of Globe Pequot, the trade division of
The Rowman & Littlefield Publishing Group, Inc.
4501 Forbes Blvd., Ste. 200
Lanham, MD 20706
www.rowman.com

Distributed by NATIONAL BOOK NETWORK

Library of Congress Cataloging-in-Publication Data

Names: Santopietro, Tom, author.
Title: The way we were : the making of a romantic classic / Tom Santopietro.
Description: Essex, Connecticut : Applause, [2023] | Includes bibliographical references and index.
Identifiers: LCCN 2022031840 (print) | LCCN 2022031841 (ebook) | ISBN 9781493071258 (cloth) | ISBN 9781493071265 (epub)
Subjects: LCSH: Way we were (Motion picture) | Romance films—United States—History and criticism. | Motion pictures—Production and direction—United States—History—20th century
Classification: LCC PN1997.W39 S36 2023 (print) | LCC PN1997.W39 (ebook) | DDC 813/.6—dc23
LC record available at https://lccn.loc.gov/2022031840
LC ebook record available at https://lccn.loc.gov/2022031841

∞™ The paper used in this publication meets the minimum requirements of American National Standard for Information Sciences—Permanence of Paper for Printed Library Materials, ANSI/NISO Z39.48-1992.

For Mimi Lines
and
Ruth Mulhall

I think that Barbra Streisand is, first and foremost, an actress, a wonderful actress, who found that fate and a giddy God had endowed her with an instrument that even she does not fully understand.

—Tennessee Williams on Barbra Streisand

Contents

In the Beginning

In the beginning, screenwriter Arthur Laurents agreed to write a movie for Barbra Streisand. And not just any movie, but hopefully a movie musical, because in the box office–driven world of Hollywood, a singing Barbra Streisand meant box-office gold. Barbra, producer Ray Stark thought, should play a Brooklyn woman who teaches blind children. And given the worldwide success of *The Sound of Music*, what if Barbra taught the children to sing? There was just one problem: as Laurents was on his way to pitch the idea to Barbra, he already knew that it was not just a bad idea but a downright terrible one. The blunt-speaking Barbra would, he felt certain, make short shrift of any idea where she'd be playing Brooklyn's answer to Maria von Trapp.

Explained Barbra: "By this point, he and I had known each other for ten years, ever since he directed me in *I Can Get It for You Wholesale* when I was nineteen," and although Laurents's original idea may not even have been worth discussing, he remained undeterred. He'd sit down and they'd talk anyway. Back in 1962, when Barbra was cast as the lovelorn Miss Marmelstein, she was little known and Laurents, the esteemed book writer of the classic musicals *West Side Story* and *Gypsy* as well as the screenwriter of the very successful films *The Snake Pit*, *Rope*, and *Anastasia*. Smart, acerbic, and nobody's fool, he and Barbra understood each other: two opinionated, fast-talking, extremely talented New Yorkers.

By now, however, the times had changed. In 1972, it was Barbra who had become an entertainment legend, an Emmy, Grammy, Oscar, and Tony (EGOT) winner, a Brooklyn-born "superstar." The power equation had shifted—which bothered Laurents not a bit. Settling into a nice chat between friends, Laurents did not even bring up the idea of Barbra playing a singing nanny. Instead, while they sat talking, it struck Laurents that Barbra reminded him of a classmate from his days at Cornell University, class of 1937. What was that girl's name? It was, he thought, almost too good to be true, but Barbra Joan Streisand reminded Arthur Laurents very much of his college friend Fanny Price—"a girl I'd known for twenty minutes at Cornell."

Working quickly, Laurents wrote a detailed treatment, giving it to Stark to read on a flight from New York to Los Angeles. Immediately upon landing, Stark called Laurents: "It's wonderful. I want to do it!" Stark didn't care that the film would feature a nonsinging Streisand. He liked what he was reading and saw box-office possibilities: "I didn't know Arthur Laurents until this film. He was the kind of writer I liked—had serious insights into his characters. He could add complexities but in the end it was a love story—with great depth to it."

That very same treatment was sent to Barbra. Sitting down to read, Barbra felt her own excitement growing and in later years recalled the words of director David Lean: "I had read somewhere that David Lean said if there were five good scenes in a script, it would make a good movie. And there were more than five in Arthur's treatment. So I knew immediately after I read it that I wanted to play Katie . . . as Arthur told me, I reminded him of a girl he knew in college named Fanny Price, who was very political, and Arthur knew I was politically active, too. He's often said that he borrowed other parts of my personality as well and gave them to Katie."

Fanny Price. One letter away from Fanny Brice, the original Funny Girl: a singing, comic legend who was, not so coincidentally, uber-producer Ray Stark's mother-in-law. The same Ray Stark who had not only overseen Barbra's electrifying Broadway and Hollywood star turns as Fanny Brice in *Funny Girl* but had also asked Laurents to write this new movie for Barbra. Never afraid to throw his weight around, Stark was soft spoken but tough around the edges, capable of standing toe to toe with the biggest stars and directors. He loved both parts of show business—the show and the business—and was, in the words of his friend, producer Don Safran, "the last of the great old world Hollywood producers."

Having shepherded and survived both 1964's *Night of the Iguana* with Richard Burton, Ava Gardner, and director John Huston and 1967's *Reflections in a Golden Eye*, starring the combustible duo of Elizabeth Taylor and Marlon Brando, little intimidated Stark. Wrote Huston about Stark, "Ray is adept at throwing people off balance. He makes a practice of starting rows among people working for him, believing that out of the fires of dissension flows molten excellence. Though he appears to swing from bonhomie to a fierce enjoyment of an open row, there is a steady, calculating intellect in command, ever watchful."

Barbra Streisand knew she owed Ray Stark; after all, it was Stark, along with composer Jule Styne, who had insisted upon casting Streisand as Fanny Brice, even when his own wife, Brice's daughter Frances Arnstein Stark, demurred. The very young Streisand, one month shy of her twenty-second birthday when *Funny Girl* opened in 1964, was one wildly talented Jewish girl from New York City who would be playing another, and Stark had been smart enough to see the similarities: "They are both intuitive women: strong, earthy, intelligent, vital and absolutely honest. . . . Both are naturals; those great talents who are imitated but never imitate. . . . They are two funny girls, different in all ways but the basic ones. I think they would have liked each other."

Yes, Barbra was grateful for Stark's faith in her, as well as for his producing skills, but their relationship remained complicated. She chafed at the restrictions he had placed upon her, reportedly casting her in the film version of *Funny Girl* (1968) only if she agreed to star in the show's West End London production. The problem was that *Funny Girl* in London would open only after Barbra had first fulfilled her two-year obligation on Broadway, all of which made for a very long time playing the same role.

Making matters more difficult, part of Barbra's commitment was having to sign a four-picture deal with Stark. Having by now starred very successfully in the film versions of *Funny Girl* and *The Owl and the Pussycat* (1970), Barbra Streisand still owed Ray Stark two more films, which is why Stark had inveigled Laurents to write a Streisand-centric movie. Ray Stark and Barbra Streisand may have had tempers, but even after all of their arguments over the past ten years, Ray Stark still wanted to be in the Barbra Streisand business: "I was very involved because I wanted to do a different kind of movie with Barbra. We had done a musical *Funny Girl* and a comedy *The Owl and the Pussycat*. I felt the time was right for a love story."

And now that Laurents was chatting with Barbra, it became clear to the writer that the fast-talking, politically liberal, defiantly Jewish Barbra Streisand, a woman who in Laurents's words, "always had a kind of fierce passion," reminded the writer of his friend Fanny Price in more ways than one. Price had been an outspoken liberal, in fact, the leader of the Young Communists League on campus, and Laurents quickly began to assemble notes for a screenplay: if he took parts of Fanny's personality, combined them with aspects of his good friend Virginia "Jigee" Viertel, a political activist in 1940's Hollywood, and overlayed the mix with elements of Streisand's own persona, he'd have a character capable of driving a full-length Hollywood movie. A woman of great political conviction. An activist and impassioned outsider. An outcast who stood up for her beliefs, and here, he felt, was the clincher—an ethnic wallflower who fell in love with the campus heartthrob.

Laurents had already written adaptations for both Olivia de Havilland (*The Snake Pit*, 1948) and Alfred Hitchcock (*Rope*, 1948), but the story taking shape in his mind would represent his very first original screenplay, a treatment of his own life and beliefs, specifically his disgust with the post–World War II blacklist, which had taken away his passport: "I believed it wasn't un-American to be a member of the Communist Party; it was un-American to be on the House Un-American Activities Committee. I still believed that and I wanted to say it through a heroine who was a Jewish Communist. In a Hollywood movie." Katie's rather desperate embrace of Communism had the potential to alienate, but her genuine enthusiasm would make sure audiences did not reject her. Strident and shrill she would be, but also passionate, genuine, and fired by a desire for a better world.

Laurents's movie heroine would be, he wrote, "like Barbra, unlike Barbra; younger, another time, an earlier time, against another background. Cornell! Frizzy hair and sensible shoes, a brown skirt and blouse, a red scarf, handing out leaflets in 1937 on the Arts campus. 'Stop Franco! Stop the war in Spain!'" And with those images churning in his mind, Arthur Laurents knew with certainty that Fanny Price was going to morph into the central character of a new movie for Barbra Streisand.

His heroine, he decided, would remain perpetually unsure of her looks, and just like that another memory popped into place: he'd borrow more than a bit from the life of Katrina Wallingford, "the owner of that Sutton Place apartment and the girl who asked a quasi-Hubbell of her own if he was leaving her because she wasn't attractive. All those component parts would finally be melded and submerged into the Katie and Hubbell I invented as I wrote." He might not have known the plot yet, but Arthur Laurents had the engine for his movie: "with Fanny's outrage and convictions, the story would tell itself. Beginning at Cornell, it would be close to me and right for her. And if it was right for Barbra it would be right for Ray."

The name mattered: Fanny would become Katie. Unquestionably Jewish. Last name: Morosky. A Jewish name, yes, but no run-of-the-mill, everyday moniker. "She was too passionate about too much. . . . The boys would call her by her last name—Morosky." Laurents's passionate Katie would be unique. Sui generis. A woman of standards who demanded better from everyone in her orbit. Admirable, but far from a saint. Loud, unrelenting, exhausting—and vulnerable.

Katie's personality would be light years removed from that of her lifelong love, a WASPy, to-the-manor-born goy for whom everything in life came easily—too easily. Name: Hubbell Gardiner, a variation on the name of Laurents's handsome friend Hubbell Robinson, the head of the ad agency Young and Rubicam: "A wearer of elegant suspenders, as comfortable with women as with a never empty glass." His full name for the movie: Hubbell Gardiner, a name so WASP that the first and last names could be reversed without missing a beat. It never would be specified exactly where Hubbell grew up, but the image of riding boots and Southern aristocracy seemed to pop into mind as soon as the name was uttered. Did Hubbell come from old money? He'd be comfortable rather than rich, raised in the tradition of cool, respectable parents who never allowed emotion to sully their proper WASP veneer.

Hubbell, in fact, would be based in part on Peter Viertel, husband of Laurents's good friend Jigee, a jock who was a first-class tennis player and skier, a published novelist at age nineteen, and later, a screenwriter. Viertel may not have been a golden boy blonde, but another of Laurents's inspirations was Bob Parrish "who was blond and Aryan. . . . I took what happened to me in college and split it between her and Redford. He was her fantasy WASP." In short, just like Katie, Hubbell would come to life as a composite of many: "part me, part a naval lieutenant named Dougal Wyatt who had a coterie of Yale buddies (all gay); and he would be part of whoever was going to play him."

How to define Hubbell's ease in life? Laurents drew on the memory of a friend from ten years earlier, "Tony Blue Eyes." When he was a child, Tony told Laurents, teachers would send him from room to room with the same note for each teacher. When Tony finally opened the note himself, it read, "Did you ever see such beautiful eyes?" Yes, Tony admitted to Laurents, he was skating through life on his charms and startling blue eyes, and while it helped smooth his path, "easier wasn't necessarily better." For Laurents, it was but a quick switch to trade Tony's Blue Eyes for Hubbell's dazzling smile, the metaphor encapsulated in Hubbell's first story: "The All-American Smile." Audiences, Laurents reasoned, would hear the opening lines of Hubbell's autobiographical story and instantly understand the dichotomy between surface dazzle and lack of inner commitment; in beautifully simple prose Hubbell would explain that "in a way he was like the country he lived in: everything came too easily to him. But at least he knew it. . . . And if, more often than not, he took advantage of everything and everybody, he knew that too. About once a month, he felt he was a fraud." Wrote Laurents, "The fraud, of course, was me; that there was some of me in him began to bring him alive. He wasn't as colorful as Katie but being less certain than she he was more complex."

Hubbell's success in his college writing class would come directly from Laurents's own experience in a New York University "Writing for Radio" class taught by CBS Director-Producer Bill Robson. Laurents had written a play which Robson proceeded to read aloud to the class, and in Laurents's recall, "I reacted somewhat as Robert Redford does in *The Way We Were*—embarrassed, pleased, I examined the ceiling, the floor—and like Redford, fought the giggles." Hubbell's ease with writing would, in fact, form another contrast with Katie because in Streisand biographer Neal Gabler's neat phrase, "She is a plodder on the page as in life."

The autobiographical words of Hubbell's story would reveal not just the golden façade but his shortcomings as well: when it all comes easily, what can any of it mean? Is the temptation to skate through life on surface charm alone unavoidable? It would be these shortcomings Katie would pour all of her love into correcting, even—especially—when Hubbell grew weary of her expectations. Loving, frustrated, flawed, and passionate—Katie and Hubbell began to come alive.

What excited Laurents most of all was the central idea of polar opposites. Hubbell, "a person who was everything she wasn't; a person who was unattainable; a fantasy; a beautiful blond goy. A jock but not just a jock. A jock who was a writer in her English class." Hubbell's talent versus Katie's tenacity. Morosky as the do-or-die Marxist and Hubbell, in Laurents's vision, the jock-novelist "who *doesn't need* to face the moral issues but is faced with the demands imposed by love and the compromises that come with love." Each would complete the other—or would they? How would the mismatched lovers end up? As he began writing, even Laurents didn't know: "I wasn't worried, I knew they would tell me."

Realizing that much of Katie's drive would be a mirror of his own, scenes began flowing from Laurents's memory bank. Having worked as a proofreader in the Linotype room of the *Ithaca Journal News* during college, Laurents would now hand Katie the same job. If Laurents had worked on an army radio show as assistant to the director, Katie could now begin her own career in much the same way. Hubbell, Laurents decided, would even stay over in Katie's Murray Hill walk-up apartment "just as I did in Eve Merriam's."

Laurents served in the army while Hubbell would spend the war in the navy. And if one night during the war, the uniform-clad Laurents had arrived at the Stork Club with his sister, only to be refused entry, then Katie would walk into the Stork Club with her boss, see a serviceman being refused entry, and lash out by calling the maître d' a fascist. It was all grist for the mill, necessary pieces in the creation of his loving but wildly different protagonists.

Part Fanny Price and part Arthur Laurents, Katie Morosky began to take shape as a lover of politics, literature, and Hubbell Gardiner. She remained recognizably human, so much so that in future years, many would claim to have served as the inspiration for her creation; as late as December 27, 2000, in a letter to author Greg Lawrence, then in the process of writing a biography of Jerome Robbins, Laurents felt compelled to point out that Madeline Lee's claim of serving as the inspiration for Katie Morosky was decidedly untrue.

Laurents wanted to ground at least half of the love story against the background of the blacklist in Hollywood, recalling it as a time when "[t]here was both terror and excitement. This was the end of the 40s, before McCarthy. I was living there. It was glamorous. Then came this inquisition." Glamorous postwar Hollywood and a powerful disturbing chapter of American history. Yes, he'd keep the love story in the foreground, but he wanted to take on the Hollywood blacklist that he had personally endured, the visceral memory of which still rankled. Scenes began to come and go with startling frequency; first deciding that a lunch he had attended at famed director George Cukor's home, complete with a guest list that included Katharine Hepburn and Ronald Colman, would provide inspiration for Hollywood luminaries discussing the blacklist, he then instantly tossed the idea aside—the more he thought about it, the more he found it impossible to imagine Katie and Hubbell at Cukor's house. The scene never made it into the final script.

He'd replace that scene with another highly charged political memory from the same era. At a soon-to-be famous meeting of the Writers Guild, one at which writer/producer Dore Schary seemingly endorsed the blacklist, Marguerite Roberts, a talented writer afflicted with a terrible stutter, forced herself to stand and speak exactly one sentence: "I don't know how Mr. Schary can look at himself in the mirror every morning without vomiting." In Laurents's recall, Schary and his "fellow toads" had run for the door, trailed by boos—a dramatic real-life Hollywood exit.

Laurents had forgotten neither the meeting nor Roberts's stutter, and it all seemed tailor made for Hubbell's Hollywood years. There were, he recalled, many stutterers on the Hollywood scene—Budd Schulberg, Jigee Viertel, and Ring Lardner all sprang to mind—and the metaphor seemed apt. At first, thinking that he would write a scene in which the stutterer tried to speak at a political conference, he quickly realized that he had no idea what Hubbell would have done during such a meeting. Hiss? Walk out with Schary and his minions? He cut the idea before it even took shape.

Other Hollywood scenes did make his final outline. As a young man, Laurents had attended a party at writer Clifford Odets's house, the starry guest list headed by Charlie Chaplin. Clowning around while impersonating a matador, Chaplin had crashed into a wall and knocked one of Odets's valuable paintings to the floor; the displaced painting had quickly revealed a microphone—Odets, a suspected radical, was being bugged by the government. The memory stuck, and Laurents decided it would now be combined with his "this-is-how-the-other-half-lives" experience of attending a party hosted by Louis B. Mayer's daughter Irene Selznick. When it came time to screen a film after dinner, Selznick had pressed a button, and her Matisse silently glided toward the ceiling as the movie screen descended. In Laurents's fact-becomes-fiction imagination, Katie and Hubbell would now attend a dinner party at producer George Bissinger's home, and as a valuable painting flies up to make room for a movie screen, it would be torn by a hidden microphone.

As for Katie and Hubbell's political difficulties, those, he decided, could come straight from the life of his good friend Jigee Viertel. A beautiful woman who had both danced in movies and worked as a story editor, Jigee's political past as a member of the Communist Party had, thanks to the FBI, made life in Hollywood very difficult for her second husband, screenwriter Peter Viertel. At Hollywood studios in the late forties and early fifties, any writer who was married to a Communist instantly became persona non grata, a fact that meant, in Laurents's assessment of Jigee and Peter, "[i]t was down to her beliefs, his beliefs, and who loved whom and who didn't. That was what it was going to come down to with Katie and Hubbell."

Jigee's past romantic life had only further complicated the picture; she had at one time been married to Hollywood prince Budd Schulberg of *What Makes Sammy Run?* fame, and yet Schulberg had informed on her after their marriage ended. To director Sydney Pollack, it would be Schulberg who served as the model for Hubbell's intellect, just as Peter Viertel inspired his athletic prowess and Robert Parrish, his WASP good looks.

For all of the script's political content, Laurents still wanted to keep the love story center stage for one crucial reason: every successful Barbra Streisand movie was at heart a romance in which she won over her golden leading man through sheer force of talent and personality. What chance did Omar Sharif (*Funny Girl*) or Ryan O'Neal (*What's Up, Doc?*) have in withstanding her desires either on-screen or off? Her looks and affect may have proved unusual, but she used that fact to her advantage. It was a motif made crystal clear in Bill Manhoff and Buck Henry's screenplay for her successful, first nonmusical film, *The Owl and the Pussycat* (1970, in which her character of hooker and "actress" Doris Wilgus, plaintively asks "novelist" Felix (George Segal), "Do you think I'm pretty?" She then proceeds to answer her own question: "I'm not really. I just make you think that I am. . . . You've got to act pretty."

It all struck close to home for the screenwriter, reminding him of his days directing *I Can Get It for You Wholesale*. Never short of chutzpah, the nineteen-year-old Barbra had bluntly asked Laurents why she couldn't play the lead, but before Laurents could answer, Barbra had, just like Doris Wilgus, answered her own question: "It's because I'm not pretty, isn't it?" Wrote Neal Gabler of the encounter, "Laurents admitted to himself that it was true." Building upon that memory, Laurents reasoned that in trying to regain Hubbell's love, Katie would self-analyze in nearly the same words: "It's that I'm not attractive—not in the right way, isn't it?"

And yet, Arthur Laurents understood, no one had ever managed the oddball/object of desire dichotomy with Streisand's dexterity, and that remained a big part of her standing as queen of the box office. Audiences had cared little about an already happily married Barbra in the highly confused, albeit interesting, feminist tract *Up the Sandbox* (1972), but let Barbra go to work on her leading man and the film inevitably proved successful: Katie Morosky would pursue her handsome leading man but this time with a dramatic heft lacking in Barbra's other movies. Laurents felt certain that he could construct a through line that would capitalize upon her unique blend of bulldozer force and genuine vulnerability and in the process, bridge the gap between female empowerment and Barbra's own genuine belief in traditional romanticism.

Bits of Barbra from Brooklyn and Barbra the politically liberal Hollywood superstar would be sprinkled throughout because Katie Morosky would in several ways play like an extension of Barbra herself. From his years in the business, Laurents knew that the biggest film stars like Katharine Hepburn and John Wayne played variations of themselves in every role and that Barbra Streisand, with her proud ethnicity, blustery Brooklyn ways, and angelic singing voice, had now established herself as the latest larger-than-life star personality in Hollywood. Wrote Laurents, "[Katie Morosky] had to be a Jew; Barbra herself had arrived as one. Not flaunting, not defying, just simply declaring at Hollywood customs: Here is a Jewish movie star."

By the time of *The Way We Were*, Streisand had morphed into an attractive, frankly sexual woman, a movie star who just happened to come in a package different from any previously glimpsed.

Katie Morosky's college years would unfold as a variation on the teenaged Streisand herself. Said Al Ramus, a producer of *PM East/ PM West*, the television talk show in which she got her start, "She was the essence of every confused, not-very-attractive girl who wanted extravagantly more out of life than birth circumstances could possibly give her." Katie would be loud, lacking in humor, and unrelentingly serious, yet at the same time, smart and compelling, her sense of injustice and passionate take on life making her attractive and worthy of an audience's total attention.

It's not that Barbra and Katie were identical but rather, reasoned Laurents, that "[t]he connecting tissue is Barbra's passion and her sense of injustice." Katie Morosky would be smart—like Streisand herself. Fast talking and with a very quick mind. The key, Laurents felt certain, lay in his belief that Barbra Streisand had the singular ability to make Katie seem completely original. In Katie's combination of right and wrong, she hopefully could and would remind viewers of the very young Streisand, about whom Jerome Robbins had said, "She does everything wrong but it comes out right."

As all of these memories flowed, Laurents felt his excitement growing. He liked these characters. In fact, he liked them too much. "One risk I wasn't as fully aware of as I should have been, considering what came later: the story was so personal, I cared about it. That was dangerous for a screenwriter." Excited as he was by the possibilities, however, the often-prickly Laurents nonetheless retained his own uneasiness about Barbra's participation: "I had doubts that she would accept the part. When she played Miss Marmelstein she was such a puritanical kid. I had now written a story about an idealistic teenager who later goes to Hollywood, is forced to get tough to survive, starts using four-letter words, and learns to fight back to retain her individuality." Katie, in fact, would start out incapable of using four-letter words—or three-letter ones either; as Hubbell would eventually point out, she can't even say "ass." Barbra's own reaction upon reading that Katie never used four-letter words until moving to Hollywood was to exclaim, "That's me!" This was a character Barbra understood, one who afforded juicy possibilities and a chance to prove herself as a dramatic actress. After all, as she repeatedly reminded interviewers, she was an actress first and a singer second: "I started singing because I couldn't get a job as an actress and I started directing because I couldn't be heard as an actress."

As it turned out, when *The Way We Were* first saw the light of day as a novel in 1972, Laurents would claim that he had intended it all along as a novel, never visualizing it as a movie, let alone a movie starring Barbra Streisand: "How I came to write a novel begins and ends with Barbra Streisand. And yet it had nothing to do with her." The basic story, Laurents went on to state, was too big for the stage, so it had to take shape as a novel. Perhaps he spoke in these terms to ensure that reviewers would treat the novel as an original work and not a mere novelization of a film treatment, but as his own papers reveal, *The Way We Were* first saw the light of day as the very treatment that excited Barbra Streisand and Ray Stark. Dated August 14, 1970, and prominently stamped on the title page as the "Property of Rastar Productions Inc.," the 114-page treatment preceded the March 10, 1971, first draft screenplay by seven months and the 317-page novel, by nearly two years.

It was early innings yet. The actual screenplay itself needed to be written, but for now, Barbra was smiling, Ray Stark was happy, and even Laurents pronounced himself satisfied. Satisfied he may have been, but the famously opinionated Laurents would still never tread lightly, even when it came to his star: "The Barbra I first knew was such a bright and alert person. She often asked me for reading lists and would pore over every book I recommended, but this curiosity was no longer there. I had told her once to read Solzhenitsyn and one day while I was working on *The Way We Were* she called me to say, 'Hey, your guy won the Nobel Prize!' 'Have you read his books?' I asked. 'No,' she replied. 'I just haven't got the time anymore.' There was a time when you could talk to Barbra for hours on any subject and be constantly stimulated intellectually. Now she was beginning to bore me."

What Barbra thought of Laurents at this juncture remained unknown, but one thing she did know with utter certainty: she was going to star in a movie titled *The Way We Were*. And as *The New York Times* reminded everyone, "Rule number 1 in show business: Never bet against Babs."

Enter Sydney Pollack

"Sidney Pollack was exactly the right director to handle both Streisand and Redford at the peaks of their careers." —Jeanine Basinger, film historian

With producer, star, and screenwriter all temporarily satisfied, one overarching question now loomed: Who would direct the film? Whoever it was had to have the strength to elicit a dramatic performance from Barbra without endangering audience sympathy, while at the same time possessing the strength to stand toe to toe with the opinionated star.

Never short of opinions himself, Arthur Laurents had admired director Sydney Pollack's *They Shoot Horses, Don't They?* (1969) and although he did not know Pollack, suggested the director to Stark. Stark liked the idea; he had also been a fan of *They Shoot Horses* and particularly liked the possibility that the thirty-eight-year-old Pollack might be able to induce his longtime friend Robert Redford to play the leading role of heartthrob Hubbell Gardiner.

Pollack had acted alongside the two-year-younger Redford in *War Hunt* (1962), and the two had maintained a friendship ever since. Recalled Pollack, "He was the only guy on the set as quiet and scared as I was. We both had wives and young children, so we didn't bounce around like a lot of the other actors. Our families spent a lot of time together and we got to be friends. Not real tight, but when he was in California he'd call me." By the time of *The Way We Were*, Pollack had twice directed Redford in major films: *This Property Is Condemned* (1966) and *Jeremiah Johnson* (1972). They may not have been the closest of friends, but they were buddies and worked well together, two strong-willed, highly opinionated men with perfectionist instincts.

Pollack, in fact, may have landed full force on the Hollywood radar screen with his acclaimed Oscar-nominated direction of *They Shoot Horses*, but his list of credits as both actor and director stretched back to New York City in the 1950s. Beginning in 1954 as an assistant to the highly esteemed Neighborhood Playhouse School of the Theatre acting guru Sanford Meisner, he then cut his teeth as an actor on television shows ranging from *Playhouse 90* and *The Twilight Zone* to *Have Gun–Will Travel.* Branching off into directing, he worked in every conceivable genre then found on episodic television, the Western *Wagon Train* interspersed with both suspense dramas (*The Alfred Hitchcock Hour*) and popular medical shows like *Dr. Kildare* and *Ben Casey*, winning an Emmy for the latter. Pollack looked upon it all as a training ground, and by the time he began directing feature films in 1965 with *The Slender Thread*, starring Anne Bancroft and Sidney Poitier, his dual careers as actor and director had helped him establish a comfort zone with actors of all stripes. He knew how to handle stars, and even on 1969's *The Scalphunters*, difficult personalities like Burt Lancaster and Shelley Winters responded to his overt sympathy and tact. Pollack listened and, strong-minded as he was, always valued the input of his stars.

Tactful and sympathetic he may have been, but he was also far from a pushover, as Ray Stark could attest. On 1966's *This Property Is Condemned*, which Pollack directed and Stark produced (albeit uncredited), the two men engaged in several protracted battles, bruising experiences that left each man wary of the other. In the words of Robert Redford, who had starred in the film, Stark had not been pleased with Pollack's work on the movie, which meant that "To him, Sydney did not smell good." Even in these early stages of his career, however, Pollack was not intimidated by Stark and with his obstinate personality, proved himself a skilled Hollywood infighter, one capable of changing alliances to get his way. He was, it seemed, an equal match for Stark.

Whatever the past difficulties between Stark and Pollack, commerce trumped all in Hollywood, and in the back of Stark's mind lay the fact that Pollack was friendly with the elusive Robert Redford. In just as calculating a manner, Pollack knew that with Stark in the producer's seat, *The Way We Were* would actually get made, a not inconsiderable factor given Columbia Pictures' shaky financial status and its general front office hesitancy over the material.

Even more to the point, as Pollack quickly learned, it wasn't as if other studios had entered into a bidding war for the rights. Period pictures—and this one required sets and costumes ranging from the 1930s into the 1950s—were more expensive to produce, and in the director's own words, "the script had been turned down by other studios—no one was interested in McCarthy politics." Even after agreeing to finance and distribute the movie, Columbia front office concerns persisted, albeit somewhat humorously. Related Pollack: "Early on when I started to work on it, I bumped into the man who had taken over Columbia, which was in bad shape. This pic really helped them enormously. He said to me half-jokingly—'you're going to do a picture where Barbra plays a Jewish communist and she doesn't sing a note—are you trying to destroy this company?!'"

Problems and all, however, the more Stark thought about Pollack, the more he liked the idea. Said the producer, "I realized Sydney was a good director. He had done a remarkable job with the cast of *They Shoot Horses*—always in control. He seemed to be perfect for Barbra." Just as importantly, Barbra Streisand liked the sound of Sydney Pollack as her director. In Pollack's own words, "Barbra was smart.

She liked my Sandy Meisner connections because she was ambitious, as an actress, to learn." At the same time, he was not unaware of the pitfalls that went with directing Streisand: "She has a tendency to take over a picture, just by the size of her talent and larger-than-life presence. It's hard for a costar to stay in the same ring with her." Aware he was, but intimidated? No.

This glossy love story, a throwback to the classic star-driven Hollywood romance of decades past, represented terra firma for Pollack, a director who liked the traditions and forms of golden age Hollywood movies. By his own admission, Pollack was interested in "a strong narrative line, craftsmanship, and visual style"; together they formed the guiding principles of the Pollack style. Leave the experimentation to Scorsese, Coppola, DePalma, and the other young Hollywood directors beginning to make their marks because Pollack was influenced most heavily not by the Bergmans, Kurosawas, and Fellinis revered by these new young Turks but rather, by classic American directors "like Stevens and Wyler and Zinnemann. Mostly I suppose, Kazan because he was a very performance oriented director."

For the time being, then, everyone involved, even the opinionated Arthur Laurents, seemed pleased by the idea of Sydney Pollack, which meant that as Laurents put the finishing touches on a novelization of his treatment, he sent the book's galleys first to Stark and then to Pollack. Pollack was not impressed, writing in a December 4, 1971, letter to Robert Redford that "Laurents is really a playwright and not a novelist. Try if you can to disregard the mistakes he makes as a novelist. There are many." Later in the same letter, he heavily underscores his criticisms: "The problem in the novel, and it's a big problem, is that Laurents has treated that whole section [about Hollywood] in an exaggerated and 'campy' way. The people are not real."

As it turned out, the novel, released in April 1972, eighteen months before the film premiered, received very mixed reviews, with *Publishers Weekly* complaining, "[W]e've seen it all before in fiction and nonfiction and, truth to tell Mr. Laurents does not bring anything particularly new to the examination of the subject." Reviews in smaller papers proved more complimentary, with the *Florida Times-Union* terming the novel "Good reading, a touch of smiles and a trace of tears," but it was dismissed in *The New York Times* by Raymond Sokolov, the paper's food editor, who informed readers that "[t]he author never grapples with his real issues. Instead, he has 'crafted' another daytime TV serial, rooted tenuously in the always exploitable milieu of showbiz leftism."

Nonetheless, Pollack remained sold on the material's potential and, in April 1972, officially signed on to direct. Contentious days with Laurents lay ahead, but for now, in these very early days, the honeymoon phase between screenwriter and director remained in full force. Said Pollack, "I called Arthur right at the start and said, 'You know what you're proposing here? This is dynamite. This will be the first-ever blacklist movie, the first one to show how it was.'"

The missing piece in the puzzle remained that of a bona fide leading man, and with Pollack's by-now ten-year friendship with Redford firmly in mind, Stark asked Pollack to once again test the waters with the star. It was, however, that very request that caused another big problem: Robert Redford was not a fan of Ray Stark, with whom he had clashed over *This Property Is Condemned.* Stark had sold *This Property Is Condemned* to Warner, which had, in Redford's words, "really dumped" the film, meaning that when Pollack first approached Redford about the role, the conversation was tinged with negative feelings. Said the actor about *The Way We Were*, "Ray Stark was the man behind it and I told [Pollack] that it sounded to me like another Ray Stark ego trip. I didn't even want to read it." Pollack persisted; having been moved by the story, he casually extolled its virtues to Redford. The actor's considered reply? "Aw, that piece of junk."

At the time of his initial conversation with Redford, Pollack had not even formally signed his own contract. With Pollack now signed, however, Redford had in effect given Stark an opening. Recalled the star, "I pushed. I said, 'If you want to even consider me for *The Way We Were*, it has to be Sydney developing it.' So, I made this noose for myself because Stark gave in and suddenly I had an outline written up for me that I hated."

Oh. Uh-oh.

Robert Redford—or Maybe Not

"No matter how any of us may feel about Redford's skill as an actor—he was sometimes terrific, sometimes terrifically bland—he was one of the great fantasy figures of American movies in the '70s: he seemed to glow gold." —Stephanie Zacherik, *New York Times*, June 3, 2011

At the very beginning of casting discussions, Robert Redford had not, in fact, been the only name mentioned. Five minutes of serious consideration had been given to Ryan O'Neal, who possessed the requisite WASPy good looks and had proven an effective foil for Barbra in the highly successful *What's Up, Doc?* (1972). The problem was, Barbra's relationship with O'Neal, which had blossomed during *What's Up, Doc?* was over, and while the duo remained friendly, it was Redford, whose career after *Butch Cassidy and the Sundance Kid* (1969) had clicked into high gear, whom everyone now wanted to play Hubbell Gardiner.

The idea of Robert Redford starring opposite Barbra certainly appealed to Laurents, who viewed them as a modern-day answer to Fred Astaire and Ginger Rogers, "but more because he had more sex to begin with than Astaire, she had more class to begin with than Rogers." Enthusiastically backed by Laurents, the relentless Stark now began to focus on landing Redford: "When this story began taking shape it occurred to me that Redford was the most logical choice—he was the exact opposite of Barbra. He was very cool and very reserved. As an actor he seemed to work introspectively rather than emotionally. Their approach was very different, their styles, background—very different—perfect because that's how the roles were written. Sydney understood that instantly."

Pollack's full-court press on his friend had begun even before signing his own contract, and in his letter of December 4, 1971, he implored, "If I knew you less well and we weren't friends I wouldn't sell so hard. I'd probably play it very cool . . . but I'm too excited about this possibility not to push. . . . Please don't rush through it and please don't read it while your mind is on too many other problems. It's important. For me it's that very rare combination of GOOD *and* commercial." To Pollack, Hubbell was far from a cipher: "Hubbell is NOT a cop-out or a weak guy, rather he is the most sophisticated character in the novel."

Undeterred by his friend's lack of interest, Pollack emphasized the role's career potential; Redford, for all of his increasing success, had not yet starred in a dramatic love story, his only significant "romance" coming opposite Paul Newman in *Butch Cassidy and the Sundance Kid* (1969). Sign on to play Hubbell, Pollack argued, and Robert Redford could establish himself as a romantic lead: "We've both talked about doing a love story. . . . I knew by the time I was halfway through it that this was the one. . . . It is not conventional. Not the expected kind of story of romance. The people are not black and white, they are COMPLICATED. They have flaws and rough edges and that makes it, for me, much more interesting. . . . I've never really felt so good about a project at this state. There is time to get it right. Seventy percent of it is there already."

Play the role, counseled Pollack, and Robert Redford could expand his stardom—and power. Not to mention make a great deal of money: "And just to show you how dirty I can play when I want something, I will drop in the fact that you can get your salary on it. 'For God, Country and Sundance!'" Pollack continued to press, convinced that Redford's golden exterior and palpable intelligence personified the male romantic figure as an object of unattainable yearning: "Katie and Hubbell are representatives of people we all have met—in college or at work. We recognize their world. The activist and America the beautiful."

It all sounded nice, but there was just one problem: that romantic image held little appeal for Robert Redford. He enjoyed acting, the spontaneity and give and take of it all, but in Pollack's words, "the glorification of him as a romantic icon made him self-conscious," which meant that as written in these early stages, the role of Hubbell Gardiner made Robert Redford self-conscious in the extreme. The character, he felt, was an object, a man who was, in Pollack's memorable phrase, "A WASP beige boy."

Pollack, who knew a trick or two about cajoling actors, would talk, back off, and come back the next day from another angle: "I don't have to say anything about the period. You love it as much as I. And the forties is really virgin territory." He appealed to the politically aware Redford's interest in the Hollywood blacklist: "The whole McCarthy thing can be a great asset if it's handled unpretentiously and un-preachy."

Pollack was not unsympathetic to his friend's concerns, genuinely understanding that despite his laid-back, golden good looks, Redford had a dark and moody side to his nature. "Bob could probably get by on his looks but he doesn't. He's not just a leading man; he's a character actor." For all his amiability, Sydney Pollack was comfortable in a war of attrition if it served his artistic purposes, and he began making promises: The role of Hubbell would be beefed up. He'd become a man with his own political opinions, a worthy foil to Katie: "His not taking part in the same way Katie does isn't from lack of understanding or consideration but rather from too much understanding and consideration. He KNOWS more than she."

Redford still didn't like the script. Well, Pollack explained, neither did he, not fully. Other writers would be brought in. Redford listened—and didn't budge. And it now dawned on Pollack that his friend was not playing hard to get but rather, "didn't like the script, he didn't like the character, he didn't like the concept of the film, he didn't think the politics and love story would mix. There was nothing about it he liked."

Redford's concerns, in fact, didn't end with just the role. He remained uneasy about working with Streisand, not about her talent, which he respected, but the fact that her previous films had either been big musicals (*Funny Girl*; *Hello, Dolly!*; and *On a Clear Day You Can See Forever*) or light comedies (*The Owl and the Pussycat* and *What's Up, Doc?*). She had yet to play a straight dramatic role, and Redford admitted, "What I was really worried about was the whole concept of basing a movie on Barbra as a serious actress. She had never been tested. I told Sydney 'Her reputation is as a very controlling person. She will direct herself. It'll never work.'" Countered Pollack, "She's unbelievably good in the right thing . . . and it's been a long time since you've had any help [on-screen] outside of BUTCH."

Pollack badgered his friend to reconsider. Reported the director, "I spent literally eight months beating him to death in order to get him to do it. His basic objection was the story was written as a woman's piece. It was not a question of ego. It was the question of not wanting to spare the time to play a weak, spineless male sex object. . . . I kept saying to Bob: 'Hubbell is an existentialist. Hubbell sees the long view. Hubbell knows that for all of this passionate rhetoric, twenty years from now the guys who are putting these other guys in prison are going to be working together with them.' Which is in fact what happened."

Redford did at least listen to Pollack; it's likely that with any other director, he would have completely shut down the conversation, but the old friends respected one another as colleagues and by this point, had shared ten years and three films together. Pollack continued to noodge him because to Pollack, this was a love story of substance, fronted by a man and a woman who lived as political and emotional opposites, their differing personalities and senses of morality allowing both men and women to identify with the characters. The college jock versus the ultra-serious striver who wanted to save the world. An unobtainable golden boy who has never experienced rejection falling for a woman so afraid of rejection that she works overtime at distancing herself from others. A man of opinions who doesn't often bother to express them married to a woman who does nothing but shout every opinion she has ever held. Pragmatic Hubbell versus idealistic Katie.

For Pollack, the two characters were "components of a single person. What I feel is that if Katie had a little more of Hubbell, she'd be better, and if he had a little more of her, he'd be better. They're invaluable to each other." (In later years, he further explained: "In the making of the film I really fell in love with those two characters in a curious way, because I think they're parts of all of us.") It all sounded fine, but Redford wasn't buying. If Hubbell had opinions, where were they? In fact, what were they? Reading the script, Redford saw a pretty boy who did nothing but glide through life. Pollack offered a counterargument: OK, that might have been the case when Hubbell was in college and the service, but as he aged and chased his Hollywood dream, the road to success grew bumpy. He was, in reality, a golden boy thrown off course, one who acquired a decided measure of complexity in the process. Sounds nice, said Redford—but why didn't he see a single one of those supposed bumps on Hubbell's road? Where were the meaty scenes with subtext? At best, Hubbell had a couple of good lines puncturing Katie's bubble: "You don't talk—you lecture."

But those lines were few and far between, and to Redford, the script represented one endless parade of "Katie—Katie—Katie."

Rewrite the character, let the viewer understand Hubbell's passions and worldview, and Robert Redford might—might—consider signing on. But for now, Hubbell remained a cipher of little interest to the actor. Even the bittersweet ending, he felt, wouldn't work because none of the emotion had been properly earned by a character who remained a straw man. He did not want to spend time portraying a good-looking cardboard cutout, yet still acknowledged one spark of interest: "I said there have to be some underpinnings that at least suggest a darker side. The darker side here was that he has not written a great novel. He doesn't want to be put up on that pedestal. And there's a certain grace from just knowing that." It still wasn't enough to make him sign on, however, because Robert Redford felt it was actually Sydney Pollack who seemed to hold a far greater interest in the Hubbell Gardiners of the world than he did; if Hubbell remained a man frustratingly incapable of lasting commitment, it was that very trait Redford found to be so prominent in his friend: "One of the reasons Sydney wanted to do it was that he identified with the character of an uncommitted man."

Yes, Pollack admitted, there was no question that the screenplay's dramatic possibilities remained heavily weighted in favor of Katie. It is she who remained a dynamo of action, a frizzy-haired voluble Snow White who awakens the literally sleeping Prince Charming in El Morocco's bar. It is, in fact, Katie who pursues, buys flowers, takes her conquest home, and after their breakup, actually uses the traditional male line "I promise I won't touch you." With the famous Streisand profile on prominent display, there might, in fact, even be a touch of Cyrano hovering over the proceedings, and yes, Pollack acknowledged to his friend, it was always Cyrano who engendered audience sympathy. He could even agree that Laurents seemed to regard strengthening Hubbell's character as an unfortunate path to "reducing the clarity, significance and correctness of Katie's character." Yes, yes, yes—but, he insisted to Redford, those problems could be solved. Pollack would bring in additional writers. Laurents would have to rewrite. In fact as far as Sydney Pollack was concerned, the script remained a work in progress, and rewriting could continue throughout the entire shoot. Beginning a film without a final script did not faze the director (six years later he would begin directing Redford in *The Electric Horseman* with "maybe 35 pages of script"). "Trust me," he pleaded with his old acting buddy. "You have to trust me."

By now, the screenplay had been rewritten repeatedly, with the first draft of March 10, 1971, supplanted one year later by drafts dated March 15, 1972, and April 6, 1972. Speeding along the path to production—albeit minus a leading man—Pollack and Stark utilized the April 6 draft for a full scene-by-scene breakdown. Estimated running time: 141 minutes. Long, but easily correctible.

And now with that scene-by-scene breakdown in mind, Pollack wrote a memo dated May 10, 1972, in which he fully outlined his laundry list of objections to the Laurents script. Based upon three days of meetings he held with Redford, the memo dispatched the elements he liked in one short paragraph, noting that he found the script intelligent, the political background provocative, the dynamic leading woman nicely matched by an appealing leading man, and the ending highly emotional. He then singled out two scenes for particular praise: the fight at a party hosted by Hubbell's best friend J.J., and Katie's tearful telephone call to Hubbell.

Praise dispensed, Pollack then moved on to quick, incisive suggestions for deepening the supporting characters. Strengthen Hubbell's friends J.J. and Carol Ann. Develop Carol Ann as a genuinely intelligent and therefore believable rival/alternative to Katie. Help J.J. exhibit a sense of humor and an actual philosophical core that deepens his friendship with Hubbell. Let J.J. be the one to ruminate about "the way we were," about life speeding by at too fast a pace. In fact, J.J.'s could be the middle-aged angst that would resonate with audiences.

Redford thawed a bit. Clearly the director was taking his concerns to heart, even suggesting strong, specific motivations for Hubbell; wouldn't it make sense if Hubbell and Katie really began to spin apart in Hollywood because Hubbell wants to write screenplays, rather than the novels Katie insists upon? Maybe Hubbell, like everyone in Hollywood, actually wants to direct, not write.

In his push to give greater depth to the character of Hubbell, Pollack attempted to cover all bases, and at times seemed to contradict himself. First, he wanted the college-era Hubbell to have much more of a sense of humor, yet at the same time he wanted Hubbell to studiously attend one of Katie's Young Communists League meetings, not exactly gatherings noted for youthful high spirits. Hubbell, he insisted, had to be Katie's equal in passion, intellect, drive, and depth of character. In fact, the imbalance in their impact could be corrected if scenes featuring Hubbell alone, without Katie, could now be added.

The September 1972 start of shooting lay only four months away, but with this memo, the seeds of discord had now been firmly planted, because in Arthur Laurents's view, the story was Katie's, not Hubbell's. Always had been. Always would be.

As deadlines loomed, Redford bent—but only a little. Ray Stark grew more impatient by the day. In Pollack's reckoning, "He liked Redford and wanted Redford but he felt out of control—he was sitting around and waiting." A Ray Stark not in total control was not a happy Ray Stark, and other names began being floated with increasing frequency: Ryan O'Neal resurfaced as a person of interest. So, too, did blonde, handsome television favorite Dennis Cole. A tennis date was then scheduled for Barbra and tall, good-looking Ken Howard. Even though Howard remained a completely unknown quantity as a leading man in feature films, according to Laurents, all went well on the tennis date until a beautiful woman arrived to pick up Howard. Wrote Laurents, "Barbra froze. Next day she told me there was no sex appeal between them, that nothing would happen up there on the screen. . . . I agreed with her one hundred percent and Howard was out." The talk turned to Warren Beatty, and while the 1970s were to represent the peak of Beatty's box-office appeal, he remained a man of such studied diffidence that underneath the dazzling surface, would his Hubbell appear to be more bored than hopelessly in love? Everyone kept circling back to Redford.

Redford may not have liked the script—in fact, he definitely didn't—but the character began to resonate for him in some undefined elemental way. The sense of things coming too easily—that he understood—not because he had led a charmed life but because his golden exterior led people to assume that he had: "I started as an actor in the theater playing a lot of character parts, and suddenly, I found myself in this place where it felt like I was getting locked into a kind of a stereotype, and it did bother me. And then I would hear, 'Well, but that's easy for you.' Or, 'You look like somebody who's educated in the East,' which I wasn't. And came from an elegant background which I didn't." A difference between assumption and reality. Redford bent a little more.

Pollack pressed harder, by now convinced that the movie actually couldn't work without Redford. He was, the director now felt, the only actor with the strength to prevent the film from turning into an all-Barbra, all-the-time festival: "I did not want to do a Streisand vehicle. . . . the essence of this picture really had to do with the relationship, which required equal footage for both characters. . . . So I kept saying the only guy I know of who could stay toe-to-toe with her, is Redford. Because he has a strength and intelligence on screen which does not rely on histrionics or what's in the role.

It's something he brings in his persona like the old-fashioned movie stars. Like Cooper did. Like Tracy did."

In his full-court press to land Redford, Pollack had one important supporter: Barbra herself. Having first seen Redford on-screen starring opposite Natalie Wood in *Inside Daisy Clover* (1965), her interest had been immediately piqued, and she found herself wondering, "Who is this man? . . . I realized there's a lot going on behind those crystal-blue eyes." So great was the depth of Barbra's interest in landing Redford that Pollack came to call her his greatest ally in trying to sign the actor: "I needed the strength that Redford brings on the screen and Barbra understood that."

It wasn't just for artistic reasons that Pollack remained determined to land Redford because he also remained acutely aware that in Hollywood, all of the film's artistry wouldn't matter one iota if it failed at the box office. Political films had never spelled big box office, and Barbra would not be singing, a fact that represented a big disappointment to her most fervent fans. There needed to be a big male star who could hold his own with Barbra, a star whose sexual charge would interest Streisand herself as well as the audience. That meant Robert Redford.

As the weeks dragged by with no sign of Redford coming on board, Barbra grew increasingly uneasy: "They were talking about other people because he had turned it down so many times. I was hoping and praying, but it didn't look good. . . . I wanted him in that role so badly." Redford continued to vacillate, and his then wife Lola was driven to distraction: "I wish he would make up his mind already. He's driving me crazy. He sits up at night and says, 'What should I do?' I don't like it. Pollack is really turned on by it. I trust him. Maybe he sees something I don't see.'"

Finally, the *Hollywood Reporter* carried an article on June 6, 1972, that Robert Redford had signed for the movie. It all sounded well and good, but that piece of news was retracted the very next day via an official statement that the part had not yet been cast. By now thoroughly fed up with Redford's indecision, Ray Stark gave Pollack an ultimatum: meet with Redford at his apartment in New York that very evening and get a definite answer. Pollack would have exactly one hour to close the deal.

Pollack hurried over to see his friend, forcefully repeating that script revisions would build up Hubbell's part. Just as predictably, Redford shot back with his objections to Hubbell's cardboard characterization: "What is this picture about, Pollack? Who is this guy? He's just an object. A nothing. He runs around saying 'Aw, c'mon Katie, c'mon Katie. He doesn't want anything. What does this guy *want* Sydney?" Pollack matched Redford's intransigence with his own, refusing to give up until he had browbeaten his friend into acquiescence: "I would not let him off the hook. I said, 'You've got it wrong. This isn't a fuzzy piece for Barbra Streisand. This is substantial and—what do you know—it's political.'" This time, Pollack rattled off the names of the additional writers he'd bring in: David Rayfiel, Alvin Sargent, Dalton Trumbo, and Francis Ford Coppola. The best of the best. Stark called. It was 11:00 p.m., and by now, he had given Pollack not just one, but three hours to close the deal. Time was up. Did he have an agreement? When the answer came back "No," Stark barked, "We're hiring Ryan O'Neal." Pollack objected—he needed ten more minutes. Pollack cajoled. Redford hesitated—and then, at last, he capitulated: it was 11:30 p.m., June 10, 1972. He acquiesced not only because Pollack had worn him down—which he had—and not because he suddenly loved the script—he didn't—but because of his trust in Pollack and in the director's promise to bring in those additional award-winning writers. In Redford's recall, "Finally I just took the part on faith."

That decision was helped by the fact that however much work he felt the script needed, as a politically involved citizen himself, he appreciated the film's attempt to mix the romance with the sordid blacklisting era. The clash of politics and class, liberals versus conservatives—in Redford's own words: "The questionable nature of free speech was a provocative notion and I attached to that." Explained the reluctant star, "The reason I finally decided to do the picture, was that I had faith that Pollack and Alvin Sargent and David Rayfiel would make something more out of that character than was in the script. As it was written, he was shallow and one-dimensional. Not very real—more a figment of someone's imagination of what Prince Charming should be like. What emerged out of the rewrites were glimpses of the darker side of this golden boy character—what his fears were about himself."

A deal was finalized, and on June 12, the *Hollywood Reporter* retracted its retraction. Robert Redford was now officially costarring in *The Way We Were*.

Then filming *Up the Sandbox* in Africa, Streisand received word via a telegram sent by her agent Sue Mengers. Recalled the star, "I was in Africa making a movie and . . . a friend of mine at the time sent me a telegram, and it said 'Barbra, Redford,' and I knew he had signed on." Streisand would be top billed, but Redford received the larger salary: $1.2 million to Barbra's $1 million. Competition. Friendly competition to be sure, but like all stars, both were aware of their exact positions within the Hollywood hierarchy.

In later years, Redford markedly downplayed the extent of his reluctance, instead explaining, "I thought it was a good script. I thought it was great for Barbra. But the character in the initial script was, I felt, one dimensional. . . . So Sydney and I got together, and we worked something that felt good to me, which was a character that appeared a certain way and people would ascribe certain things to him that he didn't really know were true." Analyzing further, "[I] wanted to work with Barbra and I felt it was a wonderful premise for a love story." With the original script weighted in favor of the female role, "the question was, could you bring a balance into things?"

In less guarded moments, he dropped the politesse and explained his reluctance in terms that certainly colored his relationship with Arthur Laurents: "I had turned it down because I thought it was overly sentimental and drippy. I also thought the politics in it was bullshit. It was knee-jerk liberalism and very arch. But there was some very good love-story writing, which read to me like an old-fashioned Hollywood movie." Deliberate snubbing, dented egos, and dustups between star and screenwriter were to burst forth during filming, all of it making for a fraught production period, but that tumult lay in the future. For now, even Laurents was happy to have Redford signed and on board.

Barbra and Bob, Katie and Hubbell, whatever the combination, Streisand was intrigued and soon after her return from Africa, expressed interest in meeting Robert Redford. There was just one problem: Robert Redford didn't want to meet. He put off the meeting. And then put it off again. This, Barbra told Pollack, was starting to feel personal. Finally, Redford agreed to a dinner at Barbra's house, but the meeting, he said, had to take place with Pollack present. There would, in fact, be only three meetings between the two stars before shooting began, but it turned out that there was a strategic method to Redford's resistance: he didn't want to meet often because, in Pollack's words, "he believes very strongly that the strangeness contributes to the chemistry in a movie. And I must agree that the fact that they didn't know each other inside out worked for what was going on in the college scenes where she was supposed to be awkward with him."

What was obvious to Pollack right away—in fact, what became obvious to everyone—was that Barbra found Robert Redford a devastatingly handsome man. Observed James Woods, who made his feature film debut in the small but key role of Katie's college boyfriend, "Barbra was very enamored of Bob. You really believe she melted for this guy—she opened that part of herself and it informed her character and the film." In the view of director Pollack, "Barbra was delighted because she had a crush on him, even before we started. It was hard for women not to have a fixation, because he was everywhere, like Elvis. He was the golden boy long before Hubbell came along."

Yes, there was the obvious physical attraction on Streisand's part, but the attraction also worked on yet another level. Said Barbra, "He always has something going on behind his eyes. He's not just an actor, he's an intelligent, concerned human being, so that whatever you see has many layers underneath." For his part, Redford displayed a decided appreciation for Streisand's protean talent: "I saw her [sing] way back in the '60s, and I thought she was really, really good. Really talented. Unusual. I found her attractive in that way."

Appreciate Streisand's extraordinary musicianship he did, but Robert Redford nonetheless delivered an ultimatum to Pollack: "I didn't want her to sing in the middle of the movie!" No, Pollack decreed, Barbra wasn't going to burst into song mid movie. *The Way We Were* was not a musical but rather, a love story, and a political one at that. But to Robert Redford, it was still a substandard political love story, and with the ink on his contract barely dry, he began pressing his director for major script changes. Pollack was amenable. Arthur Laurents was not.

The battles were just beginning.

The Script

"Film's thought of as a director's medium because the director creates the end product that appears on the screen. It's that stupid auteur theory again, that the director is the author of the film. But what does the director shoot—the telephone book?"
—Billy Wilder

With questions about the script bouncing between everyone involved, Ray Stark requested that Pollack and Laurents sit down together and work out a final version of the screenplay acceptable to all. Stark arranged for the work to be done in Sun Valley, figuring that the congenial resort atmosphere, far away from either Hollywood or New York, would help smooth the process. Besides, the producer rationalized, Arthur Laurents loved to ski, which meant that Sun Valley would put him in a good mood and hopefully make him more amenable to all of the proposed changes.

It all proved a case of wishful thinking because with two such opinionated and diametrically opposed personalities as Pollack and Laurents, the work proceeded in fits and starts. As it turned out, even supposed compliments foundered in a welter of misunderstanding, with Pollack exclaiming to Laurents,

"You don't know how everybody in Hollywood is amazed by you."

> "Why?"
>
> "Because you've written the best love story in years and you're a homosexual."

Incredulous at the comment, Laurents continued his work, but the two men held radically different visions. To correct what Pollack saw as a fatal error in Hubbell's character, the director came up with a new opening to the film: "I had this idea of starting with Hubbell on the witness stand, informing on supposed Communists as Katie watches from the sidelines. As Hubbell begins supplying names, the film would flash back to their college days." To Pollack, the setting of the hearings would perfectly justify the flashback: "You don't have to alter anything, you tell the same story, except that what's triggering her memories is watching him slowly knuckle under to this pressure and weigh his instinct for survival as a writer against his own morality." In this way, he felt, Katie and Hubbell would become part of the blacklisting action and not mere observers to the ongoing turmoil. After each set piece in the film, whether that of the college years or New York City during World War II, the movie would then once again flash back to Hubbell's testimony, utilizing his time on the stand to bookend the story line.

Pollack liked the idea of the repeated flashbacks to Hubbell on the stand, the audience uncertain whether he would name names, but recalled the director, "Arthur's position was there was no defense for naming names. For purposes of drama I wanted to shore up the other side—it can't be a black and white argument because it's not very interesting. If a guy murders for no reason, it's not interesting, but if a person has some motive, some deep-seated pain that he struggles with, and he does bad acts, you can make drama out of that."

Pollack's idea was dramatically interesting, but Laurents did not want his screenplay changed in such a fundamental manner. Ray

Stark weighed in: he wanted a love story, not a political tract—concentrate on the romance, not the blacklist. Said Pollack, "It was a tough mixture—to try to deal with the blacklist, which the film doesn't fully do, and to try to do a love story." In retrospect, he analyzed, perhaps it was better that he hadn't insisted on his idea of making the leading man an informer: "I think then I would have had trouble with the studio. They were already worried that I had a Streisand film in which she didn't sing."

Pollack's dissatisfaction with the script mounted, and he further raised Laurents's hackles by insisting that the composite real-life role models the screenwriter had utilized in creating Hubbell and Katie made the romance "too unbelievable by half." The clashes with Laurents intensified over the political sequences, with Pollack bluntly opining, "It's not that he didn't understand the House Un-American Activities Committee, but he didn't contextualize it properly. There had to be a kind of education curve for the audience and Arthur was bad at that." To Laurents, who had lived through the blacklisting period, listening to Pollack pontificate about events about which he had no firsthand knowledge was tantamount to a declaration of open hostility.

Having reached an impasse, Pollack and Laurents left Sun Valley and flew East with Stark to scout locations at Cornell University. The trip did not prove a success, with Cornell's cheek by jowl juxtaposition of modern buildings and older ivy-covered dormitories making the campus unsuitable for filming. In Laurents's typically blunt assessment, "The combination of old and new was unsightly, unbalanced contemporary America."

At the end of the scouting trip, Laurents remained in the East, first visiting his parents and then decamping to his house on the dunes of Quogue. The start of shooting on *The Way We Were* was now only weeks away when his telephone rang: it was Sydney Pollack calling to tell him that Ray Stark was going to fire him. Cried

Pollack, "Oh man, I'm sorry." Laurents did not go quietly, yelling at Pollack, "You're going to build up Redford's part because you're in love with him. I don't mean homosexually but he's the blond goy you wish you were. The picture is Barbra's no matter what you do because the story is hers. Be careful you don't destroy it trying to give it to him." Laurents may have originally pushed for Pollack as director, but by now, he ruefully exclaimed, "I got him, alas."

Laurents was furious, but the drama was not yet complete because the phone soon rang again. This time it was Ray Stark, dramatically telling Laurents, "Sydney is going to fire you." What's more, Stark told the screenwriter, "he, the producer, could do nothing." Why, Laurents asked, was he being fired? Because, Stark explained pragmatically, Pollack basically came as a package deal with Redford: "It's the two of them together and I need Redford." Laurents was out.

A veteran of both Broadway and Hollywood, Arthur Laurents was tough and pragmatic, but in working with Stark and Pollack, he was dealing with two experienced infighters, which made for a dynamic rather bluntly dissected by Barbra's makeup man Don Cash Jr.: "It's hard to talk about Sydney Pollack, because you don't know where he's coming from. You always felt there was something behind everything he did, like a master politician." At heart, the talented Pollack was a genial sort, empathetic with actors, generally soft spoken, and respectful of others. But in Laurents's mind, Pollack was anything but respectful of the script, and in some ways, the entire contretemps did in fact flow out of Pollack's own personality, as the director himself seemed to unintentionally admit: "I like to present very strongly both sides of an argument. I don't like it to be all one way. So it's really a way to figure out unresolved questions in your own life in a certain way."

By now Pollack was firmly in charge, pulling strings and controlling personal interactions. The real problem lay in the fact that as the film's original screenwriter, Laurents was well aware of Redford's discontent yet still had never been afforded a personal discussion with the star. The flow of information had all been controlled by Pollack, who offhandedly rationalized, "I think what got him angry was he never had a face-to-face confrontation with Redford. . . . It was all done through me, in a way."

Pollack felt he had reached the end of the line with Laurents: "It was a beautiful story and a real romance with wonderful dialogue, but the picture wouldn't be as good as it could be if I could not make the Redford character stronger. If Hubbell had a stronger point of view, a more positive way of arguing with her . . . I was trying to make it an even-handed argument. We had to strengthen this guy who took the long view, who found a virtue to waiting, someone who, unlike Katie, felt you can't know with certainty so fast about significant issues."

In Laurents's own words, "Hubbell can see both sides of any problem—that's why things are much more difficult for him," but for Pollack, Laurents still favored Katie too much: "The problem was that Arthur was so protective of the Katie character. . . . I wanted to bring in someone with fresher eyes who didn't have the possessive sense and to that end David Rayfiel and Alvin Sargent came in; there was very little work on Katie—it was dealing with Hubbell."

A furious Laurents felt that his script, the very events of his own life, was growing distorted. Pollack, of course, disagreed: "I did not alter Laurents's story line 'manipulatively,' as Arthur accused. I did it because I had a hunch Bob and Barbra would be magical together, and I knew I had to engage Bob's intelligence."

The film's assistant director, Howard Koch Jr., a veteran of previous films with Streisand, Pollack, Redford, and Stark, provided a unique perspective on the question of authorship. Now known as Hawk Koch, he was one of Pollack's first hires on the film: "Sydney and I knew each other. My father, Howard Koch, had given Sydney his first feature to direct—*The Slender Thread*. I had been an assistant director on *This Property Is Condemned* in 1966, having worked my way up from production assistant to second assistant director. Sydney called me and said, 'You got along with Barbra on *Up the Sandbox*. You worked with Redford when we did *This Property Is Condemned*. I'd like you to come on board.' Redford, in fact, had even asked me to do *Barefoot in the Park* in '67 and at one point, he drove me to his place that eventually became Sundance, so we had spent time together.

"For her part, Barbra and I had worked on *Sandbox* and my father had produced *On a Clear Day*. At that time he would screen movies at home for Barbra and Elliot Gould and I'd be there as well, so she knew me. I liked both Barbra and Bob and they each trusted me—it's important that there be a sense of trust between the actors and the first AD. I always used to say there was no room for a woman named 'Miss-communication' on the set. We're all in it together—you become a team, a family. When Sydney told me that it was Bob and Barbra in a love story, I knew it was going to be special and I definitely wanted to join.

"I was fortunate in that I was hired four months before shooting began so I was around during a great deal of the preparation and pre-production. I had seen firsthand on *This Property Is Condemned* how labor intensive the script process was with Sydney. There's a scene at the end of that movie where Redford and Natalie Wood have broken up, and that scene was rewritten four or five times before Sydney was satisfied. Francis Ford Coppola and Jim Bridges had worked on it and Sydney also brought David Rayfiel down on location to work on it until he was satisfied. So—I wasn't surprised that Sydney brought in Rayfiel and Alvin Sargent on *The Way We Were*. I never met Arthur Laurents, but during prep, Sargent was working on a rewrite and I thought it made a huge difference to the final outcome. I felt it was that draft that made the story into a movie. It really came to life when I read that draft and I always felt he should have received a credit along with Laurents."

It wasn't, however, just Rayfiel and Sargent who were now summoned by Pollack. Contributions were solicited from a veritable who's who of Hollywood screenwriters: Dalton Trumbo, who had lived through the blacklisting and actually been denied his rightful "Story By" Oscar for *Roman Holiday* (1953); Paddy Chayefsky, Judith Rascoe, Francis Ford Coppola, and Herb Gardner were all brought in with instructions to give more heft to Hubbell. Make him less passive. Let the audience discover his beliefs and passions.

The writers went to work on Laurents's script of April 6, 1972. Among the numerous scenes Pollack and Stark disliked were the following:

- Katie seducing boyfriend Frankie McVeigh after the senior prom. The scene was never to be shot.
- Katie's father meeting Hubbell's parents at the time of Katie and Hubbell's wedding. The wedding sequence remained unfilmed.
- A meeting between Katie, Hubbell, and blacklisted screenwriter Brooks Carpenter in which Brooks asks Hubbell to put his name on a screenplay actually written by Carpenter. Hubbell sadly refuses; his name, he tells Brooks, is all he has left, a decision that Katie supports; she is pleased that he still cares about his status as a writer. It was a touching scene, explained the stranglehold the blacklist held on many screenwriters and showed a loving bond between Hubbell and Katie. The scene was never to see the light of day.

Instead, with Coppola, Rayfiel, Rascoe, Sargent, and Pollack himself, all writing, scenes and pages came and went at a dizzying pace; on May 15, 1972, the script ran 151 pages. By June 22, it clocked in at 144 pages, with the length and number of scenes continuing to change on a near-daily basis.

Pollack remained adamant that changes in the political sequences had to be made, that the subject couldn't be raised and instantly dropped or the film would sink into a miasma of ill-defined rhetorical arguments: "My original fear when I took the picture was that you couldn't open up a can of worms like the blacklist and not deal with it." Continuing in that vein, he actually drew analogies to those who witnessed the Holocaust: "I'm going to make a terrible exaggeration here, but I said it's like dealing with Dachau through two people who are neighbors of Dachau. They live next door and see people coming in and they jabber at each other at the terrible things—or the good things, depending on how they see it—that are going on at Dachau. Because the two leading characters seemed to be observers and nonparticipants, it seemed to me to be a terrible cheat. Which is why the first act works so much better than the rest of it. Because she's in the throes of it in the first act, she's in the Young Communist League, she's hawking the leaflets, she's on the barricades. He's observing all this."

To better understand the rationale of those who gave names to the HUAC, Pollack turned to those who had actually been caught up in the Hollywood Red Scare: "I began talking to people like Dalton Trumbo and Abe Polonsky, and I read over and over *Wanderer* by Sterling Hayden, who had been an informer." Hayden, a tall, handsome leading man from the late forties and early fifties, who was also a decorated Marine Corps veteran, had served as a sympathetic witness to the committee and tormented himself ever after over the betrayal. Wrote Hayden in his autobiography, "I don't think you have the foggiest notion of the contempt I have had for myself since the day I did that thing." Explained Pollack, "When I read *Wanderer* and spent time with Hayden, one sentence in the book stuck: 'A stool pigeon should never be tall.' He, Hayden, was taller than everyone around him—the guy was obviously so frightened of what his life would be like without work he did something he paid for the rest of his life. Hayden had a tragic life from then on—he became a big drinker. I didn't want to excuse what they did—I just wanted to make drama out of it."

With the arc of Hayden's life story in his mind, Pollack and his writers began reshaping the script. Said Pollack, "The reason I have been so hung up on Hayden's book is that I keep finding tiny character clues within it that seem like starting points for Hubbell. I think the blacklist should be dead center to the drama rather than keeping it to one side. This in turn makes the political material less talky and more dramatically immediate. Secondly, it fulfills the metaphor of Hubbell as America. And thirdly it gives him something *to do*."

Working with his team of writers, Pollack added a scene in which Hubbell begs the studio head to let him keep his screenwriting job; by this point in the film, he was older, no longer the golden boy, and incapable of effortlessly skating through life. This scene, Pollack felt, finally provided a glimpse of how Hubbell had changed, how even the Hubbell Gardiners of the world can be battered and bruised by life.

A second newly scripted scene took place in Union Station after Katie returns from the Washington, DC, HUAC hearings. Katie and Hubbell would launch into a titanic fight, with Hubbell at last giving as well as he got; this time, it was Hubbell who'd get angry, yelling that none of it matters—that after all the protests, absolutely nothing would change: "I'm telling you—people, people are more important than any goddam witch hunt. You and me—that's what matters more than any principles." Katie would push back: "Hubbell, people are their principles." A battle of determined equals—or at least that's how Pollack viewed the scene—one that Redford felt finally gave Hubbell a strength of character to match the golden-boy looks. Said Redford, "I gave full credit to Sydney. And he did honorably respond to my script concerns. An important last-minute addition came.

Alvin Sargent and Rayfiel wrote Hubbell up finally as someone with a point of view. Until then he was Katie's stooge, the guy who won't either support her Communism or name names."

At times, it seemed as if there were enough writers on *The Way We Were* to form a Writers Guild quorum, with Coppola, Rayfiel (an occasional date of Streisand), Sargent, Chayefsky, Gardner, and Trumbo representing a veritable who's who as well as a who's-writing-what. And while Pollack spent hours, days, and weeks wrangling his writers, he also faced another rather pressing piece of business: casting the entire multimillion-dollar film, from the biggest supporting turns down to the smallest one-line bit: College classmates from the thirties. Katie's political activist friends in the forties. Hubbell's 1950s Hollywood crowd. Phones rang, recommendations were made, and decisions were handed down. Decisions that were then reversed. And then reversed again. But in the end, all of those casting decisions came down to Sydney Pollack.

Which was exactly how he wanted it to be.

Casting the Film

"*Casting is 65 percent of directing.*" —Director John Frankenheimer

When Sydney Pollack looked at the script breakdown, the biggest of the supporting roles and the one requiring immediate attention was that of J.J., Hubbell's best friend from college through the Hollywood years. As it turned out, a favorite for the role emerged quickly: the patrician-looking Bradford Dillman. Explained Pollack, "I looked for a long time for someone to play Redford's sidekick. We read a lot of actors and he emerged very early on as the favorite. He had the Brahmin look."

Dillman was, in fact, to the manor born, having attended Hotchkiss prep school and Yale University, after which he had enlisted in the United States Marine Corps. He was also an actor of substance, having played one of the sons in the world premiere of Eugene O'Neill's *Long Day's Journey into Night* (1956) and winning a Tony Award in the process. In Hollywood, his most notable credit remained a leading role in *Compulsion*, a 1959 film version of the Leopold and Loeb case, in which one of his costars was Orson Welles. Married to the beautiful model and actress Suzy Parker, Dillman understood the privileged world of J.J. and Hubbell and happily signed on for a film that, thanks to its two stars, was generating buzz even before shooting began.

In a surprise move, the beautiful and unknown Lois Chiles was tapped to play Carol Ann, a college classmate, J.J.'s paramour, and Hubbell's adulterous bedmate. With near-perfect features capped by blue eyes and a knowing half-smile, she certainly looked the part of a gorgeous young woman who was cool, reserved, and certain of her place—one who resembled a female version of Hubbell. She was also, at this point in her career, a complete unknown.

A native of Houston, Chiles came from a well-to-do family in the oil business and had been discovered by *Glamour* magazine while attending Finch College. Interested in an acting career, she enrolled in classes with Sandy Meisner, but it was really thanks to Ray Stark that Chiles landed the role; in later years Pollack even admitted, "I met a lot of different girls for that role. I don't remember how I found Lois Chiles. It was actually her first role—with billing of 'introducing Lois Chiles.'"

Pollack may not have remembered how Chiles was cast, but Chiles certainly did: "I had actually starred opposite Clifton Davis in a low budget—$350,000—feature called *Together for Days*, directed by Michael Schultz. The movie then opened in two theatres—in Houston where I grew up, and in Detroit—but it died at the box office. Ray, however, remembered the film, and remembered seeing me in it. That's what made him interested in casting me as Carol Ann.

"I was, at this point, young, living in New York City, and definitely not savvy. The phone rang one day and after I picked it up—something I didn't usually do—I heard a voice saying: 'This is Ray Stark.' I have to admit I didn't know who Ray was. And then Ray said, 'Do you want to be a movie star more than anything?' I was pretty cheeky in those days and I instantly shot back: 'Is this an obscene phone call?' Ray just said, 'No—I'm at an Italian bar with Arthur Laurents and Sydney Pollack—we're casting a movie and would like to see you.' I met the three of them, and they gave me the part. There was no screen test, and I really think it was Ray pushing for my casting that did it. He actually ended up signing me to a three-picture contract—the sort of contract that was just then going out of fashion. I wasn't focused on becoming a big Hollywood star, but I was very interested in being a part of such a major Hollywood film."

For the role of Bill Verso, Katie's hard-driving but nice-guy boss at the radio station, it was Redford who suggested his friend Herb Edelman. The 6'5" balding Edelman, a native New Yorker who had originally enrolled as a preveterinarian major at Laurents's alma mater Cornell, seemed to personify the quintessential New York personality of a radio man in the 1940s. By this time, Edelman had worked consistently in television and appeared in the feature films *In Like Flint* (1967) and *I Love You, Alice B. Toklas* (1968), but he scored most prominently with two nicely judged supporting roles in Neil Simon's *Barefoot in the Park* (1967) and *The Odd Couple* (1968). Said Pollack, "Herb Edelman and Redford were pals from *Barefoot in the Park*. Redford suggested him for the role. He was great in the role and he and Barbra worked very well together—they had a nice camaraderie."

Edelman's Bill Verso would appear prominently in the 1940s World War II section of the film, as would the oddly named Pony Dunbar, Katie's coworker and friend. Just as he had sensed Edelman and Streisand would work well together, Pollack intuited that Sally Kirkland, a native New Yorker who was energetic, talented, and slightly eccentric, would make Pony Dunbar a good friend to activist Katie Morosky. Deepening the connection on a personal level was the fact that Kirkland had been a fan of Barbra ever since seeing her at the Bon Soir in the early stages of Barbra's career: "As a kooky personality, she presented herself in such a charming, loving ballsy way. She had the guts to be a comedienne just by being a person. Sometimes when people see performers like Cyndi Lauper or Madonna they don't realize that Barbra started that, in a way." Kirkland had booked very small roles in four films (the most prominent being *Blue* in 1969, starring Candice Bergen) but alongside her rather prominent personality, lay a substantial talent, and she was quickly signed.

The role of George Bissinger, Hubbell's director in Hollywood, had been based on the still-living but already legendary Irish actor–director John Huston and was soon assigned to the equally Irish Patrick O'Neal. O'Neal, who in fact starred in Huston's 1969 film *The Kremlin Letter* and even named his son after the director, had established his acting chops as far back as 1961 with a starring role on Broadway in Tennessee Williams's *The Night of the Iguana*. He followed that with prominent supporting roles in films ranging from Sean Connery's *A Fine Madness* (1966) to the William Holden–led *Alvarez Kelly* (1966). With O'Neal's firsthand knowledge of Huston as both friend and director, he would, Pollack felt certain, bring authenticity to the role of Huston's fictional counterpart. (As it turned out, O'Neal's one problem was knowing Huston too well. Said the actor, "I think Huston is very easy to play. He's a very theatrical person. My problem isn't how to play him but how to keep from playing him too much. Sydney keeps saying 'A little less John, please.'")

Part of the Hollywood crowd surrounding Hubbell was to be his agent Rhea Edwards, who begins as a friend and ally before ultimately turning informer. The role was seemingly modeled on Meta Rosenberg, who worked in the story department at Paramount and about whom Dalton Trumbo said, "[She] behaved like most informers when called before HUAC: she gave the names of communists she probably did not like and withheld the names of communists she probably did like, my name among others, though I was in jail when she testified." To play this complicated character, Pollack quickly cast one of his favorite actors, Allyn Ann McLerie.

McLerie, an acclaimed musical theater performer who had danced for both Jerome Robbins and George Balanchine, had actually worked briefly with Streisand when cast as a Ziegfeld Follies friend of Fanny Brice in the stage production of *Funny Girl*, but her role was cut during the show's tumultuous out-of-town tryouts. By then, she was based in Hollywood, having moved there in the 1950s and amassed a wide range of credits stretching from the Doris Day vehicle *Calamity Jane* (1953) to television guest spots on *Bonanza* and *The Waltons*. Said Pollack, who also cast McLerie's husband, George Gaynes, in the role of the maître d' at El Morocco, "Allyn Ann is a sensational actor as is her husband George Gaynes. She was in *They Shoot Horses* and *Jeremiah Johnson*—she's a wonderful, versatile actress." Having happily worked with Pollack and Redford on those two previous films and being especially interested by the juicy scene in which Rhea tries to justify her supplying of names to the HUAC, she quickly signed on.

Cast in the role of Katie's Hollywood friend Paula Reisner, a socialist writer modeled on screenwriter Salka Viertel (Peter's mother and rumored lover of Greta Garbo) was Viveca Lindfors. A native of Sweden who was now an American citizen, she was a member of the Actors Studio and had starred on Broadway in *Anastasia*. Lindfors brought a foreigner's sensibility to the role of Katie's lone Hollywood female friend, a fellow outsider who despised the pretensions of the film world as much as did Katie.

Another small but flavorful Hollywood role, that of blacklisted writer Brooks Carpenter, was to be filled by Murray Hamilton, a trusted character actor who had started as a Warner Brothers messenger boy before graduating to the starring role of Ensign Pulver in Broadway's 1948 smash hit *Mr. Roberts*. Film credits ranged from Billy Wilder's *The Spirit of St. Louis* (1957) and Otto Preminger's *Anatomy of a Murder* (1959) to *The Hustler* (1961) and *If It's Tuesday, This Must Be Belgium* (1969). The role of Carpenter had been created to give a sense of the writers who refused to cooperate with the HUAC, and in these early stages of the script's development, the character was slated to give a stirring speech in defense of individual liberties at a large-scale political rally. It was a role that could easily be handled by Hamilton, who had recently acquired a certain type of recognition as Mr. Robinson, husband of the adulterous Mrs. Robinson (Anne Bancroft) in 1967's *The Graduate*.

The roster of the remaining supporting roles was notably filled out by the then completely unknown James Woods, who landed the small but interesting role of Frankie McVeigh, Katie's college boyfriend and fellow member of the Young Communist League. Said Woods, "I was appearing in a bad play in East Hampton that was not well received by the audience. I didn't know it at the time, but Arthur Laurents came to see the play and thought I did a good job. I had never done a movie, aside from a strange sixteen millimeter film directed by Elia Kazan that never really saw the light of day, but Arthur recommended me to Sydney Pollack. When I received the offer for *The Way We Were* I was startled—no question about it. The part originally had only five lines but I didn't care—I wanted the role."

He signed his contract instantaneously and later laughed, "I was so unknown to Pollack that when I got to Schenectady for the start of location shooting and was standing with the extras, Sydney walked by and said, 'I bet you're the guy playing Frankie McVeigh.' He wasn't even sure!" (Pollack applied a similar casual approach to the extras. Recalled Andrew Richman, then a student at Union College, "I was chosen as an extra and Sydney Pollack had everyone who wanted to be an extra meet at Memorial Chapel. As he walked down the rows of Memorial Chapel, I shouted out to him, 'How about a part for a Jewish kid from Brooklyn.' I knew that he was Jewish and had grown up in Brooklyn and he said to me 'Go and get a costume.'") Woods's name would be buried among the credits, running well after those of Dillman, Chiles, O'Neal, Lindfors, McLerie, Hamilton, and Edelman, but it represented a first feature film role, and one he felt could get him noticed.

Pollack continued to juggle these casting demands with the signing of his production designer, cinematographer, and costume designer. In turning to men and women with whom he had not yet collaborated but whose work he admired, Pollack knew that in the hands of his award-winning team, *The Way We Were* would be suffused with the period detail crucial to the film's appeal. Production designer Stephen Grimes, cinematographer Harry Stradling Jr., and costume designer Dorothy Jeakins. Hollywood A-listers. Team players. When to begin?

Yesterday.

Designing *The Way We Were*

Steven Grimes—production designer

> *"He must have knowledge of architecture of all periods and nationalities. He must be able to visualize and make interesting a tenement or a prison. He must be a cartoonist, a costumier, a marine painter, a designer of ships, an interior decorator, a landscape painter, a dramatist, an inventor, a historical and, now, an acoustical expert."* —Academy Award–winning production designer William Cameron Menzies defining his job

The look, the physical settings, and the very texture of the film would all begin with one man: production designer Steven Grimes. The forty-five-year-old Grimes's trademark skill, one that made him sought after by directors ranging from David Lean to Peter Yates, was his ability to prepare beautiful and extremely detailed, atmospheric sketches that provided invaluable road maps for directors and cinematographers alike. Eventually collaborating with John Huston on no fewer than fourteen films, Grimes amassed a list of credits stretching from *Lawrence of Arabia* (1962) to his Academy Award–nominated work on Huston's *The Night of the Iguana* (1964). He first collaborated with Pollack on *This Property Is Condemned* in 1966, and shortly before *The Way We Were*, had provided extraordinary work on Lean's *Ryan's Daughter* (1970). Enthused Pollack about the designer, "Steven Grimes—I stole him from John Huston!

Grimes stayed on when I took over *This Property Is Condemned.* He worked mostly with John Huston and David Lean. He was an ex-pat—and he was an artist."

William Kiernan—set decorator

Signing on with Grimes was the five-time Academy Award–nominated set decorator William Kiernan, whose career stretched back to 1943. Kiernan, Grimes, Pollack, and Redford had all worked together on *This Property Is Condemned*, and Kiernan had worked with Streisand on William Wyler's *Funny Girl.* With five Academy Award nominations for films ranging from the musical extravaganza *Pal Joey* (1957) to Robert Wise's *The Sand Pebbles* (1966), Kiernan was now on the verge of retirement but intrigued by the challenges afforded by the decade-spanning material, signed on for what was to prove his last feature film production.

Harry Stradling Jr.—cinematographer

> *"A period film is a gift for the cinematographer."* —Academy Award–nominated cinematographer Rachel Morrison

Hand in hand with Grimes's and Kiernan's decisions would lie the choices made by cinematographer, Harry Stradling Jr., selected by Pollack for an expansive vision capable of capturing the sought-after balance between the nostalgia-laden romance of 1930s college life and the light/dark reality of 1950s Hollywood.

Stradling, a forty-seven-year-old veteran director of photography and Oscar nominee for his work on *1776* (1972), was particularly known for his work on Westerns, eventually shooting no fewer than eighty-seven episodes of *Gunsmoke.* The year 1971 had found him working with Hawk Koch, the assistant director of *The Way We*

Were, on the Western *Something Big* in Durango Mexico, an experience highlighted for Koch by Stradling's setup of six cameras for a big action sequence; with all the cameras positioned and the lighting finalized, someone asked Stradling to take a picture of the setup only to find out, in Koch's recall, "one of the biggest cinematographers in Hollywood had no idea how to operate an instamatic camera!"

What Stradling did know, however, was how to glamorize stars by highlighting assets and disguising problems. He possessed one additional asset when it came to photographing *The Way We Were*: his recently deceased father, Harry Stradling Sr., had photographed Barbra Streisand's first four films—*Funny Girl*; *Hello, Dolly!*; *On a Clear Day You Can See Forever*; and *The Owl and the Pussycat.* It was Stradling Sr.'s particular talent to photograph female movie stars in the most flattering possible manner, adjusting lenses and lighting in order to best capture each star's attributes. In the words of his son, "He made [the women] look good. . . . You've got to want them to look good."

Barbra had formed a close bond with Stradling Sr. (Oscar winner for both *The Picture of Dorian Gray* [1945] and *My Fair Lady* [1964]), one informed by a decidedly mutual respect; the cinematographer had endeared himself to the star by answering her endless questions and treating her palpable intelligence with not just respect but also admiration. Stated Stradling of the star at the time of *Funny Girl*, "I like the nose. No, you can't make Barbra look like Marilyn Monroe. But she does have a beautiful face—because she's got something back of it."

Such praise, explained Stradling Jr., was not just for the purposes of puff-piece publicity: "He liked working with her. He thought she was a fantastic woman. Brilliant. I'd talked to my father a great deal so it was almost like I knew her. . . . He used to talk about her a lot. He'd say how soft she was; how fast she would pick things up; how she'd ask why aren't you doing this, why did you do that?"

As a result, even before filming on *The Way We Were* had begun, Stradling Jr. was armed with the knowledge that Streisand favored her left profile. He approached her with great care, photographing her differently outdoors than in: "[Y]ou can never photograph her outside. You have to build something over . . . with daylight coming down on her nose, it looks awful . . . so you shade that all off, and light it. It's very difficult to do. . . . There's a mental strain there. At the end of the day you're exhausted. But that's what you're there for. And that's what she's there for as well." In fact, as filming progressed, the rapport between star and cinematographer progressed to the point that when Barbra humorously but pointedly said of one lighting setup, "Your father never did it like that!" Stradling Jr. simply answered, "That's because I never showed him how."

That attention to detail informed the strong relationship between Streisand and Stradling Jr., and after editor Margaret Booth complained that Streisand was looking overexposed in the dailies, Barbra called Stradling directly in order to express her support. Said Streisand to her cinematographer, "Harry, I saw the film and I thought it was very good." Added Stradling in gratitude, "She didn't have to do that at all. She could have said it the next day. She need not have said anything." A sympathetic Stradling protected his star, explaining, "[My main goal] was to make Barbra Streisand look good. . . . Every now and then Robert Redford would get a little grumbly because every shot was always lined up to suit Barbra. But she was the only person I had to please. If she was happy that's all that mattered."

Pollack and Stradling decided that in keeping with Pollack's preference, the film would be shot in the traditional Scope 2:35:1 ratio. Explained the director, "My feeling has always been that Scope is my favorite way to shoot. I don't think of Scope just as a big outdoor form—a way to get more information than any other on-screen in seconds. Scope helped a lot in this movie—in terms of being close to a person and still having a sense of environment, place, and mood around you. It's particularly good in a two person scene. You can have the tightness of a close-up and still have both people."

By now, Grimes was signed and hard at work, and Stradling had outlined his requirements for film stock and cameras, which left one key design element to be finalized: who would and could realistically clothe Barbra Streisand from dumpy, youthful Communist radical to 1950s Hollywood sophisticate? Who was also capable of designing an appropriate wardrobe for Robert Redford that ranged from college and the wartime navy to postwar casual California lifestyle? And, oh yes, outfit hundreds of extras in period clothes?

The answer lay in the extraordinary talent of three-time Academy Award–winner Dorothy Jeakins, a sensitive soul, who by this time had lived a life that made Katie Morosky appear to have been raised in the lap of luxury.

Dorothy Jeakins—costume designer

> *"Her special talent is to make costumes look real and not like costumes."* —Robert Wise

Born in 1914, Jeakins had been abandoned by her parents at an early age; her father took the five-year-old Dorothy away from her mother and over the next several years, proceeded to hide the youngster in a succession of foster homes. At one point, young Dorothy survived only by begging on the streets of Los Angeles alongside her abusive foster mother. Describing herself as "pathologically shy and neurotically modest," Jeakins discovered her talent for drawing at an extremely young age and began in the film industry by painting cells of Mickey Mouse for $16 per week. She soon married, and with her husband stationed in Paris during World War II, found herself raising two children on her own. Still dealing with the psychological ramifications of having been deserted by her parents, she suffered a second severe trauma when her husband decided not to return home from Paris.

She supported her family with work as a wardrobe illustrator at 20th Century Fox, and when director Victor Fleming (*Gone with the Wind* and *The Wizard of Oz*) looked through her portfolio, he was so impressed by her abilities that he instantly made her co-designer of his epic film *Joan of Arc*. Starring Ingrid Bergman, that 1948 film won Jeakins the Oscar for Best Costume Design in the very first year the award was given. She followed that triumph by winning a second Oscar the next year for Cecil B. DeMille's *Samson and Delilah*. Her talent for bringing long-ago times to life had in fact been informed by a personal life molded by her own sense of abandonment; she lacked any sense of roots and in her work, found an "affinity for the past"—a past that she could design and control herself.

She felt most at home with period clothes that required the attention to detail she loved to provide, in the process forming an artistic sensibility that made her ideal for the decade spanning *The Way We Were*. Said Jeakins, "I'll let my imagination work for me, seeing a character as a person I might know. . . . I'll place swatches of color around the floor, colors for background and foreground, all the while I'm sifting for a unifying theme. To me, all the world's like a Cezanne painting, brimming with color." On *The Way We Were*, production designer Stephen Grimes's detailed paintings provided a wealth of information for Jeakins, who insisted on authentic details in all of her designs; if period-accurate clothes required buttons, then buttons it would be, even if no one would ever see them.

Actors felt safe with Jeakins, and in the words of actor–producer John Houseman, "She very seldom tries to impose her own quirks or ideas on the actors. She works for the script rather than the flash." Asked for her own philosophy of design, she murmured, "The canvas is the script and the designer is the painter."

All of which made Jeakins ideally suited to design for Streisand and Redford, the 1970s incarnations of larger-than-life golden-age stars. With her soothing personality, Jeakins would be able to calm fears and answer the endless questions lobbed her way by the opinionated Streisand. They would work well together.

Or so it seemed at the time.

John Burnett and Margaret Booth—film editors

> *"The notion of directing a film is the invention of critics—the whole eloquence of cinema is achieved in the editing room."*
> —Orson Welles

There was one key member of the production team—or as it turned out, two—still to be set: editor. The ever-controlling Pollack wanted to exercise total power over the cutting of the film, a fact he made crystal clear when explaining his conception of the editor's job: "They're really paid to execute. They're specialists in their own field but none of them are paid to conceptualize in any way. And there's no way that I wouldn't edit every frame of my own picture, because what is the alternative? The alternative is that somebody could make it into a whole other film. They could change the rhythm of what you did, they could be on the wrong person at the wrong time, they could cut an acting moment in half."

And to fit that rather high-handed description, Sydney Pollack had chosen John F. Burnett, then in the earliest stages of a distinguished Emmy-winning career, who had already edited Streisand's *The Owl and the Pussycat* (1970). Skilled, but capable of taking his marching orders from Pollack, Burnett had worked his way up the Hollywood ladder after beginning his career as an uncredited assistant editor on Billy Wilder's *The Spirit of St. Louis* (1957). He had followed up that oftentimes deliberately claustrophobic Jimmy Stewart vehicle with a trio of expansive musicals, *The Music Man* (1962), *Gypsy* (1962), and *My Fair Lady* (1964), and after branching out on his own as sole editor of the well received *The Heart Is a Lonely Hunter* (1968), he cut *Suppose They Gave a War and Nobody Came* (1970) and Blake Edwards's interesting Western *Wild Rovers* (1971).

Just one potential fly in the ointment loomed; even though he would retain sole credit as editor, Burnett would be working alongside another editor, and not just any run-of-the-mill-cut-it-together-and-move-on journeyman. Instead, courtesy of the dictatorial Ray Stark, John Burnett would now be working alongside the revered Margaret Booth. Sydney Pollack was not well acquainted with Booth, but he realized, how could he possibly object? By this time, Booth had been cutting films for fifty years and already was, in the director's words, "a legend in Hollywood."

Born in 1898, Los Angeles–native Booth had literally grown up with Hollywood itself. She started her Hollywood career as a "patcher," editing films directed by D. W. Griffith while learning the language of film alongside her fellow pioneers: "When I cut silent films, I used to count to get the rhythm. . . . If I was cutting a march of soldiers, or anything with a beat to it, and I wanted to change the angle, I would count one-two-three-four-five-six. I made a beat for myself."

Her official list of credits at MGM, including *Romeo and Juliet* (1935) and the Garbo classic *Camille* (1936), only hints at the dozens of films on which she consulted in her capacity as "supervising film editor"; her enormous impact on the industry lay in her work as a pioneer of "invisible cutting," a style in which one image seamlessly blends into another to further the forward momentum of the story. So acute was her influence that the *Village Voice* newspaper referred to her as "the final authority of every picture the studio [MGM] made for 30 years." In the Booth style of editing, narrative remained dominant, which in Ray Stark's worldview, meant that she was an ideal fit for Pollack. Pollack, a mere whippersnapper compared to Booth, was in no position to question Booth's role. It was, he said, the first time he had not picked his own editor, but thanks to Stark, Booth was signed, sealed, and delivered. Booth and Burnett it would be.

The last pieces of the team were now put in place: Streisand's hair would be handled by Kaye Pownall, who had worked with Barbra on previous films, and her longtime makeup artist Don Cash Jr. would once again be on board. Said Cash to Pownall, "Knowing Barbra like I think I do, this is the *perfect* part for her. If she plays it right, she'll win an Oscar."

Oscars, however, were not paramount on anyone's mind at the moment. Instead, with the scouting trip to Cornell University having proved a failure, where exactly was this multimillion-dollar production going to film? Yes, interiors could be scheduled for the Burbank Studios, but authentic-looking period locations needed to be locked in for the 1930s college sequences as well as World War II–era New York City and sun-drenched 1950s Hollywood. It wasn't just that the Cornell campus of 1972 could never pass muster as an ivy-clad university from thirty-five years earlier. It was that with all of the ensuing script delays and the start of a new academic year, second-choice Williams College, which had provisionally granted permission for three weeks of filming from August 14 to September 5, was no longer available. Finally, further scouting trips resulted in the decision to film at Union College in Schenectady, New York, a small liberal arts institution that with careful shooting and set decoration, could comfortably pass as an Eastern college campus circa 1937.

No physical transformation of the Union College campus would prove necessary, and the production team instead made use of the arboretum, gymnasium, track, and sorority houses. Seven hundred fifty college students, one-third of the Union College student body, were now drafted as extras. Whether or not that high number was just a piece of Hollywood press-agent puffery, what was certain was that the student extras, cast by Jack Saunders, were to be paid a mere fifteen dollars per day plus lunch. The female students would be outfitted in saddle shoes and long skirts, while male students, sporting pleated pants and period haircuts, were required to shave off any beards, mustaches, or long sideburns.

Two weeks of location shooting in Schenectady, New York, wouldn't make anyone soon forget Paris, but *The Way We Were* had found its on-screen home. Laying heavily on the minds of all the designers, however, were the very specific requirements of a period film: one misplaced television antenna, one modern car or item of clothing, and all believability would fly out the window, squashing Katie and Hubbell's romance with a reminder of the bitterly divided Vietnam-era America waiting outside the movie theater's front door.

Like an invading army, *The Way We Were* production team geared up to travel cross country, the location work in Schenectady to be followed by a peripatetic week of shooting in New York City during the first week of October. Permits were now secured for Manhattan locations:

- Grand Central Station
- The 5th Avenue main branch of the New York Public Library
- The streets outside of St. Patrick's Cathedral
- 18th Street and 3rd Avenue
- A cocktail lounge at the top of Beekman Tower
- Sutton Place

After the completion of location shooting in Manhattan, *The Way We Were* company would return to Los Angeles for the bulk of the interior scenes as well as additional exteriors. Los Angeles locations were to include the University of Southern California, Malibu Beach, and such historic sites as Marion Davies's estate. Golden-age studio mogul Jack Warner's office on the Warner Brothers lot would double as George Bissinger's office, hopefully lending the film additional layers of authenticity given Warner's real-life status as a friendly witness during the HUAC hearings.

New York's El Morocco nightclub, complete with two hundred extras in period dress, was to be re-created on Columbia Pictures Stage 21 in Burbank, and while Jeakins and her assistants could handle the grand-scale costuming of so many extras, frustration had set in for the designer when it came to designing Katie's fifty plus costumes. The genteel Jeakins, who after her crushing experience with the autocratic Cecil B. DeMille on *Samson and Delilah*, religiously eschewed any overt conflict, had reached her limit: "Barbra would say yes to a design, then no, then approve a second version, then change her mind again." After designing three-quarters of the costumes, Jeakins was replaced at her own request, telling her successor Moss Mabry, "I can't stand all this confusion and indecision."

The fifty-five-year-old Mabry, under contract to Columbia Pictures since 1968, had a resume nearly as complete as Jeakins's, having designed *Dial M for Murder* (1954), *The Manchurian Candidate* (1962), *Mutiny on the Bounty* (1962), and *Bob & Carol & Ted & Alice* (1969). A three-time Academy Award nominee, Mabry was also the man who had put James Dean into the famous red jacket he wears throughout *Rebel Without a Cause*. After signing his contract in July of 1972, Mabry enthused, "I haven't been this excited about a film in a long time. Barbra wears sixty-two changes of wardrobe ranging in feeling from 1937 to 1952. If this isn't a designer's dream—I don't know what is."

Used to working with the biggest of stars, Mabry quickly developed a rapport with Streisand, who asked for designs that emphasized her breasts and rear. Said the designer, "She's got wonderful buns. And one of the most beautiful busts in Hollywood. And beautiful skin."

When it came to the costumes, second assistant director Jerry Ziesmer related exactly how the differences between Redford and Streisand played out. Trying on his white naval uniform, Redford placidly stood in front of a mirror as Dorothy Jeakins, Sydney Pollack, and Pollack's brother Bernie, the film's set wardrobe man, all worried about the fit, the medals chosen, and the color. Redford's response? A laconic, "Guys, it's fine. A uniform's a uniform, OK?" When Streisand entered for her wardrobe test, however, the questions began: "What color's the set in the El Morocco? What am I wearing? The blue? With the white and the hat? What do I wear when we meet again? Not the darker blue? Could I have changed? I don't want to wear the same thing the whole picture!"

Her questions were not meant to cause difficulties, but instead, she simply worried every detail into the ground in pursuit of the best possible performance. Said assistant director Hawk Koch, "Barbra is . . . funny, smart, passionate about her work, and a consummate professional. She brings you in, and she wants to discuss and ask questions about the work. She wants to make sure that what ends up on film is exactly what you came there to get." To Jerry Ziesmer, her approach was reminiscent of Al Pacino's: "Both Al and Barbra stopped only when the director convinced them they had done their best." Without the director calling halt, both actors would gladly have continued to film take after take in pursuit of their perfectionist visions.

Including all of the newly designed Moss Mabry costumes, the final budget for the movie now came in at $5 million ($36 million in 2023 money), with filming scheduled to wrap on December 3, 1972, right before the opening of Streisand's *Up the Sandbox*. The planned release date for *The Way We Were*: October 24, 1973.

And while the designers completed their work and new pages arrived in a continuing flurry on August 28, September 5, and September 11, Pollack spent time rehearsing Redford and Streisand. Utilizing a combination of walk-throughs on an empty soundstage taped out to resemble the El Morocco set, with discussions in his office, Pollack's methods led Jerry Ziesmer to observe, "Redford could be given direction, and he'd act on it immediately. Barbra got the direction from Sydney and then would have to chew on it while she'd talk of other things, like wardrobe or the set dressing or the lines. But finally she'd come back to the point where the direction had been given and the rehearsal could continue."

With college locations prepped, it fell to Jerry Ziesmer to organize travel plans for cast and crew, plans that began with Streisand and Redford flying East ahead of the crew, each star accompanied by a friend who doubled as hair or wardrobe assistant. Next came some seventy members of the production team who all flew together, with the camera crew lugging a substantial amount of their equipment onto the plane as "extra luggage." Yes, equipment could be rented in New York City and transported to Schenectady, but the camera department wanted no surprises on location when it came to cameras and lenses, so along for the ride went the very expensive equipment.

Even before takeoff, however, the trip got off to a bumpy start, when two agitated members of the hair and makeup team insisted to Ziesmer, "We are with Barbra." In status-conscious Hollywood, those words meant exactly one thing: whether on the same plane with the star or not, by virtue of association, they felt themselves deserving of first-class accommodation. As the argument on board the plane gathered intensity, the sudden appearance of Sydney Pollack walking back from first class quieted everyone. Praising the hair and makeup styles seen in the wardrobe tests, styles engineered by these very same malcontents, Pollack carefully asked if that same wonderful look could be duplicated during filming. Feathers smoothed by the director's flattery, the proud answer came back that yes, in fact they could. Said the director as he exited back to first class, "You two are the greatest!"

Take off cleared, the seventy-odd members of the cast and crew were now winging their way to Schenectady, New York, for the September 18, 1972, start of filming. Barbra and her five-year-old son, Jason Gould, would be living in a Victorian house near the Union College campus, with the crew lodged at a local hotel and Redford and Pollack staying in suites at the Holiday Inn.

The Way We Were had already survived the firing of its screenwriter, a star who hated his role, and power struggles between producer Ray Stark and a director who publicly confessed to doubts about the very viability of the film's political content. Barbra Streisand staying in a rental house in Schenectady? Robert Redford living in a Holiday Inn? Ready or not, *The Way We Were* was about to begin.

On the Set and Ready to Roll

"Pollack was very much in control—I'd even say controlling."
—Production assistant Art Smith Jr.

As the crew readied the very first shot of *The Way We Were* on the Union College campus, Barbra Streisand, cocooned in her trailer, grew nervous. The start of any film represented a leap into the unknown, but here was her long-sought-after dramatic debut and one that found her starring opposite Hollywood's leading man of the moment, a man about whom she had developed feelings that only increased the mixture of trepidation and excitement. Said makeup artist Don Cash Jr., "She would never say it, but Barbra definitely had a crush on Redford."

As Barbra's nerves grew, Sydney Pollack asked Redford to go speak to Barbra and calm the waters. Redford's answer: an emphatic no. "I said, 'It feels like that's appropriate. If she's nervous, that's good. We'll meet on the set in the scene. To me, that was more organic. And then, of course, as Barbra and I started to work together, it did become organic." Redford's cautious approach worked. Observed fellow cast member Sally Kirkland, "There was almost a mystery about Streisand and Redford in the way they were together. It was almost like they held onto that mystery in order to keep the romantic sexual tension between them in the film."

Right from the start, the stars reacted differently to the quirks of location shooting. Recalled Andrew Richman, a student extra from Union, "Robert Redford, as I remember, was very friendly and you could find him outside with the extras. The boy or male extras were mostly from Union, and I remember him tossing a football around. Barbra Streisand for the most part would be in her trailer and would come out when she had to shoot." Explained Bernard R. Carman, a production liaison, "Extras and bystanders were repeatedly warned not to talk to the stars, not to ask for autographs, and not to engage them in any way. In Streisand's case the rules were strictly enforced and a few extras who indiscreetly violated the sanctions found themselves dismissed. . . . Between takes, Streisand spent most of her time inside the Winnebago camper that served as her mobile dressing room."

Art Smith Jr., who worked for a short period of time as an East Coast production assistant, found the atmosphere often tense: "At the time I was just out of the army and in college, where one of the professors said we could receive credit for working on a film. I had already worked on *Sesame Street* so a week on *The Way We Were* sounded good to me. It was a very interesting experience; Pollack was very much in control—I'd even say controlling.

"He sat back and analyzed everything. Barbra Streisand was tense—maybe because she was making the transition from singer to dramatic actress. She was often unhappy because she wanted things done just so—she made demands on the art director. Redford was more laid back, a nice guy—kind of an adult California kid. It seemed like there was confusion on the set and that crew members seemed unhappy with all of the constant changes."

And yet according to Jerry Ziesmer, even though Streisand struck a note of separation, "[t]he extras loved Barbra, and they felt they needed to help her. . . . The extras admired Barbra's intense work ethic and the quality of her performance. When Barbra was acting

. . . everyone saw a working actress struggling through rehearsals and trying every avenue of performance before capturing what was best. They struggled with her and rooted her on to her final victory. They felt they were a part of her labors."

Those extras, it seemed, had eyes only for the stars, with proximity the ultimate goal. Said Ziesmer, one of whose responsibilities entailed wrangling the students: "If I had extras for a classroom, they all wanted to sit next to Barbra or Redford. If there was a scene with our stars walking down the street, all of the extras wanted to walk down the same side of the street. About the fourth day with the extras, I noticed that more and more of them were dressing and fixing their hair exactly like Barbra and Redford. On some days of filming I felt I had six or seven clones of our stars."

It was, however, the starkly different acting methods of the two stars that quickly became most noticeable to everyone on set. Barbra would arrive two hours before the shooting call and spend the time studying the scene, getting into hair and makeup, and discussing the day's filming with Pollack. Acutely aware of every element involved in the day's shoot, she had already seemingly developed a director's overview, asking assistant director Ziesmer, "Jerry, let me know when Robert arrives, will you? If you see props send them to me, and set dressing, and I have to talk with Sydney."

By way of contrast, in Ziesmer's recall, Redford "would arrive barely ten minutes before he was due on the set. When Redford arrived he was tanned, handsome, well groomed, charming, and basically ready to perform. . . . He got out of the car, went into his dressing room for five minutes of makeup and then two minutes to get into his wardrobe, and he was ready. The Redford smile came with him," not that he was any less aware of the details than Barbra. Related Ziesmer, "Redford was a lot of fun for the crew, and we enjoyed him even though he'd put us through every kind of testing during the making of the film. He knew a little about everyone's job, and that was very dangerous." It all fit in with the method of working together that Pollack and Redford had honed through previous experience, with the director explaining that the nuts-and-bolts work actually came during preproduction: "The way Redford and I work—we practically live together. Hang out. Sit around. Talk, talk, talk. Then no more talk. He doesn't like to rehearse. He's always been a very intuitive actor."

The quick-speaking Barbra analyzed a scene as meticulously as she did a song in the recording studio, talking it over, examining nuances in forensic detail—and then talking some more. Redford took the opposite approach, noting, "I suppose I have a small anti-intellectual bias. I resist directors who want to intellectualize scenes to death. I want to get in there and do it."

Of his work with Streisand, he analyzed, "Barbra would talk and talk and talk and drive me nuts. And the amusing thing was that after she'd talk and talk and talk, we'd get down to doing it and she'd do just what she was going to do from the beginning."

So all-encompassing was Barbra's eagerness to talk that her makeup artist, onset observer Don Cash, dropped the news that Redford and his entourage took to calling her "Blah-Blah"—"'So how's Blah-Blah today?' That's what he called her all the time—Blah-Blah." It was never done maliciously, explained Cash, and "Even though he had some harmless fun calling her Blah-Blah behind her back, he treated her with respect and she was blown away by that." Out of their different approaches, however, a chemistry evolved: Streisand and Redford really were opposites in every way, qualities that seemed to infuse Katie and Hubbell with an extra layer of meaning. The two stars liked each other, and that, Redford explained, helped them "create an inner life of enjoyment between the two characters."

Robert Redford was simply more self-contained than Barbra, and that difference fed an extra charge into their performances. There was a sensual energy between them that played out in every shared scene, whether drinking beer at a deserted outdoor café or in silent glances suffused with erotic longing. Said Laurents, "She was simply mesmerized because she found him so beautiful, and he was ever so pleasant because he thought he was stealing the movie away from her."

When it came time for a night shoot in the nearby town of Ballston Spa, all of the street's parking meters were removed and the store windows redressed with 1930s fashions. (The period setting included a nicely judged inside joke, with second assistant director Jerry Ziesmer acknowledged as "J. Ziesmer Optician" on the front of one of the stores.) A dozen antique cars loaned by the New York Historical Society completed the set dressing for the two scenes slated to be shot over the course of three nights: the first found coffee shop waitress Katie having to serve Hubbell and his friends. (Figuring that the point of Katie's incessant work was already being made, Pollack cut a scheduled scene showing Katie in her additional job at the local newspaper.) The second scene, involving only Streisand and Redford, featured Hubbell coaxing Katie to cross the street and share a beer to celebrate the sale of one of his short stories.

In that first scene, as Hubbell and his entitled posse of friends enter the coffee shop (Ballston Spa's oddly named "Good-Whip Restaurant and Bakery" on Front Street), the stark differences between the always-struggling Katie and the ever-smooth Hubbell are made abundantly clear: Katie and her boyfriend Frankie work while Hubbell and gang haven't a care in the world. Under Katie's surface disdain lies a decidedly growing interest in Hubbell, and she steals glances at him at the exact same time Frankie jealously eyes her. Remembered Woods, "The coffee shop is a wonderful sequence. Bob said to Barbra, 'Don't look at me. Look down, make me have to bring your eyes up. You're a bit nervous around me—it's first love.' It works very well in the finished film—they found a way to make this a part of falling in love."

It was not Laurents but David Rayfiel who came up with the idea of Hubbell and his friends playing a game of "Best Of" in the coffee shop. For the purposes of *The Way We Were*, it seemed natural that Hubbell and company would debate the best parts of life because they accepted the best as their due. What, they would ask each other, is the Best Bourbon? The Best Ice Cream? Best Ever Saturday? That the idea came from Rayfiel was unsurprising because by the time of *The Way We Were*, he had long since secured his position as Pollack's "go-to" man for rewrites, having supplied uncredited rewrites on both *This Property Is Condemned* and *Jeremiah Johnson*. Writer and director would eventually work together on no fewer than eight films because Rayfiel, in Pollack's estimation, possessed the key asset of "writing elliptically, so that it comes out organically, the way you would know something about someone in real life." So highly did Pollack value Rayfiel's talent that he ultimately used one of Rayfiel's lines in no fewer than four different movies: "You think not getting caught in a lie is the same thing as telling the truth."

What makes the "Best Of" device particularly effective is that it recurs at other key points during the film, most notably ten years later when Hubbell and J.J. play the game while sailing in California. A decade out of college, are they still carefree, or are they rudderless in both the literal and metaphorical sense? Are they content to drift wherever the tide takes them? One can never be quite certain, but by establishing the game as far back as this coffee shop scene, when heard again on the sailboat, it functions as a perfect lead-in to one of the film's most memorable pieces of dialogue. Hubbell and J.J. debate which is the best ever year: 1944? . . . 1945? . . . 1946? . . . , but they cannot arrive at a definitive answer, and as the wind dies down and the boat lazes along without direction, what remains crystal clear is what the audience has known all along: without Katie, Hubbell loses his moral compass, drifting through life on the tarnished aura of his golden charm. It is only now, still meandering on the sailboat, that J.J., in a character-defining bit of dialogue, analyzes the prospective loss of Carol Ann with disinterest—"She wasn't much. I just liked her, having her around"—before offering a surprising but heartfelt comparison to Katie, with whom he has so often been at odds: "It's not like losing Katie—now that would be a loss." It's Katie, the perennial outsider who was never asked to play the "Best Of" game in college, who has come to represent the "Best Of" nearly every aspect of their lives.

For Lois Chiles, whose character of Carol Ann was prominently featured in this college coffee shop sequence, her arrival on set in Schenectady had proved somewhat bumpy: "It would have made my life easier if Ray had shown my first film, *Together for Days*, to Sydney. Sydney didn't know me or where I came from. He hadn't really cast me, so he was looking at me with suspicion at first. It was a tough atmosphere for me. But we got through that and became very friendly. I understood what it was like for Sydney: he was dealing with two of the biggest stars in the business and the script was still being rewritten every day. I was not a priority and I understand that—but I still also felt it at the time. The good thing is that after that rough beginning it all got resolved. Sydney realized that I was really working and really trying."

Having completed the coffee shop sequence, attention now turned to the first genuinely intimate scene between Hubbell and Katie. There were, in fact, three hundred movie fans standing in the street for a glimpse of Streisand and Redford, but they were out of view, utterly quiet, and caught up in the stillness of the moment. That sense of privacy permeated the sight of Hubbell drinking alone at a sidewalk café (newly constructed by the crew directly in front of Ballston Spa's Medberry Inn) before he insists that Katie cross the street to join him. For the first time ever, they banter as equals:

Hubbell: I'm celebrating.

Katie: Why?

Hubbell: I got you to cross the street.

Katie: Do you always smile?

Hubbell (breaking into a grin) No—no!

He breaks down her reserve, and when he tells her the real reason for the celebration—that he has sold one of his short stories—she is thrilled for him.

It's a turning point in their relationship because he has not told any of his own crowd about his good fortune. Instead, he chooses to tell Katie—the outsider, the strident young Communist—and the woman who believes in his talent. They are all alone in the quiet night, and Stradling's carefully detailed lighting increases the sense of intimacy.

It is here that any audience's knowledge of Streisand's own life story lends an extra layer to the proceedings. If Barbra Streisand, the kook from Brooklyn, has spent her life searching for her own over-the-rainbow prince, then she is here living out her fantasy alongside Hollywood's own Prince Charming, and in technicolored thirty-foot-high big-screen splendor no less. It does not matter that Redford didn't want the role of Prince Charming either on- or off-screen; he is here playing it out on-screen for Barbra Streisand and the wallflowers of all stripes relegated to the sidelines out of nerves, jealousy, or insecurity. Streisand may have been a powerful, steely force in Hollywood, but she also maintained a genuine vulnerability that endeared her forever to her hard-core fans. The outsider who demands her own place at the table could still be hurt, and that softer side never would leave her.

In a beautifully judged bit of acting, Streisand conveys Katie's uncertainty through both giggles and a social awkwardness that forces her to fill in the not totally uncomfortable silence by twice repeating the news that the Duke of Windsor has married Mrs. Simpson. What anchors the scene in memory is a telling bit of action courtesy of an Alvin Sargent rewrite: in an understated but highly erotic interlude, the simple act of Hubbell tying Katie's shoe registers with surprising impact. With Katie's shoe resting on his leg, Hubbell reties the laces and looks are exchanged until, in what will become an oft-repeated refrain, Hubbell tenderly exclaims, "Go get 'em Katie." Here, on the eve of graduation, a wistful Katie replies with what will turn into her own oft-repeated mantra, "See you later, Hubbell."

Said Barbra, "It was that little extra pat—he held it a little longer—that's what made it so touching." Pollack himself credits Sargent with the sensitivity that informed the scene so subtly: "That's a certain style of writing. The situation was Arthur's but details like that were Alvin's."

For all the stresses and strains inherent in filming three thousand miles from home, location shooting proceeded quite smoothly, with some unexpected pleasure arriving when the local teamsters invited the production team, including Streisand, Redford, and Pollack, to be their guests at a home-cooked Italian dinner. In Hawk Koch's description, as the drive to the dinner destination grew longer and longer, "Barbra began to worry. . . . She said with a Brooklyn edge, 'Where are you taking me? The food better be good!'" Eventually arriving at a luncheonette on a deserted street, Barbra's concerns did not dissipate: "Are you sure this place is safe?" In Koch's recollection, "'Of course, it is,' I lied." Laughed the assistant director years later, "Those Schenectady teamsters were tough customers. They played Liar's Poker but not with one dollar bills—they played with one hundred dollar bills!" The luncheonette, of course, was completely safe;

everyone enjoyed a terrific home-cooked dinner; and the denouement to the evening only arrived the next week, when the teamsters turned in weekly timecards that included the hours spent preparing the evening dinner. Writing decades later, Koch smilingly explained, "Needless to say, that was one expensive dinner. The lesson I learned was this: clarify, always clarify, or be prepared to eat it."

After two weeks in Schenectady, during the first week of October, *The Way We Were* caravan made the three-and-a-half-hour trip back to New York City for exterior shots before heading to the Burbank Studios in California. The locations had changed, but the daily barrage of new script pages did not, as evidenced by Judith Rascoe's October 5th five-page, single-spaced memo to Ray Stark. In detailing Katie's desperate desire to hold onto her marriage, it was Rascoe who suggested a line for Katie, which Laurents came to particularly dislike: "I like Hollywood. I like Alice Faye. What's not to like?" Laurents never approved of the line, which nonetheless survived the final cut as part of Katie and Hubbell's late-night reconciliation. In fact, in the midst of writing new dialogue for Katie, it was Rascoe who delivered a cogent analysis of exactly why the Hubbell–Katie marriage could not survive: for all their mutual love, their marriage splinters because each possesses an essential element of personality that is harmful to the other.

The New York City location shoot, sometimes smooth, occasionally tense, still produced moments of levity at odds with Streisand's fearsome reputation. In Sally Kirkland's first scene, her character of Pony Dunbar, a friend who has not seen Katie in a long time, spies Katie on West 75th Street, runs up to her, and exchanges a hug. Related Kirkland, "Barbra and I were walking down a street, quite near Central Park West. Barbra is pouring her heart out—we both have tinnitus and there was a lot of traffic noise. We had great difficulty hearing each other, and we kept bumping into each other.

Anyway—we had to hug each other at one point and we had earrings falling out—we both found it funny and she gave me a hug and said 'Sally, I like you—you're just like me.' So by the time the scene was perfect—they cut it. God knows why. . . . I still don't."

Cut scene or not, Kirkland retains a fond memory regarding the dropped earrings: "I'll never forget it because here I made this incredible faux pas and she just laughed. . . . She was vulnerable enough to pick up on my vulnerability." Chatting with Barbra between takes, Kirkland grew increasingly interested. Barbra, she analyzed, "has one of the most insatiable curiosities I've ever seen in anyone."

As location shooting in New York City drew to a close, two scenes remained: a pair of parties in J.J.'s apartment meant to showcase increasing tension between Hubbell and Katie. A fabricated set on a Burbank soundstage might serve handily as Katie's Murray Hill apartment, but for J.J.'s apartment, Pollack wanted an actual New York City location with a view of the East River. Given the twelfth floor location of the apartment in Beekman Towers rented by the production for these scenes, the crew had to unload their equipment trucks on the street and then pack all of the cameras and cables into the building's elevator. Actors went through hair and makeup in trailers parked on the street until, with the apartment readied, the crew departed and the supporting actors familiarized themselves with the set before the arrival of Streisand and Redford.

Actors' director that he was, Pollack walked all of the actors around the apartment, familiarizing them with the setting and discussing the character each was playing. Only then would he block the scene, which for these two party sequences included confrontations and fights among the characters. Ever analytical, Barbra posed a lengthy series of questions, challenging Pollack until she felt comfortable. Recalled Ziesmer, "She had to be convinced that Katie was in the right place for the scene. . . . Was that where Katie would be? Why? Would she be eating? Drinking? Barbra's questions would go on until she was comfortable with Sydney's blocking of the scene." With Barbra and Redford reassured, Sydney would then ask all of the actors to read through the scene—"Don't act. Just try the words"—and with each reading, he would change blocking until each actor felt at ease.

It was only now that the crew was brought back, with the actors rehearsing the scene for the crew's benefit—master shot, establishing shot, close-ups, coverage—the lengthy and confrontational party ate up a great deal of time before both Pollack and the actors were satisfied. The scenes proved crucial because it was here that the antipathy between Katie and Carol Ann would burst into the open; in filming the sequences, Lois Chiles proved particularly admiring of Pollack's approach: "Sydney as director was the general of this collaboration. Barbra kept more to herself but with Sydney—and with Bob—I felt like I had by now fit in, into the whole of the movie and to Sydney's style of directing. I just wanted to keep improving under Sydney's direction."

For this scene, indeed for all of the location sequences, one overarching question lingered: Had Pollack captured the performances he needed from his two stars? It was a doubly pertinent question at this relatively early stage because while Sydney Pollack already knew how to operate with and around Robert Redford, he was still feeling his way with Barbra. The rhythm between Pollack and Redford had been established on their three previous films, and they each knew when to push and argue and when to acquiesce and let go. If they weren't always in agreement, they still worked well together, and for the most part, enjoyed each other's company.

By way of contrast, Streisand had quickly developed a difficult reputation when it came to directors, and early on in the filming of her first feature, *Funny Girl*, one crew member was supposedly heard to quip, "Don't be hard on Barbra—it's the first film she's ever directed."

Was she controlling or just a perfectionist? Argumentative or inquisitive? Three weeks into the East Coast shoot, Pollack was in the process of figuring out those answers, but as the crew packed up for the trip back to Hollywood, the director realized that he had made an unexpected discovery: Barbra Streisand, whom he memorably characterized as possessing "extreme intensity like a dial turned all the way up," was proving to be the least of his problems.

How to Direct Superstars? Carefully

> *"There's a creative way to talk to actors and there's a clumsy way, and Sydney knows the creative way."* —Barbra Streisand

Barbra Streisand, she of the fabled temperament, was proving to be no problem for Sydney Pollack for the simple reason that he was open to discussion with his intense but thoroughly dedicated leading lady. They would, in Pollack's recall, "discuss what this picture was about, where we might have trouble, what was moving to me and what was moving to her. I think it's safe to say she trusted me." Pollack understood not only that Streisand was smart but that her questions and worries came from a place of caring. "When I hear an actress talking to me with an understanding of a role that's so close to my own understanding, that makes me feel confident that we're not going to have a problem. And we didn't. The least of my problems was Barbra, funny enough."

Of Streisand's talent, Pollack possessed not the slightest doubt: "I was knocked out by Barbra's performance in the film of *Funny Girl.* I was so impressed by the reality of her acting so I just wanted to get the best possible performance—I didn't think I was taking her to new ground." Pollack's gaze was fixed on the inherent Streisand acting ability that he felt had sometimes been overwhelmed by the superstar persona. He wanted no falling back on trademark mannerisms and vocal tics but rather the delivery of a clear dramatic performance—"I really wanted to get her back to a kind of simple truth in her performance which I knew she was capable of." From their in-depth talks, Pollack gleaned that Streisand did in fact "want to go straight with this movie and not rely on what we normally expect of her—the timing, the gestures, the facial expressions. She didn't want to use any tricks. She and Redford fed each other. It's really a combination of two rare talents with charisma and acting ability as well."

In short, Sydney Pollack wanted to banish all traces of the larger-than-life musical personality performances that had made thirty-year-old Barbra Streisand an entertainment legend. It was, he felt, his mission to channel her prodigious musical gifts into the dramatic arena: "She has a passion that you can hear in her singing. And her musical talent extends right directly into the acting—I'm talking about rhythms, and hearing even a choice of words that's better than another choice of words. . . . she's not a big girl but she has this ability to create the impression of being much bigger than she is, on-screen, which happens to a lot of stars who're special like that. . . . You can't compare her to anybody. That's a blessing and a curse for her. Makes it tough to cast her, but when she's cast properly . . . I mean there isn't anybody else who could play that part with the same power and impact."

That huge talent came with its own set of problems, and Pollack remained wary: "Of course a dynamo hooked up wrongly is dangerous. There are dangers with a talent on that scale. I think the biggest danger that happens to people like that is that there isn't anybody for them to listen to . . . ninety-nine percent of the people Barbra Streisand deals with are inferior to her in terms of talent." Barbra, he felt, was "like any other enormously talented person. They are never a problem if you can create an atmosphere of trust." There was an analogy, in Pollack's view, to the situation that had always faced

Streisand's acting idol, Marlon Brando: "He knew, like any genius knows, that in his little finger he knew more about acting and theater than these people who were ostensibly telling him what to do. Well, that not only makes you cynical, but it makes you tough on the other people and tends to insulate you from growing."

Barbra Streisand could, in fact, be tough on other people. In her own words, "I'm blunt. It saves me a lot of time but also costs me friends," but Sydney Pollack never did lack belief in his ability to control the entire set and elicit a first-rate performance. In his reasoning, if he felt happy with the performance, then so, too, would the audience: "The only thing I could go by—and it seems arrogant but it isn't—is to assume that, if *I* like it, I can make somebody else like it. Because my passion for it will somehow get on the film."

And that is precisely why, in pursuit of that sought-after dramatic performance, Sydney Pollack would, after a full-day's shooting, talk with a voluble Barbra Streisand. And then talk some more. Before talking some more again. There was no detail too small for gimlet-eyed analysis, which made perfect sense, because part of Streisand's performing genius—and she was, as singer and stage personality, a genius—was her obsessive attention to detail. Nothing escaped her eye, and on the last night of her starring role in *Funny Girl* on Broadway, she was still giving notes to the prop man that there was too much dust on the plastic flowers. . . . Determined to make her dramatic debut work, she was now worrying over every detail—hair, costumes, the tiniest bits of business—it all fed her nightly calls to Pollack: "She'd call at 11 p.m. Oh! My God! Every night! Should I do this? What d'you think if tomorrow, I . . . Suppose maybe I should wear my hair down? When we get to the bed scene, what might be nice, suppose I feed him some grapes or bananas or something?' It was all pushing and testing and trying to cover every base and being a perfectionist, being totally thorough about it, worry it, worry it, worrying it.... Robert Redford's a little like that too. This isn't a problem really. It is just time-consuming."

Streisand was a world-class worrier, but the lengthy discussions with Pollack were just that—discussions, not arguments—a healthy give-and-take among colleagues. Said Barbra, "A lot of directors don't know what they want or how to communicate what they want. They deal in results: 'Do it faster.' But Sydney knows ways to talk to actors that somehow make them feel they're arriving at a new place by themselves. There's a creative way to talk to actors and there's a clumsy way, and Sydney knows the creative way."

Director and star might disagree, but rancor and anger never intruded. They were, Pollack felt, "healthy arguments. They were never ego arguments." As director, he listened carefully, impressed by Streisand's intelligence, and for the most part, happy with his star's input. (In fact, both Streisand and Redford cited Pollack's self-effacing side as something that made them comfortable. Said Jerry Ziesmer, "Sydney was a very quiet person. I never heard him raise his voice.") But even Pollack, it turned out, had his limits: "She's inquisitive, extraordinarily curious, enthusiastic and a very, very hard worker. But sometimes I'd want to say, 'Will you just relax?'"

Unsurprisingly, Barbra worked best with extensive rehearsal, and in fact, her performance deepened with every take. Said Hawk Koch of the filming, "Redford preferred fewer takes but Barbra liked to keep going." Used to repeated takes in the recording studio, where she could change or control any instrument, arrangement, or orchestration, rehearsals on *The Way We Were* allowed her a similar combination of control and freedom. By way of contrast, Redford's approach was more "spontaneous and improvisatory." In fact, Redford never performed the same take twice, which in Pollack's words, "made hell for me and it made hell for the editor to match continuity. Over the years with Bob, I learned to make adjustments, like running five angles on a scene to cover my ass so that it will cut in the editing."

The trick for Pollack was to strike the proper balance between Streisand's love of rehearsal and Redford's preference for improvisation and fewer takes. The goal was a meeting in the middle without undergoing the stress suffered by Joseph Mankiewicz while attempting to find the balance between Marlon Brando's constant rehearsing and Frank Sinatra's one-take approach on *Guys and Dolls* (1955). In that regard, Pollack succeeded, with *The Way We Were* set proving far more collegial than that of *Guys and Dolls*. The nightly viewing of rushes, in fact, was already offering evidence that Redford/Hubbell's lower-key yet appropriately exasperated response to Streisand/Katie's determination actually worked to the film's benefit.

Part of that success may also have been attributed to Pollack's somewhat looser approach to the traditional scene-starting cries of "Speed—Sound—Roll Camera—Action!" In his own telling, "The terrible tragedy for every director is to watch an actor do what you want and not have the camera rolling—and never get it back again. So I always try to roll the camera before anybody's really ready." That is not to say that Pollack was not ever firmly in control. Analyzed Robert Redford, "There's no one more interested in control than Sydney. He's a careful person, he cares about how he's thought of, and he doesn't take chances."

Sydney Pollack was, of course, shepherding two actors whose career goals already included the ultimate means of artistic control: directing. The groundwork for that directing was being laid on the set of *The Way We Were*, with both stars observing Pollack closely. Camera placement, lighting, exploration of character, occasional disagreements—it was all grist for the mill, and within the next decade, each would direct feature films on subjects that seemed to have thematic roots in *The Way We Were*: Redford would win an Oscar on *Ordinary People* (1981)—for directing a story about WASPs—and

Streisand nabbed a Golden Globe for directing her exploration of cultural and religious traditions among Jews in *Yentl* (1983). Both stars had decided opinions, but it was not just Barbra who questioned and cajoled regarding lighting, camera angles, and appearance. Just as Streisand refused to cut her fingernails, Redford would not trim his hair to period-appropriate military length. Said Pollack, "Each of them was a pain in the ass from time to time because they both knew how they liked to be presented."

Beginning with *Funny Girl*, Streisand had always favored being photographed with the left side of her face in profile, insisting, like Claudette Colbert in her heyday, that she had only one good side. Redford rolled with the punches: "A discomfort about her nose from one or the other angle. Fine by me. I acknowledge that kind of thing, when it affects that actors' confidence. I said, 'Okay, whatever works.'" At the same time, Redford himself also liked being shot from his left side. Said makeup artist Don Cash Jr., "In Bob's case he has moles on the right side of his face that sort of pop out on camera. Very distracting." The mutual preference for left-side profile shots made for a problem in face-to-face close-ups, one that Stradling solved by shooting dual close-ups—most notably when Katie and Hubbell dance slowly at the college prom—with "some sort of soft light behind them so there were no harsh shadows on their faces." By staying flexible, Pollack and Stradling had arrived at a practical solution to a potentially troubling artistic problem and had managed to do so without any diminution of quality.

That, though, was not to say that *The Way We Were* was a problem-free set, not by a long shot and not with Arthur Laurents and Ray Stark involved.

In the Heat of Battle

"It's what always happens. It's simply last minute nerves and jitters." —Ray Stark to columnist Joyce Haber regarding *The Way We Were*'s army of screenwriters.

Sydney Pollack's plate, it turned out, was overflowing, and not always with joy. The problems, in fact, started at the very top with a financially shaky Columbia Pictures. As days turned into weeks, the bean counters in the front office grew restive in the face of cost overruns, additional location shooting, and an ever-increasing roster of expensive screenwriters. In Pollack's own blunt assessment, "Truthfully, nobody had any faith in the picture."

At the same time that he was attempting to keep his two stars happy and negotiate the right mix of politics and love story, Pollack was also dealing with the fractious Ray Stark. In Pollack's forthright assessment, "Bob didn't get along with Ray Stark, and neither did I." The mix of three such determined personalities as Redford, Stark, and Pollack was not an easy one, and it was small wonder that Streisand proved to be the easiest of the film's heavyweight presences. Considered Pollack, "Ray was a strong producer, very involved. I'm a rebellious guy with this strong producer; Ray and I have always gotten along but we've always fought—I've done four films with him. We fought hard. . . . He let me do my cut and my shooting but he was very involved." That, in Hollywood-speak, translates as "he was a pain in the ass."

Adding to the problem was Redford's continued unhappiness with the script. Get along with Streisand he did, but Robert Redford was still agitating for more development of Hubbell Gardiner, an on-set reality that Pollack acknowledged: "Bob was worried he would end up as a lump of a sex symbol—he wasn't really happy working on the picture. . . . he was worried about his part." According to one commentator, it got so bad that Redford likened filming to "doing overtime at Dachau."

October 11, 1972, found Pollack himself rewriting the confrontation between Katie and Rhea, and more changes followed on the 13th and 24th, with a key scene between Hubbell and J.J. arriving on the 26th. That extended sequence found the two best friends drifting in Hubbell's sailboat and drinking beer while talking about J.J.'s problems with Carol Ann. It all led to a half-hearted fight between the two men; forced and trite, most of it did not work, but for the time being, into the script it went. With script changes arriving daily, the fact that the script dated October 26 came to be labeled "Shooting version of the screenplay" seemed more of a wish than reality.

The pace of script changes only continued to accelerate, the records revealing that new pages arrived in quick succession on October 28, November 2, November 3, and November 6. Fired by Stark and Pollack, Laurents was no longer a presence on set, but he remained the screenwriter of record and in that position, continued to comment, often acidly, on the script changes with which he was presented. Barely holding onto his temper, on November 6 he wrote a Columbia Pictures inter-office memo to both Stark and Pollack in which he strongly objected to two recently shot scenes concerning politics. The first was the Pollack scripted showdown between Rhea and Katie, and the second a recently written scene of Hubbell and J.J. talking about the Hollywood Ten.

Hollywood veteran Laurents understood that daily script changes sometimes represented the norm on a major film but, he felt strongly, not when submitted by eleven different screenwriters. Aside from Coppola and possibly Trumbo, Laurents was the most well known of the writers, and to have nearly one dozen screenwriters whacking away at his work and distorting the political intent of his movie only served to bring him to the boiling point. This, he felt, was personal. The blacklist scenes were drawn from his own life and in his mind, the new writers, Trumbo excepted, were dealing with a witch hunt about which they knew little. Particularly disgruntled about the proposed cutting of political talk between Katie and Paula (Viveca Lindfors), Laurents felt that the very guts of the film, the politically motivated blacklist designed to ground the entire second half of the film, were being destroyed.

By now, the open secret of a platoon's worth of writers contributing to the screenplay forced Ray Stark to downplay the situation when interviewed by columnist Joyce Haber: "It's what always happens. It's simply last minute nerves and jitters." With eleven writers having rewritten, deleted, and invented sequences and lines of dialogue, the rewrites and rewrites of rewrites had caused holes in the story and the unthinkable happened: Stark called Laurents to ask him back onto the film, exclaiming, "You win, pal!" Wrote Laurents, "Ray was eating crow with enthusiasm."

Why ask Laurents to return at this particular time? Because, in Laurents's retelling, Barbra was now unhappy, and Redford remained displeased: "They wanted me to repair the damage, cover it and make sure that what remained to be shot was kept on track." Secure in the knowledge that he was in the driver's seat, Laurents asked for a great deal of additional money—and received it. He had one more requirement: he would write what he wanted and if others interfered, he'd leave for good. Wish granted.

When the self-admitted "nervous, not even very confident," Laurents arrived back on the set, the first person to greet him—in his recounting complete with a hug and tears—was Lois Chiles. Chiles recalls events differently than did Laurents, but by this time, her immersion in the shoot was thorough, her self-admitted enthusiasm for such a major-league Hollywood experience likely coloring Laurents's recall of hugs and tears. Said Chiles, "I wasn't so focused on looking at this as 'I want to be a movie star.' I was in the right place at the right time. I was a kid, fascinated by the whole process of it all. It was like being a part of a carnival and a circus—the way all the different departments collaborated. That was what I found fascinating, more than thinking about 'oh this is my chance.' I was just so interested by the art of it all."

As to Laurents's on-set reunions with Barbra and Redford, their reactions, like Katie and Hubbell, could only be described as polar opposites. His meeting with Barbra proved a happy one—they were friends of long standing, and after the highly frustrating experience of watching eleven writers work over his script, he loved seeing how zealously Barbra had guarded the character of Katie. Barbra, he felt "had been a wonderful pest, dredging up a scene here, a line there from my early versions, lugging them to the set and utzing Sydney to put them back. She knew Katie Morosky better than he did and fought like hell for her."

The Laurents–Redford relationship, however, remained problematic, and resentments lingered on both sides: Redford was still upset with Hubbell's lack of substance, and Laurents remained convinced that Redford's demands were upsetting the balance of the film. The reaction when star and author actually saw each other again? In Laurents's retelling, Redford fixed him with "a stare of ice that could sink a Titanic and before I could open my mouth, walked by, cutting me dead. . . . Redford glared at me the first day I walked on the set and didn't say hello until a decade later. I had absolutely no idea why and finally thought, 'Oh, fuck him. My money was on Barbra anyway.'"

It did not help matters that neither man ever proved shy in criticizing the other. Redford outlined his objections to the character of

Hubbell bluntly: "As it was written, he was shallow and one-dimensional. Not very real—more a figment of someone's imagination of what Prince Charming should be like." The always combative Laurents gave as good as he got, opining that "Redford does not want to be an actor, he wants to be a 'movie star.'" What's more, Laurents seemed to feel, Redford exemplified exactly what was wrong with all of Hollywood: "Redford glared at me the whole time. I thought the reason was that I was not building his part up. He behaved badly, but that goes with the territory. You can't expect decent behavior from a movie star or anyone else in the industry who stays and lives in Hollywood. They stop being human beings. They're too insecure. They're afraid."

Even while avoiding each other at all costs, both Redford and Laurents got along well with Streisand. In fact the only reported instance of conflict between Barbra and a fellow cast member came from Marcia Mae Jones. A former child star whose career stretched back to 1931, she was here cast as Peggy Vanderbilt, a radio actress cum Hedda Hopper figure, a role that the then fifty-year-old actress called "a good bit, nothing more." Although virtually cut out of the film, she still received billing yet remained disgruntled with Barbra: "Streisand never came over to speak to me—the usual courtesy when an older performer is in a film. . . . Very cold. The set had a chilling feeling. I had never experienced anything quite like it. I was relieved when it was over."

By way of contrast, as the filming of interior scenes progressed smoothly at the Burbank Studios, a second scene between Streisand and Sally Kirkland was scheduled, and this time the scene did make the final cut. It's a brief scene but one developed with a nice sense of rhythm as Katie and Pony are shown working the Office of Information switchboard during the war. Katie, wondering why Hubbell hasn't called her—"It has been a week!"—chats with Pony in rat-a-tat fashion as they field constant calls to the switchboard. Call, response, and physical action at the switchboard all quickly develop the feeling of a bond between Katie and Pony, and while Streisand and Kirkland had not seen each other since that first brief and aborted scene back in New York, the warmth between the two women remained. Explained Kirkland, "And again, it was 'Sally, how are you? What have you been doing?' She couldn't have been more warm. All of these people complain about her rudeness or temper and I never got any of that in *The Way We Were*. What I got was that she was curious about me, really looked, really listened."

For Pollack, it continued to be Streisand, she of the legendary temperament that had supposedly caused people to run for cover on various film sets, who assumed the role of "easiest to deal with because she was very happy with her part." Pollack's viewpoint was echoed by Arthur Laurents's own observations: "There are all those stories in magazines about how Barbra demands this and that, but it never happened in *The Way We Were*. She insisted on little things, like getting her good profile in the close-ups, but otherwise she was letting them maneuver things to be played Redford's way."

There were, in fact, moments of Streisand-centric levity mixed in with the long hours. Relates Hawk Koch, "When I worked with Barbra on *Sandbox*, if she was late coming out of her trailer I'd remind her that her company, First Artists, was producing the film and controlled the money—if she was tardy it was costing her money. I'd say that and she'd laugh and move quickly to the set. On *The Way We Were*, when she was slow coming out of her trailer, I'd say, 'Barbra—c'mon. We're all set and now we're running late.' She'd laugh and say, "It's Ray Stark's money—screw him!"

The El Morocco nightclub, which was to feature so prominently in the first ten minutes of the movie, was now built and decorated on Stage 16 in Burbank, with over one hundred extras in period garb and hairstyles portraying servicemen and couples out for a night on the town. The extras would be called on to dance, and while unlike the college prom, there would be no jitterbugs, they were nonetheless drilled by a choreographer on Stage 12 in the decorous style of dancing suitable for a swank nightclub of the 1940s. So meticulous were production designers Stephen Grimes and William Kiernan in their re-creation of El Morocco that they crafted exact replicas of the club's original matchboxes. Would the matchboxes be seen on camera? No one knew, but for the designers, that wasn't the point—the set had to look, feel, and play authentically.

On the day before shooting the El Morocco sequence, Pollack quietly instructed Ziesmer that no matter how many extras filled the screen, the focus would always remain on the two stars: "Jer, keep the bar area filled with a bit older folks, you know? . . . put the young beauties in the back, over in the dining area; keep the folks around Barbra and Bob . . . well you know . . . a little plainer. Put the prom queens in the back."

The shooting of Katie and Hubbell's reunion in El Morocco proceeded without incident, but it was three weeks later that a highly unexpected moment came on that same soundstage. By now it was November, cast and crew were all tired, and there was a delay as cinematographer Harry Stradling Jr. lit the next shot in Katie's apartment. The El Morocco set had vanished, and nothing remained but the piano. Talking quietly among themselves, those present were at first unaware that Barbra had walked over to the piano and was playing Marvin Hamlisch's theme. Relayed Jerry Ziesmer, "The sounds were pure tones, simple and beautiful, coming across the cold and dreary soundstage. Barbra was lost in her thoughts unaware that we were watching her." Even Sydney Pollack was captivated, and when one person began to speak, the director forcefully whispered, "Shhh! Maybe she's going to sing!"

She didn't—but as the group quietly listened, she became aware of the quiet and in her best Brooklyn-ese, queried the group, "What? What are you looking at?" The crew laughed, as did Barbra, but the memory lingered. Wrote Ziesmer of the moment, "I'll never forget Barbra's playing on the soundstage that day. The impact of the pure, simple tones of her music reaffirmed to me why I left teaching to be in film and to make movies like *The Way We Were* with people like Barbra Streisand."

Several days were spent filming at Marion Davies's old estate in Malibu, and when relating those days at an awards ceremony honoring Redford years later, Streisand cracked wise, "When he offered me a ride on his motorcycle I asked, 'Where are the seat belts?' He knew I wasn't your motorcycle type of gal," but "I wasn't scared at all because I did feel safe with him, perfectly safe—the same way I did every day on the set."

Barbra felt safe with Redford, but Jerry Ziesmer could not always say the same. In his position as assistant director, it was Ziesmer's job to make sure that all of the actors, including Redford and Streisand, always remained ready to film on a moment's notice. While in Malibu, however, Redford begged Ziesmer for just ten minutes on the beach away from the production. Reluctantly, Ziesmer gave in—and was rewarded with Redford's absence for two and a half hours. Pollack fumed at the delay, and when Redford returned and saw Ziesmer, he simply turned on the charm: "Sorry Jer—what are you mad at? I couldn't help it. How am I supposed to know you needed me? I'm here! You're the assistant director, Jer, you should've done something!" It was all said with a grin and a chuckle and led Ziesmer to vow that Redford would "never get to me again, but of course, he did."

Now deep into production on this second film with Barbra, Ziesmer maintained great respect for the star, but she, too, presented her own set of challenges, and Ziesmer humorously wrote of his own Malibu location encounter with her. "'Jer, how are you?' Barbra began, and again I heard bells and saw red blinking lights of warning. A superstar was asking about my well-being! . . . Whenever Barbra began and ended a sentence with my name I knew there was big trouble for me, because Barbra had thoroughly thought out whatever she was after. Barbra at times reminded me of General Patton."

Barbra, in fact, was requesting that Ziesmer call Redford to the set first because problems ensued when she arrived first: "You know what the wind and salt air and all does to my hair and makeup, right Jer?" Ziesmer acquiesced, calling Redford to the set, only to have Barbra still arrive first, with Redford nowhere in sight. Finally, deciding that the only way to solve the problem was to provide Barbra and Redford with walkie-talkies on which he'd summon them to the set, Ziesmer turned on the walkies, called the two stars to the set, and watched as the trailer doors opened: "Out of Barbra's motor home stepped Barbra. Out of Redford's motor home flew his walkie-talkie." Ziesmer forever after remained convinced that Barbra and Redford had worked in humorous tandem to make his life difficult.

Pranks and all, the days of shooting were drawing to a close, and as Thanksgiving of 1972 approached, Ray Stark provided an unexpected gesture; abrasive and tough he could be, but at the same time, he often proved a walking, talking contradiction, leading Ziesmer to state, "He could be the most unique, creative producer I've ever encountered and he could also be the most stubborn, hardheaded, and uncompromising person I knew in the entire film industry." That Thanksgiving found him giving play to his generous side, and while the company filmed the Armed Forces Radio sequences, Ray Stark had two hundred frozen turkeys delivered to the soundstage—one for every member of the cast and crew, from actors and cameramen to secretaries and security guards.

And now, after all of the rewrites, delays, and wrangling of egos, only one scene remained to be shot: the very ending of the film. Needing the proper wintertime atmosphere for Katie and Hubbell's final farewell, Pollack had scheduled a November return to New York City for two days of shooting. Said Hawk Koch, "Shooting on a college campus was easy compared to trying to film in New York City in a period accurate way. Anything could intrude and remind you of the present day. In fact, when the film came out, Sydney received praise for a low shot of Bob talking to Barbra in front of the Plaza, but the shot was really just to avoid the intrusion of modern day New York!"

The company flew back to New York on November 27, 1972, with shooting scheduled for the next two days. Explained Hawk Koch, "I remember those dates very well. My wife and I were about to have a baby and she was not thrilled that I was traveling 3,000 miles away when she might very well go into labor. We started shooting on the 28th and during a break a bell boy came out of the Plaza—remember there were no cell phones in those days—shouting 'Mr. Koch. Mr. Koch. You've just had a baby girl!' I flew home the next day."

Laurents had always felt that Katie and Hubbell's bittersweet reunion in front of the Plaza would provide a powerful finish, one that might just gloss over all of the preceding story holes. The sequence would begin with Katie running across Fifty-Eighth Street to man her "Ban the Bomb" leafleting table until she stops short after spying Hubbell in front of the Plaza Hotel. Hubbell looks once and gazes elsewhere before suddenly registering that it really is Katie standing nearby; they hug, with Hubbell's appropriately glamorous, coolly distant, and decidedly WASPy girlfriend silently observing. News is exchanged—Hubbell is in town writing for television, and without another word spoken, both Hubbell and Katie know what a betrayal of his talent this represents. The unspoken subtext: he has never lived up to his potential, preferring instead to take the easy way out. Still, no criticism is voiced, and Katie informs Hubbell that yes, she is still married and invites him over for a drink: "It's the only Dr. David X. Cohen in the book." They part with smiles, and in Laurents's smart handling of the scene, they have upended audience expectations. The audience has eagerly anticipated a final reunion, and now it has registered as a near anticlimax.

Until.

Until Katie, bending over a table of leaflets, senses someone nearby; Hubbell has crossed the street to speak to her once again.

Hubbell: You never give up, do you?

Katie: Only when I'm absolutely forced to.

Hubbell quietly explains that he can't come to visit, and Katie smiles in understanding—"I know." It is time to say goodbye, and in a silent declaration of her love, Katie brushes Hubbell's hair off his forehead one last time.

They hug, and it is only now that Hubbell can finally ask about the daughter he doesn't know:

Hubbell: How is she?

Katie: She is just beautiful. You'd be so proud of her.

Hubbell: Is he a good father?

Katie: Yes. Very.

And then comes one final wistful expression of their signature banter:

See you, Katie.

See you, Hubbell.

With that, Hubbell is gone, and Katie returns to the all-consuming business of stirring up the masses to ban the bomb. Katie and Hubbell have come full circle.

Borne ceaselessly into the past.

Fade-out.

The End.

It's a lot of emotional punch to convey in a short three-minute scene, but Streisand and Redford were ready. The crowds of spectators eager for a glimpse of the stars were now roped off, and the assistant directors repeatedly called for quiet before the cameras could roll. Of that day's hubbub, Pollack contemporaneously noted, "The scenes we shot today involved a quiet and intimate farewell and it's hard to keep out extraneous noise. And even though actors are basically exhibitionists, they become shy and embarrassed with a sea of strange faces staring at them."

With the location locked up, the traditional cries for the start of shooting on *The Way We Were* rang out:

> "Sound rolling"
>
> "Speed"
>
> "Action!"

Take completed. One more. And then another.

One day of shooting now remained: close-ups of both Barbra and Redford. The gentle touching of Hubbell's hair. The lingering hug before parting forever. And just like that, with one last shot, *The Way We Were* had wrapped. Second director Ziesmer received a megaphone with messages written on it from cast and crew, and Barbra, "wonderful, as always, gave me three of her record albums nicely autographed." At the same time, in a humorous and perceptive analysis, Ziesmer summed up his three months of interactions with a smiling Redford, who pointedly asked him, "'What exactly do you do, anyway?' We had good times together. His good times were then, and my good times were looking back on it a quarter of a century later." Like the characters in the film, Ziesmer and Redford had their own disparate ways of looking at the way they were.

With all filming completed aside from a very few days of retakes, Laurents let loose in a blistering December 7 memo to Stark. Famous for his take-no-prisoners approach on both Broadway and Hollywood, Laurents hit new heights of frustration with what Stark and Pollack had wrought, objecting both to his work being rewritten by others, and also to what he viewed as an overt attempt to gain screenwriting credit for Alvin Sargent. In fact, he sarcastically suggested, since so many others already appeared to have had a hand in the rewrites, why not also list the four apostles of the New Testament as co-screenwriters?

As it turned out, what infuriated Laurents all the more about the rewrites was the repeated insertion of dialogue describing Hubbell's attempts to draw Katie's face in the sand. As Laurents logically pointed out, the entire movie hinged on Katie dreaming of Hubbell, not on Hubbell obsessing over Katie, but in the quest to build up Redford's role, a line had been crossed. In the end, the rather labored dialogue, which did nothing less than reverse the essence of both characters, would fortunately be eliminated.

Laurents proved equally dismayed by cuts to the fireside scene when Katie and Hubbell make love for the second time. In light of Katie's bewilderment as to whether the drunken Hubbell even remembered their first night together, the script called for Hubbell to now gently tell her, "It'll be better this time." Redford and Pollack, however, had cut the line, which infuriated Laurents. Why, the screenwriter wondered, was the line being cut when Stark himself admitted to crying after first reading the line? Was there any reason besides Redford's ego?

Laurents was fuming, but now, with retakes completed, after all of the agonizing, after Streisand's worry, Redford's indecision, and Stark's interference, the ultimate question had to be answered: Was *The Way We Were* going to be a romantic masterpiece or a period snooze? Sydney Pollack sequestered himself in the editing room with John Barnett and Margaret Booth and found himself staring at a very big surprise.

Editing the Film

> *"Margaret Booth turned out to be a magnificent lady. Her loyalty was to the picture and she didn't play politics. She was a very hard working and amazing woman."* —Sydney Pollack on editor Margaret Booth

The surprise, Pollack quickly realized, lay in the fact that *The Way We Were* was both wonderful and well, there was no other word for it, terrible. On the plus side of the ledger, the chemistry between his two stars was blazing forth in widescreen technicolor, but at the same time, the movie as a whole seemed to move in wildly uneven fits and starts. It all felt too long—occasionally exhilarating yet sometimes downright boring. Swinging between despair and elation, Pollack began looking for scenes to cut.

Small scenes were the first to hit the cutting-room floor:

- Arthur Laurents's personal story about his friend "Tony Blue Eyes," transformed for purposes of the movie into Hubbell's rueful admission of coasting through life on the strength of his smile, had been intended to demonstrate Hubbell's willingness to lower his guard during that first nighttime conversation with Katie. Redford played the subtext well, but when projected on the screen, his confession only seemed to elongate the buildup to the scene's climactic gesture of tying Katie's shoe. Gone.

- Katie planting a victory garden in front of her apartment; as originally written, the scene was to represent the audience's very first glimpse of Katie. Barbra, the most popular female movie star in the world, planting in the dirt as her star entrance? Out it went.
- J.J. and Hubbell on a crowded wartime train—unnecessary.
- Katie manning a Bryant Park bloodmobile and thinking she spies Hubbell. By this point, her desire for Hubbell had already been made clear, and the scene never saw the light of day.
- Katie trying on dresses at Saks? No need—everyone knew she wanted to look her best for Hubbell.
- Katie strolling through Central Park, ogled by a group of four sailors? Adding nothing to the love story, the scene was excised.
- Katie and Hubbell walking through the pigeons outside of the New York Public Library. To what end? The entire scene was cut, as were atmospheric shots of Katie and Hubbell visiting an art gallery, drinking at the Palm Court of the Plaza Hotel, and eating lobster at Lundy's restaurant in Sheepshead Bay.
- A publicity photo of Katie and Hubbell's wedding day, both of them immaculate in white, was released, but the wedding scene itself was never filmed. With the deletion of the wedding (plans had called for the ceremony to be shot without any dialogue), gone, too, was the chance for viewers to meet Katie's father and Hubbell's parents. Katie's relationship with her father? Loving. Hubbell's relationship with his parents? Complicated. In an earlier draft of the screenplay, he simply said, "My folks were always easier with my brother and sister. With me they behaved as though I were on loan."

With the wedding ceremony deleted, so, too, was a nicely constructed montage showing Katie and Hubbell's move to Hollywood.

Married life lay in Los Angeles, not New York, and their move was to be shown by means of a jump cut from empty apartments and a deserted broadcast studio to gleaming Los Angeles. Pollack, however, was in a rush for the movie to leap forward into Hollywood, and in the final edit of the film, the entire montage would be replaced by a single quick cut to a view of the Pacific Ocean.

Moving on to more substantive scenes, Pollack, Booth, and Barnett attacked wholesale sequences the director felt slowed up the narrative:

- Out went a scene centering around Hubbell's reaction to sleeping with Katie. As originally scripted and filmed, Hubbell was to get up in the middle of the night, unable to even remember where he was, before finally realizing that he was in Katie's apartment; holding his head in a moment of "Oh my God. What have I done?!" Redford underplayed beautifully, but Pollack felt, it actually hurt the movie: "It gave people too much, put them ahead of the characters." Without the scene, Hubbell's anxiety and need to escape Katie's apartment as quickly as possible would now keep the audience more fully engaged, wondering where the next turn in the romance lay.
- Excised in toto: Five full pages of script featuring talk of protests against the HUAC as well as disagreements between Bissinger and Hubbell over the direction of the movie.
- Shots of an incredulous Katie visiting the set of Hubbell's movie and watching twelve tap-dancing girls shoehorned into a story that had nothing to do with musicals. The point of Hollywood's superficial excesses and Hubbell selling out could, Pollack felt, be made in half the time without such detailed explanation, and scene 169 was cut.
- Snip! Gone, too, was the Union Station setup for Katie and Rhea's fight, in which Hubbell would tell Katie that Rhea had

informed on Brooks Carpenter and also named eight others as members of the Communist Party. Along with it went Allyn Ann McLerie's "big payoff scene," in which Rhea, running into Katie at the butcher's, tries to justify her willingness to inform. It's not that the scene didn't work, because it did, in fact, land nicely, with Rhea wondering aloud, "It'll be years before I know whether I did the right thing. And by then, it won't matter," only to be informed by Katie, "I can tell you now, Rhea, you did the wrong thing. And if it matters, I think you're a shit. And I never used that word before." With this cut, Rhea's screen time was by now so thoroughly diminished that the audience can be forgiven for wondering why Hubbell and Katie ever asked her to be their child's godmother—did they even know her?

The cuts continued, thirty seconds here, one minute there, and slowly the movie began to take on a more streamlined shape.

- Scene 127—filmed but now largely trimmed. As Katie and Hubbell lie in bed, she feeds him a grape before putting a second grape in her own mouth and kissing him. Erotic in nature, the scene was to be woven around Katie's asking Hubbell, "How am I for you?" Faced with his reply, "You surprised me—again," Katie interrogates her lover: "Good surprise or bad surprise?" Yes, the scene generated heat, but between the grapes and Katie's insecure questioning, it all seemed a case of too much, registering as on the nose and devoid of any mystery. The cutting-room floor beckoned.

What was missed in the same scene, however, was the quick post-love-making dialogue that would have deepened characterization with a minimum of words:

Katie: Was the Pacific awful?

Hubbell: Yes . . .

Katie: I saw the scar on your back.

In three lines, Hubbell's golden façade would have been revealed as less than perfect, and the viewer would have learned that Hubbell did not, as seemed apparent in the final cut of the film, spend the entire war in Washington, DC, in a sparkling white uniform. As it turned out, it is only in the postwar Hollywood section of the film that the viewer is even informed that Hubbell was "an officer on landing craft in the South Pacific."

- Scene 132—Writing in Katie's apartment, Hubbell can't find the right words, grows increasingly frustrated, and wants to escape by going to the movies. Katie insists he finish the chapter, and while he may growl, "We've been cooped up here for two days!," for Katie, the situation is nothing short of wonderful: "I love being cooped up with you." Nice sentiments to be sure, but by this time, Katie's belief in Hubbell's talent had been as thoroughly established as his reluctance to finish the new book. To Pollack, Booth, and Burnett, it all seemed like gilding the lily. The pile on the cutting-room floor grew deeper.

In all of these decisions, editor Margaret Booth was turning out to be an unanticipated but highly welcome colleague for Pollack, her uncanny instincts for what helped push the story forward aiding immeasurably in trying to find the proper balance between politics and the love story. In Pollack's own words, "Margaret Booth was a legend in Hollywood. I didn't know her that well—she had worked with Ray before and it was the first time I didn't pick my own editor—Ray did. She turned out to be a magnificent lady. Her loyalty was to the picture and she didn't play politics. She was a very hard working and amazing woman. A helluva good friend to me on that picture. Everyone wanted their hands into the cut on that picture and she wanted what was best for the movie."

The flow was improving and the movie gaining momentum, but occasionally the decisions veered offtrack and began to resemble a case of throwing the baby out with the bathwater. For his own reasons, Pollack deleted scenes (now available for viewing as a DVD extra) that actually would have deepened the audience's understanding of the unbalanced love affair. To wit:

- Scene 135 in which Hubbell imagines introducing Katie to his father: "My father would say . . . I don't know what he'd say." Katie digs deeper, bluntly asking Hubbell, "Do you love your father?" A stumbling Hubbell tries speaking the words aloud: "I love you, Dad. Mother—I love you." His delivery is stilted because, the subtext runs, in the WASPy Gardiner household such sentiments are never spoken aloud. (Explains Hubbell in another draft of the screenplay: "It's a quiet house. We're very nice people. The lawn is cut.") The beautifully wrought capper to the scene came when Katie openly admitted, "I love you, Hubbell," only to have him gaze directly at her, look down at his typewriter, and fail to reply. Katie's quiet rejoinder? "It's all right." It's a first-rate scene and a heartbreaker in its display of Katie's vulnerability, but Pollack seemed to find it a drag on momentum, and out it went.

Even with these stumbles, the editing process revealed one indisputable fact: Barbra Streisand and Robert Redford possessed a genuine on-screen connection, his cool and her passion combining to invest the film with not just heat but also a palpable rooting interest for them to end up together. Said Ray Stark, "We were aware of the chemistry between Redford and Barbra, but it really hit us in the rushes." It was, Stark emphasized to one and all, that electricity between the stars that should be displayed front and center. Forget the politics. Ray Stark wanted a love story.

In fact, that mutual on-screen attraction between Streisand and Redford had been instantly recognizable to the stars themselves even while watching the unscored daily rushes. It was also a recognition that blossomed right alongside a healthy competitive streak. Watching the daily rushes, Streisand wondered aloud to Sydney Pollack, "How does Bob *do* it? I stink, don't I?" And when Redford would watch the rushes, he'd lean over to his director and ask, "How does she do it? She is just so goddamn great and I'm so goddamn *lousy*."

In fact, they were both turning in first-rate performances, Redford investing what could have been a cardboard character with surprising depth; even in later years, Streisand lavished praise on Redford's characterization, forthrightly stating, "I thought he was great in *The Way We Were*. I thought it was his best performance to tell the truth." For her part, Streisand had consistently dug deeper dramatically than ever before. Old-time Hollywood star power, it seemed, was alive and well, and as the rough cut of one hundred twenty-eight minutes firmly took shape, Pollack's thoughts turned away from the temporary soundtrack he was utilizing and toward the permanent score forthcoming from the film's composer, an up-and-coming, relatively unknown twenty-nine-year-old by the name of Marvin Hamlisch.

How unknown?

Four months earlier he had, at Ray Stark's request, composed a theme song before the film had even been shot.

On spec.

What about a Title Song?

"Most of the time a title is all I need to get me going, like The Way We Were." —Marvin Hamlisch

Ray Stark, who had worked with Marvin Hamlisch on the John Huston film *Fat City* (1972), had first called up the composer in late spring of 1972 and asked him to write a theme song for an upcoming movie. The initial work, explained Stark, would all be for free; Hamlisch, logically enough, asked why. Replied Stark, "I think this is up your alley and I'd like to give you a chance. . . . You haven't got the track record yet, Marvin, and the director wants you to do this on spec." If Stark did not like the song, the end result, in Hamlisch's own words, would be one of "no harm, no foul. I'd be here today, gone tomorrow." But continued Stark, the upside was enormous: if he liked the song, Hamlisch would be allowed to score the entire movie.

Only now, at the end of the conversation did Stark tell Hamlisch that the director was Sydney Pollack, the film was *The Way We Were*, and the stars were Robert Redford and Barbra Streisand. Hamlisch was in: "I must confess that I sensed from the beginning that this was going to be my watershed in the movies. The intimidation of writing for Barbra Streisand was matched by the remarkable challenge."

Hamlisch and Streisand, separated by only two years, had first met on the stage production of *Funny Girl*, for which Hamlisch had served as the rehearsal pianist. Said Barbra, "We met when I was twenty-one and he was nineteen. I always loved Marvin." Recalled the composer, "We used to go to the automat all the time and eat like crazy. We both loved their pea soup and those fabulous cupcakes with the chocolate on top." Two fast-talking, smart, young Jewish New Yorkers had instantly bonded over a love of food, a wild talent for music, and enough mutual ambition to power the entire New York City grid. Now, nine years after *Funny Girl*'s premiere, while Hamlisch carefully climbed filmdom's ranks of music supervisors and composers, Streisand reigned not only as American's premier vocalist but also as Hollywood's biggest female box-office attraction. Hamlisch was excited by the challenge of writing for his old friend and immediately went to work.

In his own retelling, Hamlisch worked for weeks on multiple versions of the title song until he finally arrived at a turning point: the film may have had an unhappy ending, but counterintuitively, he would write his song in the major mode, trying to "give a sense of hope to this tragic story." Ruminating further he explained that "if it were in the minor mode, it might tell you too much in advance that Streisand and Redford were never going to get together. I wrote a melody that was sad, but it also had great hope in it."

He went to work, writing for three hours each day, with Barbra's voice always in his head, even as he remained determined "not to write something drippingly sentimental." After dozens of attempts, he finally arrived at his "eureka" moment with a theme that seemed to encapsulate the bittersweet nature of a romance filled with yearning and regret. How did he know that he had found the right theme? Because in his own words, "one day I wrote a melody that just got to me. . . . I either respond or I don't. . . . when I react the way I hope the audience will, then I know I've got it."

A very nervous Hamlisch now played his melody for Pollack and assistant director Howard Koch Jr. In Koch's description of this audition, "A tall, gangly, awkward, and visibly nervous young guy entered the office. 'Hi, uh, hi, wow, Sydney Pollack, it's so exciting to meet you.'" Explaining to Koch and Hawks that he couldn't afford to hire an orchestra, he instead had taped himself playing the piano: "I'll play the horns with my mouth, but you'll have to imagine what real horns would sound like." Hitting the play button on his tinny little tape recorder, the melody swelled, and wrote Koch, Hamlisch "pressed his lips together and out came a pretty impressive horn sound. From the moment I heard the first notes . . . chills ran up and down my spine. It was hauntingly beautiful."

With the melody set, attention turned to prospective lyricists. The number-one choice: the husband and wife team of Alan and Marilyn Bergman. Formidable talents and longtime friends of Streisand, the pair's Hollywood credits ranged from songs written with Quincy Jones for *In the Heat of the Night* to their Oscar-winning "The Windmills of Your Mind" from 1968's *The Thomas Crown Affair*. It was a sign of the Bergmans' stature in Hollywood that they had now been nominated for the Best Song Academy Award five years in a row, and Sydney Pollack knew the duo would deliver: "Marilyn and Alan Bergman are *unique*. Their lyrics do a remarkable thing: They somehow combine the overview of the director, the subjective involvement of the actors and the dramatic intention of the screenwriter." Alan Bergman returned the compliment, saying of Pollack, "He was a great director. He was one of the few who really understood the value of a song, that the title song was more than just a song—that it was part of the whole film."

Hamlisch presented the Bergmans with his finished melody, a "music first" approach with which they felt comfortable. To the Bergmans, the theme served as "the spine" of the movie, and "in the case of a ballad—unless you have Richard Rodgers, who can write the music to the lyrics—it's best to have the melody first."

Seasoned pros that they were, the Bergmans maintained a clear understanding of where the true power lay when writing for the movies: "[I]n film if the lyric writer or the screenwriter or the composer thinks he can compete with the visual image, he's wrong—it's like a Sherman tank rolling over you." They understood exactly how and when to pick their spots; on their Oscar-winning "The Windmills of Your Mind," they wanted their theme to complement, not compete with, the drifting, unsettled atmosphere pervading the on-screen action. Working from composer Michel Legrand's melody and fired with a determination to "go deeper," the Bergmans had then drafted lyrics of "anxiety and circular emotions," feelings that Marilyn, in a nice bit of imagery, described as "the kinds of things you feel just before you go to sleep."

By this time, Streisand had known the Bergmans for years and recorded many of their songs, from the well-known "The Summer Knows" (from *Summer of '42*) to the relatively obscure "Ask Yourself Why." That familiarity meant that the Bergmans could begin setting their lyric to Hamlisch's melody with Streisand's voice in their minds: "If we are writing for her only, we can't help being nourished by what we already know about her, just as a composer knows where her voice is most effective, how to best use it, the kind of intervals she likes, where her voice sits most beautifully and more importantly, where it is most comfortable emotionally."

They began mulling over lyric ideas drawn from a close reading of the script. Analyzed Marilyn, "The challenge was to write the song for the way it was going to play at the end of the movie. The first time was a plant for the end scene outside of the Plaza." Explained Alan, "The song is a corridor back in time, taking you back to the college years. That was the function of the song." They began sketching in ideas . . . hazily recollected times gone by.

Daydreams—light the corners of my mind

A nice start.

Fine-tuning each phrase, they captured an entire mood in just three short words:

Misty watercolor mem'ries.

Digging deeper, they played with the shapes and sounds of words, distilling the idea that memories can simultaneously summon emotions both painful and joyous:

Can it be that it was all so simple then?
Or has time rewritten every line?

They capped the song with a universal truth, capturing the precise tone of regret that infused the entire film:

What's too painful to remember
We simply choose to forget

The Bergmans were happy, and Hamlisch was thrilled with how snugly their lyrics fit his melody. All well and good, of course, but the real test remained: How would Barbra feel about their effort? D-Day arrived, and in May 1972, off the trio went to Barbra's home, filled with excitement as well as a palpable sense of trepidation. Hamlisch started to play; Alan Bergman, the possessor of a pleasant, lightly swinging voice, began to sing—and Barbra Streisand smiled. She definitely liked the song, but also had two suggestions. The first concerned the melody: "In the documentary on the 1999 DVD, Marvin describes coming to my house with the Bergmans to play the song for me. You can hear the melody he originally wrote, and then he explains how it changed after I made some suggestions which he loved and immediately incorporated into the song."

In Hamlisch's own explanation, that first melody possessed "a long A section. . . . The third line of the melody I had written brought the notes down the scale but Barbra's infallible instincts made her want the melody to take off and rise. We tried it and she was right. It was one of those rare, exciting moments when a collaboration works perfectly."

Barbra's second suggestion concerned the lyric, which Hamlisch himself already termed "luscious." Said Barbra, "As I was looking more closely at the lyric, I asked the Bergmans if they could change the first word from 'daydreams' to 'memories,' since that's what the song is about. And they wholeheartedly agreed." Beginning the song with the words "Daydreams light the corners of my mind" meant that the crucial word "mem'ries" followed in the second line—"misty watercolor mem'ries"—and to Barbra, that "just didn't feel right." Her request was instinctive: "I don't know why I suggested that. The word 'mem'ries' is so distinctive that I thought it would be great to begin the song with it." It was, the writers agreed, a terrific suggestion, and with that one change, Barbra Streisand nudged a good song toward greatness. Said Alan Bergman, "It was an excellent suggestion. It meant that we would be using the word 'mem'ries' twice in the first two lines, but we overcame our hesitancy about that."

And yet, on the way home, Alan Bergman suggested writing a second version of the song, wondering aloud "maybe we could do even better." Hamlisch had his doubts—"I can't beat this melody. I don't think I have another magical one in me," but in Alan Bergman's recall, "We said to Marvin she won't record for two or three months. Let's write a couple of songs called 'The Way We Were.'" A surprised Marvin replied, "They loved it. Why do that?" Because, Bergman felt, it was a chance to exercise their creative muscles and explore new opportunities: "After all, we don't always write just for them." Marilyn Bergman agreed: "It was such a wonderful title—there were many other ways to approach the title."

Barbra, in fact, confirmed that the second "Way We Were" "came about only because they had finished the first song so quickly that there was a lot more time before the movie came out. So Alan said, 'Why don't we write another song?' It was almost like a challenge to themselves, to see if they could top the first song."

Hamlisch may have been surprised by Alan Bergman's request, but with several months remaining before Barbra recorded the song, he went back to the piano. A second melody was written, one floating alongside lyrics that struck an even more reflective tone—in short, a more complex song:

When I wander through my mind
In corners I can find

The result was, in Barbra's apt description, "very French." (In fact, with the Bergmans' lyric translated into French, this second version could have nestled nicely into Barbra's "Je m'appelle Barbra" album.)

Barbra in fact liked both versions (in Arthur Laurents's recall, she sang both songs over the phone to him)—so what did Sydney Pollack think? He had, in fact, held one reservation about that first version: "I was concerned that maybe the song was not complex enough—that it was white on white." The new version was played for the director. His verdict? Thumbs-up. Which song to use?

In the midst of editing, Pollack hit upon a way to settle the question: Each version was recorded with Barbra accompanied by solo piano, and both versions were then played against the film's silent footage of college life—the exact spot where the song would be heard in the movie. Hearing both songs against the footage, Barbra herself knew exactly which version should be utilized: "This was not a difficult decision. The first version of the song fit the film perfectly and was the most memorable melody. That's why I named the second version 'The Way We Weren't.' . . . But it was the first one that captured the mood of the movie, to such an extent that they're irrevocably connected. Still, both songs are beautifully written, so it was like an embarrassment of riches."

Said Alan Bergman, "The only way to test a song is to see how it feels with the images—music, lyrics, and images all together. The second song didn't work with the images. It was too cerebral a song. The first song really worked beautifully. Comparing the two versions with the film gave us our answer—plain and simple." Recalled Pollack about the second song, "I liked that song. It had a wonderful melody and lyrics—but never would have been the hit this one was."

Barbra liked the song; Sydney Pollack liked the song; and so, too, did Ray Stark and Barbra's manager, Marty Erlichman. Recalled Alan Bergman, "Marty named the day it would be the number one song in the country! It's a very nice bonus if that happens but you never know when a song may become number one. We never were in the business of writing hits. It's not what we wanted to do."

It was time to orchestrate. Knowing Barbra's reputation for perfectionism, Hamlisch took the unusual step of preparing three very different orchestrations for the fifty-five-piece orchestra: "I called these versions A, B, and C." In each version, the opening piano chords would give way to the sound of Barbra humming the first phrases—humming as if trying to recall a half-forgotten melody. Only after the hummed introduction would the opening words of "Mem'ries light the corners of my mind" be heard, an understated way in which to shift the film backward from 1940s New York City to 1930s college life.

The musicians began playing version A; Barbra Streisand began humming; and for composer Hamlisch, the impact proved seismic: "I suddenly heard that incredible voice in my earphones. I realized she had even surpassed, right there in front of me, what I had heard her do inside me. I doubt any other singer could have done that."

Hamlisch was thrilled. Barbra was not. She was having trouble with the orchestration and asked for a ten-minute break. No need, replied Hamlisch, "just give me ten seconds, Barbra." Turning to the orchestra, he simply said, "Plan B, boys." This time around, Barbra felt pleased with the orchestration: spare, not overwhelming, but with a fully cushioned string-ladened sound capable of inducing a romantic reverie all on its own. The recording was complete.

Would anyone like it? Who knew, but with any luck, the song might even garner a bit of airplay on adult contemporary radio; any additional popularity the song gained would merely prove to be icing on the cake. For now, Streisand, Hamlisch, the Bergmans, and Sydney Pollack knew that they had a theme song that nestled snugly inside of a very romantic film. Marvin Hamlisch had earned his chance—the movie was his to score.

Hamlisch, it turned out, was certain of only one element: the movie's theme was going to be heard. A lot. "You can actually manipulate people's emotions with theme music. I knew exactly what effect I'd create with *The Way We Were*. I played that theme until it drove you crazy."

With a complete rough cut of the film now available as a guide, Marvin Hamlisch and Sydney Pollack sat down to mark all the appropriate moments for music cues. Turning on his tape recorder, Hamlisch began noting the exact moments where the music should start and stop. How long should each cue last? Which period songs would be used? Where could his own lush compositions be used effectively without overwhelming the audience? Most crucial of all, where was *The Way We Were* theme going to be heard?

Composer and director analyzed the rough cut while listening to the temporary score Pollack had inserted. Said the director, "It's the only way I can tell if a scene is going to work. . . . I fell so in love with one cue in the temp score that I asked Marvin to copy the texture of the orchestration. He was a good sport and he gave me what I wanted. It's a score that helps the picture enormously."

Noted Hamlisch, "If you score exactly what is up there on screen, you're putting white paint on white paint. I look for what the scene is about and what the subtext is." It proved a painstaking process; with no thunderous special effects to cover up plot shortcomings, one misjudged musical cue could yank audiences right out of their reverie and thrust them back into the tumultuous, decidedly unromantic year of 1973. Hamlisch remained grateful for Pollack's efforts to strike the appropriate balance and not draw attention to directorial flourishes: "It's such an intricate balance between the music, dialogue, and effects. . . . This score really could have been buried underneath the dialogue—just disappeared. I was very grateful to Sydney Pollack because he really picked a good balance."

Hamlisch now began assembling a list of the full-bodied romantic period songs that would lend a nostalgic sheen to the love story, settling on "Red Sails in the Sunset," "Wrap Your Troubles in Dreams," and "Let There Be Love"—all of them wistful Tin Pan Alley paeans to golden dreams of an untroubled past. Meticulously constructing each cue, Hamlisch decided that the film's opening shots of New York City would carry the sounds of the big-band era, alerting the viewer to exactly which time period they were entering. Five minutes into the film, when Katie first sights Hubbell in El Morocco, the nightclub band would be softly playing "Let There Be Love." It would only be then, as tolling bells brought the viewer back to Katie and Hubbell's college days, that Barbra's humming, the gentle segue into time past, would widen into her title-song vocal. It was all timed out to end just as Katie begins to speak at a students for peace rally. (Said one of the student extras, Philip Macero, of filming the peace rally, "We spent 14 hours just on the rally. I was in a scene on the track wearing track shorts, and it was freezing—45 degrees."

Hamlisch proved particularly concerned with how best to utilize the title-song melody to cue the film's bittersweet moments of emotional truth telling. Spots were painstakingly picked—the theme would well up while Katie and Hubbell made love and then again as they literally sailed into the sunset, but there was one cue Hamlisch felt particularly strongly about: the melody would not be heard under or after the final scene. In Hamlisch's reckoning, by that time he would have "overplayed my hand with this theme. I'm going to play a second theme," a new theme to let the drama speak for itself. A slow fade-out on a pair of mismatched lovers without any distracting title tune could only help the film.

Of that Hamlisch was certain.

Forget the Critics: What Did Arthur Laurents Think?

> *"I was always surprised that people liked the picture. They keep crying, they sit through it over and over watching on television."*
> —Arthur Laurents

As editing and scoring entered their final stages, no one involved in *The Way We Were* was really sure what they had. More than anything else, Pollack was simply relieved that he'd have a completed print ready for a first sneak preview, while the Columbia Pictures executives vacillated in their reactions, alternately anxious, cautiously optimistic, and doubtful that anyone would want to see a movie about political blacklisting. There was, however, one person who remained unquestionably dissatisfied with the film: Arthur Laurents.

Sydney Pollack had flown East to show Laurents a rough cut of the film, and Laurents, never shy about expressing his opinions, found this most personal of films, a few good moments excepted, to be an unquestioned mess. Surprisingly, his first line of criticism was with the leads, two superstars whose larger-than-life personae, he felt, prevented total assimilation into the roles:

"He was Bob Redford playing Redford playing Hubbell Gardiner. She was Barbra Joan Streisand paying Streisand playing

Katie Morosky." Barbra's accent, he felt was unnecessarily "grand," emblematic of a phony speech pattern used by New York actors to elevate their status. (Barbra wasn't the only actor he found generally guilty of the faux elocution, citing Al Pacino and especially, Lauren Bacall as fellow offenders.) It's a curious criticism given the decidedly Brooklyn speech patterns Barbra employs throughout, especially when wishing Hubbell "Happy Rosh Hashanah!" or humorously contemplating naming their daughter "Rakhael Gardiner." Nonetheless, Laurents deemed her guilty, bluntly declaring, "It damaged Barbra's performance."

Neither was Redford spared Laurents's caustic commentary. In his screenplay, Laurents had written a short scene of Hubbell stroking crew (the scene was filmed on Pittsfield Massachusetts's Lake Onota, with the Williams College crew standing in for Union College's nonexistent crew). It was a throwaway, intended only to establish Hubbell's athleticism. Instead, given Pollack's knowledge of Redford's athletic ability, the director had also filmed Hubbell tossing the shot put, throwing the javelin, and sprinting to glory—in Laurents's barbed words, "a decathlon man, a thirty-year-old undergraduate who rows, races, shot-puts, throws a javelin, and plays football."

It was, however, two dramatic scenes that Laurents singled out as particularly galling. The first concerned one of the arguments between Hubbell and Katie in J.J.'s Beekman Place apartment. In actuality, Pollack had cut the scene, but when Laurents grew vehement that the scene had to be included, it was shot at a later date on a mockup of the original set. The problem, Laurents explained, lay in the fact that he had written the scene to be an impassioned argument between Hubbell and Katie in J.J.'s apartment but away from their friends. Instead, Pollack had staged the scene with Katie and Hubbell's quarrel detonating directly in front of the Beekman Place gang. The emphasis had now changed for the worse, wrote Laurents, "making her a shrill, insensitive harridan while he is a strong, true gent who takes no crap. One way of building up Hubbell—the purpose, I suppose—but achieved at Katie's expense."

Laurents felt it essential to reshoot the scene, a plan immediately vetoed by Stark as too costly. As it turned out, Laurents's assessment proved correct: in the final cut of the film it remains a jarring scene, one that would have landed more gracefully if the originally scripted mitigating touch of Katie joining the others in singing "Paper Doll" had actually been included. Instead, by casting Katie in such an unflattering light, the scene causes one to wonder why Hubbell would stay with someone so aggressively angry. She does not register as a woman of principles but instead as an unreasonable, near shrew.

Such criticisms were symbolic of Laurent's visceral negative reaction to the entire film, and in a nine page single spaced typed letter to Ray Stark dated "Xmas weekend" of 1972, he let loose, about the actual footage he had viewed as well as the rewrites he was still being asked to provide: By now, Laurents felt, it all came down to a question of money, because artistic satisfaction seemed unattainable. Pay him enough money and he'd provide the rewrites—end of discussion.

So upset was he at this point that he even laced into the Streisand-Redford pairing, bluntly stating that the Katie-Hubbell pairing would have proved more emotionally satisfying with Ryan O'Neal playing Hubbell. Criticizing the directing and the cinematography as well, he found fault with all of the supporting performances with the exception of Brad Dillman's.

Laurents might have occasionally been frustrated by Barbra, but his more severe criticism was reserved for Redford—it was clear that the star's demands for constant rewrites still grated and for Laurents, the film could only be helped by one essential action: cut as much of Redford's footage as possible. The character was weak, and, he felt, so was the actor's performance.

The screenwriter pressed on with his enumeration of the film's shortcomings, many of them directed at Pollack:

- The introduction of Hubbell at El Morocco struck the screenwriter as unbelievable because Redford was, rather too noticeably, acting.
- The scene in Dr. Short's class wherein Hubbell's story is read aloud—ineffective due to faulty direction.
- The college peace rally—flat—as were the nighttime scenes of Katie and Hubbell sharing a beer.

Not surprisingly, however, it was the scenes written by others that caused Laurents to erupt most loudly in frustration:

- After fighting with Hubbell at J.J.'s, why, he asked, would Katie look for Hubbell in her living room when he had not even gone home with her? Where was the logic in such action?
- Hubbell and Katie's breakup at the radio station: flaccidly played thanks to both poor direction and Barbra's sub-par performance.

If not exactly angry, he was, however, most disappointed by the tearful telephone scene in which Katie begs Hubbell to return and help her fall asleep. A sequence which Laurents had written as sure fire Oscar bait for Barbra was, he felt, now ruined by what he termed Barbra's obsession with her appearance. Pollack and Barbra both liked how the scene played, but to Laurents, Barbra underperformed, her concern with looks taking precedence over depth of characterization.

Playing directly after Katie's tearful telephone call, the "Pill Scene" in which Hubbell comes to Katie's apartment and gives her a sleeping pill was, he railed, poorly acted, but he reserved his fiercest criticism for the Sargent–Rayfiel scripted scene set at Union Station, after Katie returns from the Washington, DC, HUAC hearings alongside the blacklisted Hollywood Ten. As anti-Communists hurled insults at Katie and her famous friends, Laurents had exactly one thought: this is absurd. Stars like Bogart and Bacall, he knew, had flown to Washington for the hearings and never would have wasted three days traveling by train. Furthermore, he felt certain that larger-than-life golden-age Hollywood stars would have been greeted by fans, not protestors, upon their return.

In Laurents's estimation, Sydney Pollack had included the scene for only one reason: Hubbell, aka the heroic Robert Redford, could greet Katie and swing into action when a protestor screams, "Shut up you Commie bitch!"; Hubbell punches the man, is grabbed by a policeman, and is socked in the jaw. In fact, Laurents so disliked this scene that it registered as the one political sequence he actually wanted to cut, finding the action phony and cartoonish.

Immediately after action hero Hubbell ends the Hollywood 10 homecoming scene by belting Katie's tormentors, he and Katie would now reach a political breaking point when, alone in a deserted train station restaurant, they engage in their most pointed political argument. "Hubbell—you are telling me to close my eyes and to watch people being destroyed so that you can go on working." People, Hubbell informs Katie, are more important than witch hunts or principles, to which Katie retorts, "Hubbell, people are their principles." Pollack, it turned out, had now cut Katie's riposte, one which was, in Laurents's viewpoint, the lynchpin of the entire movie.

Furious when he realized that Pollack had deleted the line, Laurents made it clear to Stark that he took the cut personally: "I knew why he cut it, I knew he and Redford were fed up to the teeth with me." By now, when it came to the endless battle of adding or deleting lines in the script, Laurents felt as if he were engaged in a constant fight against the duo of Redford and Pollack, with Barbra caught in the middle: "She was infatuated with Redford. That itself was obvious to everyone on the picture, not excluding Redford who handled it well, neither encouraging her nor using her crush to his advantage." In trying to get Barbra to side with him about the necessity of keeping the line that "People are their principles," Laurents was surprised that the usually assertive Barbra didn't want to upset either Redford or Pollack, claiming that the director should always be in charge. Laurents insisted that the line be reinstated, and in the end, Barbra pushed in support of her old friend: "I pushed her hard and like Katie Morosky she stood fast: the line stayed."

Pleased that "People are their principles" would stay in the film, Laurents was nonetheless devastated by Pollack's cutting of another line in the very same scene. What, an exasperated Hubbell asks, does Katie want? In a terrific exchange she cries, "I want us to love each other!," to which Hubbell instantly replies, "But we do. That's the trouble, Katie. We do." It's a beautifully wrought insight into why their union can never last, but Pollack cut Hubbell's lines, much to the film's detriment. In Laurents's apt phrase, the line showed that they loved each other "despite, not because."

Equally troubling to Laurents was the excision of the lines in which Hubbell explains the political motivation behind his studio troubles to a pregnant Katie: "The studio says they are going to fire me because I have a subversive wife." It was a scene filled with deep personal resonance for Laurents, based as it was on the end of the marriage between his old friends Jigee and Peter Viertel; the fact that Peter, still in the Marine Corps Reserves, was living with Jigee, a known former Communist, had greatly interested the FBI and damaged Peter's chances of finding a job in Hollywood. The end result? Jigee actually informed in order to help Peter, an action that Laurents interpreted as her way of showing Peter how much she loved him.

For the movie, however, Laurents had changed the heroine's decision. Katie can't conceive of ever informing, and the marriage ends because of politically motivated moral differences, with Katie quietly asking, "So if we get a divorce and you don't have a subversive wife?" Pollack, however, cut the line, a deletion that Laurents rightly felt represented a big loss in coherence and logical reasoning: "That's where the two stories came together. Barbra knew that. Katie could never betray her friends or her beliefs. And she would have to leave Hubbell after he made such an unconscionable request of her." With the excision of Katie's line, the audience is left to assume that Hubbell's one night of adultery with Carol Ann causes a marriage of nearly a decade to unravel. Laurents wasn't buying it and neither, he felt, would the audience. To the screenwriter, the cumulative effect of all these excised lines lay in narrative incoherence.

And yet, even as his frustration with the rough cut grew, by the end of the screening, Laurents experienced an unexpected sense of pleasure. The film's very last scene, the unexpected reunion of Katie and Hubbell in front of the Plaza Hotel, delivered, and delivered big time. Maybe, he felt, the film could still be a success through sheer star power; the more he thought about that final scene the more he liked it, even coming to completely reverse his earlier angry statement that Redford was too cold to create any onscreen sparks with Streisand. Maybe, just maybe, those last five minutes would send the audience out of the theater nursing a pleasant, if bittersweet romantic hangover, one filled with enough emotion to overcome all of the film's preceding faults.

After sending his memo, Laurents continued to stew, and on December 27, 1972, a mere three days after his nine page catalogue of angry complaints had reached Stark, he sat down, and in addition to sending some final scenes written for retakes, announced his decision to remain in the east, far from the turmoil of retakes and editing. He was tired of fighting with Sydney Pollack and tired of feeling powerless. What's done was done and good luck to everyone.

Arthur Laurents may no longer have been actively involved with *The Way We Were*, but the controversy over screenplay credit continued. Would the credit read "by Arthur Laurents" or "By Arthur Laurents and Alvin Sargent"? The issue grew heated enough for arbitration by the Writers Guild, and on May 21, 1973, five months before the film's release, a verdict was reached. In a ruling addressed to Rastar Pictures at Columbia, with copies to Arthur Laurents, David Rayfiel, and Alvin Sargent, the Writers Guild of America West ruled that credit remained solely with Arthur Laurents: "Written by Arthur Laurents" it would be.

Laurents's day-to-day involvement with *The Way We Were* was now at an end, and Pollack, Margaret Booth, and John Burnett continued to edit without his input. Fine-tuning throughout the spring and summer of 1973, they arrived at a two hour and eight minute cut just in time for two sneak previews. Laurents had wished Stark a very muted "good luck" back in December, but the true test had now arrived: over the course of the next two nights, everyone involved was about to find out whether good luck—or disaster—lay straight ahead.

Sneak Previews

"To say a movie is in trouble because of a bad screening is like looking at a building when it's still all raw steel girders and scaffolding and saying it's going to be ugly. You really can't tell until it's finished." —Director Barry Sonnenfeld

Columbia Pictures had by now arranged two September sneak previews in San Francisco, a test screening before the sophisticated urban audiences who comprised Streisand's most devoted fan base. Pollack liked sneak previews and believed in listening to the audience: when they laughed and where they grew restless would tell him what fine-tuning remained.

The lights dimmed, the Columbia Pictures logo of a robed woman with a torch appeared, and images of 1940s New York City flashed on-screen. As the opening credits rolled, the audience remained utterly quiet, seeming to lean into the film as they wallowed in the old-fashioned romance of it all. Sydney Pollack and Ray Stark began to exhale. The title song seemed to instantly resonate with the audience, smoothly bringing the audience back in time to Hubbell and Katie's college days. In fact the only criticism of the song came from the Bergmans themselves, who squirmed just a bit when the words "misty watercolor mem'ries" were heard exactly as Hubbell was glimpsed rowing. It was all a bit too on the nose for the lyricists, but as Alan later admitted—"no one else is noticing that." Laughter was coming in all the right spots; there were no rustling sounds of boredom and no quick mass exits for a smoke.

Here was the biggest of musical stars underplaying effectively and in just three simple words—"Oh boy, Hubbell"—delivered when Hubbell shares the news of selling his story, conveying not just her delight in his success but an entire world of pent-up emotion. The audience held a rooting interest in the outcome because only now, in the fully scored and edited version of the film, could the full extent of Redford's remarkable contribution to the movie be glimpsed. Robert Redford was a born film actor, able to convey acres of information with a single glance; Barbra's may have been the flashier role, but it was Redford's attitude, his skill at conveying internalized emotion, that made audiences understand why the romance could never work: Hubbell Gardiner was a golden boy who never fully grew up, a man/child unable to take the hard but necessary path in life.

And then, just as Pollack and Stark allowed themselves a moment of happiness and dreams of success, the roof fell in. Exactly two-thirds of the way through the film, at the precise moment when politics pushed through to the forefront, the audience grew restless, restless as in leaving the theater to buy popcorn and make a phone call or two. Pollack and Stark exchanged looks: they had lost their audience.

Oh yes, when the love story resurfaced, especially with the final farewell in front of the Plaza, the audience's interest returned, but somehow even that ending lacked the powerful emotional impact everyone had anticipated. Furthering the uneasiness was Sydney Pollack's knowledge that audiences during a film's regularly scheduled commercial run would not be quite as forgiving as those at a sneak preview, where a feeling of being the first to see the newest film resulted in a certain generosity of reaction. All of this meant one thing: as the pleasantly entertained but not exactly thrilled audience filed out of the theater, Sydney Pollack knew he was going back to work.

With a razor blade. Literally. Radical surgery was required before the second preview on Saturday night, and Sydney Pollack was going to cut entire sections out of the answer print in less than twenty-four hours. In Ray Stark's recollection, "The love story and political scenes strengthened each other. But it became obvious to us that the audience was more interested in our two stars than in any message. During the first preview we borrowed Francis Coppola's editing room and worked all night with the editing with John Burnett and Margaret Booth. We cut fifteen minutes—the political scenes." Said Pollack, "We didn't have a movieola—we had scissors and a razor blade. We didn't change anything. We took out five scenes, and they were all politics."

The first sequence to hit the cutting-room floor:

- Scene 199—In their Malibu beach house, after a pregnant Katie sharply reminds Hubbell that his fraternity in college would not allow Jews to join, she argues with him about her trip to Washington, insisting, "I'm going to Washington because it isn't fair to let our friends take a beating for the rest of us and not do something." Ever distanced, Hubbell replies, "It's a gesture, Katie. A pointless, futile gesture that can cause a helluva lot of trouble."

  Katie: I'm not afraid of trouble.

  Hubbell: Not even for us?

  Structurally, the scene nicely foreshadowed their final argument after Katie's return from Washington, but Pollack found it lacking in impact. Enough already with the politics. Gone.

- Scene 219—Slated to run immediately after Hubbell and J.J. drift lazily on the sailboat, the sequence featured a pregnant Katie driving past a college campus and glimpsing a

> college student protesting against the Truman loyalty oaths. This undergraduate, clearly representing a younger version of the still-passionate Katie, causes Katie to pull over to the side of the road, where, with the title theme playing in the background, she sobs—for everything she has lost and the inevitable compromises she has made. Said Streisand in later years, "It's a scene about what has happened to me as Katie—how have I sold out. . . . It makes one rethink one's life and purpose in life." In later years, the director allowed as how the scene did work: "Everything about the scene is wonderful and she is very good in it." He even smilingly acknowledged his disagreement with Barbra over the deletion: "Barbra and I have had a 30-year discussion about a couple of scenes which she loves. . . . It's thematically right—everything about it is wonderful—*The Way We Were* is really playing in the background. Barbra is crying."

And yet, in September 1973, for a director who had just witnessed a disinterested audience's reaction to several of the film's political sequences, here was yet another message intruding upon the love story. It all represented one too many scenes of a tearful Katie Morosky: "By itself it was a very moving scene, but for me it was one beat too many of her crying. She cried in the projection room when she said, 'I want us to love each other.' She cried when she said, 'Stay with me until the baby comes.' At the hospital she cried and then there's the final scene. By then I felt there was too much crying. So I took the scene out."

Fifty years later, Streisand herself explained why she felt so strongly that the deletion of the scene hurt the film: "That scene was the very definition of the title—*The Way We Were*. It was a defining moment for Katie, because she realized how far she had come from her younger self, who was willing to speak out and fight for what she believed in. Then, when she finds out she's been informed on, she's suddenly forced into a decision. It's the moment, as Arthur said, when the politics and the love story come together, and it's Katie who makes the selfless choice to end their marriage, in order to save Hubbell's career in Hollywood . . . and reclaim her own ideals.

Without those two scenes, you've lost the climax of the story, and the essence of her character as well as his, because Hubbell was willing to stand by her. I've been trying to get those two crucial scenes back into the film for 50 years, since 1973."

Barbra's dedication to the political elements earned her praise from the hard-to-please Laurents: "She fought for certain scenes, the political scenes. It was because she understood intuitively what they meant to Katie. She was wonderful about that."

Ironically, in the long run, the excision of that crucial scene actually proved an impetus to Streisand's directing career. Reported Rachel Montpelier on the Women and Hollywood website, Streisand felt "horrified" when Pollack cut "scenes that [she] felt illustrated why her on-screen relationship with Robert Redford's character ultimately disintegrated." Barbra, like Laurents, felt the political sequences were crucial to the love story at the heart of the film: "The political background of this beautiful love story is what sets it apart from other love stories. That's why you can't ignore the political ramifications of why they broke up." If the scenes of Katie weeping over the sight of a younger more radical version of herself were going to be cut, and if ten minutes of crucial political footage were going to be edited out, then Barbra Streisand wanted to be the one making those very decisions. In her own blunt assessment, "I directed because I couldn't be heard."

Next to hit the floor was the scene of Katie and Hubbell attending a conference on civil liberties at the Beverly Hills Hotel, with the keynote speech delivered by their friend Brooks Carpenter. This was to be Brooks's shining moment as a representative of all the principled writers who, unlike Hubbell, spoke out loudly in defense of freedom of speech. Speaking to a sympathetic audience, the impassioned Brooks cried out, "The government, my government is now threatening to imprison a writer for what he writes or thinks. I do not understand that and I deplore it. That is not the way to defend democracy, that is the way to destroy it."

Ironically, in Pollack's memo four months earlier regarding script deficiencies, it was this very scene that he had singled out as the most effective political sequence in the film. And yet now, in the wake of audience indifference at the test screening, it was, insisted Pollack, all too much with the politics: out went the political conference and along with it, the scene of Katie secretly writing a check to help fund the conference.

Even so, not every unfilmed or deleted political scene represented a big loss. No one missed the lengthy scene of a fundraiser for Carpenter's freedom of speech committee, one in which a comic master of ceremonies droned on about the Hollywood Ten while Katie argued with both Bissinger and Hubbell. The scene did feature the energizing sight of Hubbell exploding: "Goddamit, Katie, you are not in college! . . . Fuck the Bill of Rights! We never had free speech in this country and we never will because people are scared!" But—and it was a big but—the tone was bitter and undercut the love story. Only the highlights of the scene eventually resurfaced, albeit in different form, with both Hubbell's passionate assertion about the Bill of Rights (minus the word "fuck") and Katie's climactic cry that "People are their principles" emerging in their Union Station fight.

What's most interesting about the deleted scenes is that they reveal how very differently Laurents and Pollack viewed the reasons behind the dissolution of Katie and Hubbell's marriage. If, to Laurents, the couple broke up because of the moral differences reflected in their political beliefs, Pollack strongly disagreed: "[T]he implication was that [politics] caused the break-up, but that's not true and that's why the scene is not in the movie. Everyone accepts the break-up without it. The problem was structurally that it created a new possibility of hope and yet another ending: we had an ending in college, an ending and break-up in NY, an ending and break-up in Hollywood when we found out he was cheating on her, then the story started again—and that's when you could feel the audience thinking 'Oh, no—it's not going to start again, is it?'"

The toughest cuts of all, however, came in scene 219b, an extended political sequence that went a long way toward explaining Katie and Hubbell's final breakup. James Woods recalled that in a very early version of the script, Frankie McVeigh did inform on Katie during the Red Scare. That scene was not filmed, but the nugget that remained found Katie more surprised than angry when told that Frankie has informed on her:

> *Katie: He what? . . . That's crazy—he was my date at the senior prom and you cut in for ten seconds. What could he tell them? I left the party during the war for God's sake.*
>
> *Hubbell: They don't care about that.*
>
> *Katie: But I'm a nobody. I haven't been near the studio in months. Because I'm your wife?*
>
> *Hubbell, there is no justification for informing.*
>
> *Hubbell: Is that what you think I want you to do?*
>
> *Katie: I don't know, I don't know, I don't know. All I know is that if I don't name names you can't get a job in this town.*

The dialogue went on to further ground the inevitability of their breakup, with Katie stating hopefully, "If we got a divorce you wouldn't have a subversive wife—that would solve everything, wouldn't it?" But Hubbell, always the more realistic of the two, ruefully replied, "No. No, it wouldn't."

Katie and Hubbell's political differences have finally come home to roost amidst the paranoid atmosphere of the blacklist, and in a carefully planned mix of character, plot, and political background, the question of informing was to represent the dramatic peak of the film. Yet now, the frustrated Laurents railed, the divorce flew at the audience out of nowhere.

It's a viewpoint shared by Barbra herself who recently analyzed as follows: "There was a void at the center of the story, because of a last-minute cut that eliminated two crucial scenes—the UCLA scene and the Frankie McVeigh scene, where Hubbell tells Katie she's been informed on. Without those scenes, you don't understand why they broke up."

Out the Frankie McVeigh scene went, however, because if Pollack felt that the political editorializing got in the way, it didn't matter how much it deepened understanding of the characters—it was bound for the cutting-room floor: "The problem was that the breakup was inherent in the picture right from the beginning . . . so it wasn't necessary to stop everything for this new development."

As far back as his December 1971 letter to Redford imploring him to take on the role of Hubbell, Pollack had viewed the love story as the absolute focus of the film: "The political and social areas should only be background, with their story always the foreground." Eighteen months later, as he edited the film, his perspective had not changed: "I didn't want to lose sight of the fact that the romance was what people cared about. Audiences would say 'Oh yes, this is all very interesting. But let's get back to 'Is he going to kiss her?' Or 'Are they going to fall in love?' Or 'Are they going to get together?'"

It was, he felt, all a matter of timing: "I could feel that the problem wasn't the politics—they didn't want any more—but the biggest problem was that it came at the very end when timing-wise we couldn't start over again with another chapter. . . . once he cheated on her and once they saw that, when we tried to start it over again with the two of them, the audience got up and went for popcorn."

In the process of wholesale trimming, Hubbell and Carol Ann's entire affair now registered as a "blink-and-you'll-miss-it" moment. As originally scripted, Katie was to arrive at the studio to apologize to Hubbell, only to see him making love to a woman on the projection-room floor. Now, however, the scene jumped from an insinuating encounter between Hubbell and Carol Ann on the studio backlot to Katie plaintively asking Hubbell, "Why her—why did you have to go back to Beekman Place?" Katie has seen nothing, Carol Ann and Hubbell have exchanged no more than three lines of dialogue, and all of a sudden Katie and Hubbell are getting divorced? Audiences, understandably enough, would have a very tough time connecting the dots.

For Sydney Pollack, however, the deleted scenes did not fulfill the most important function of all, that of pleasing the audience: "[W]e had to emasculate the picture by taking out an awful lot that was political in it that was quite good I thought, but boring for the audience." Much to his pleasure, the film now transitioned directly from Hubbell's affair with Carol Ann to Katie asking him to "Stay with me until the baby is born." Analyzed the director, "From the end of the screening room scene ("I want us to love each other") to the break up—("Will you stay until the baby is born")—I knew they'd watch the hospital scene so I wanted to delete the politics and have the movie play straight through." Razor blade and all, it was worth it to Pollack: "It was the first time the movie worked."

A trifle defensively, he rationalized his decision: "I think it dealt very well with politics, but it's hardly the definitive film about McCarthyism just as *Casablanca* is hardly the definitive film about World War II. It was never intended to be. . . . What I basically like about the film is what attracted me in the first place. When I read it, I cried, and I managed to get that on the screen."

Streisand herself maintained an appropriately nuanced understanding of just what was lost in the wholesale editing of the political scenes: "Hubbell really belonged in Hollywood. He didn't belong in France writing a novel. He was happy there in Hollywood. And that's why my character says, 'Will you stay with me until the baby is born?' It's accepting reality. And it has strength and it has character and intelligence in that decision. The way it is now, without those two scenes, it makes it seem like they broke up because he slept with another girl once."

In retrospect she was struck by how many others noted the missing narrative pieces: "I had to look at the reviews while writing my own book, and it's interesting to see that several critics noticed the gap in the storyline. They were missing the missing scenes! Sydney let me put those scenes on the 25th anniversary DVD and clearly other people missed them as well because years later someone put them on YouTube and the comments are basically all the same—now they understand the movie for the first time!

"People still love the movie. Obviously it works, because it was a big hit. But it felt incomplete to me."

In Arthur Laurents's view, "The climax wasn't there—and no one cared. No one knew and no one cared. I think the person who cared the most about the film is Barbra." It seems no accident, then, that when the deleted scenes finally saw the light of day as an extra on the twenty-fifth anniversary edition DVD, the credit at the end read, "Deleted sequences courtesy of Barbra Streisand."

Exactly how much footage was cut remains subject to debate; on the twenty-fifth anniversary special edition DVD, Ray Stark refers to cuts totaling "fifteen minutes," while other accounts put the amount of deleted footage anywhere from five to eleven minutes. What remained unquestioned, however, was the fact that when shorn of the offending political footage, the film played to a much better audience response at its second sneak preview. As Hubbell and Katie's marriage began to crumble for good, no one rushed out for popcorn, and the hundreds of spectators remained silent, engrossed in the end of a mismatched love affair. Recalled Pollack, "When we previewed it the next night, the audience absolutely loved the picture. All of a sudden everybody was ecstatic." Stark went even further, claiming that with the film's running time now fixed at one hour and fifty-eight minutes, all of the cuts had helped strengthen the remaining political content: "Actually what we cut helped the politics that remained in the film because it provided the background. We made the point and then moved on. That's the best kind of storytelling."

Pollack and Stark pronounced themselves happy, but one disgruntled member of the creative team remained: Marvin Hamlisch. Hamlisch was not, in fact, unhappy with Pollack's choices but with his own. Sitting through the first preview, Hamlisch realized that his decision to delete the title theme from the ending of the film was misguided in the extreme: "Rationally that made perfect sense. . . . Emotionally . . . big mistake."

Afraid of overusing the melody, Hamlisch had cheated the audience of its own catharsis; without that familiar theme, the audience had remained emotionally distant as they watched Katie and Hubbell part forever. No one was crying, few seemed particularly upset, and the overriding reaction seemed to be one of "ho-hum, I guess they broke up for good."

It remained for arranger Leo Shuken to deliver commonsense advice about the use of the theme song: "Marvin, if you play it twenty times, the audience may think they've only heard it three or four times. Remember, while *you* are listening to the clarinet and the oboe, *they* are listening to the dialogue."

Realizing that Shuken was correct, Hamlisch came up with what he regarded as an easy fix. He needed just one final version of his melody to conclude the film and felt certain that the reprise would send the audience out of the theater in a heightened state of emotion.

A quick recording session would do the trick: one new ninety-second version of the theme song, complete with Barbra's vocal, would now be played over the final fade-out and credits. Calculating rapidly, he arrived at a figure of fifty-five musicians, each to be paid for three hours of work. It was, he felt, well worth the money it would cost Columbia Pictures. Their reaction? Nothing doing.

Undaunted, Hamlisch decreed that he'd pay for all fifty-five musicians himself: "This picture had everything going for it, and I wasn't going to sit by and let it slip away for a mere ninety seconds. So I went back to the head of the music department and told him that I'd pay for the rerecording myself." The startled executive acquiesced—it was, after all, Hamlisch's money.

The theme would now underpin the entire farewell scene; it would first be heard via a plaintive harmonica as Katie spies Hubbell in front of the Plaza Hotel. It would next swirl in again right after Katie brushes Hubbell's hair off his forehead one last time. Swelling to full strength after Hubbell utters a final "See you, Katie," it would only be after the camera pulls back that Streisand's vocal would float onto the soundtrack. The recording session was booked, and the new theme quickly dispatched and edited. At the next screening Hamlisch attended, he braced himself as Katie and Hubbell said goodbye and the orchestra swelled. He waited tensely—until he heard the sound of a single woman crying, and then another, and yet one more, until crying jags broke out throughout the theater. The song worked and the movie worked. Wrote Hamlisch, "And knowing it was right made it worth every penny."

It was time to face the critics.

Screenwriter Arthur Laurents. His own life inspired the script. PHOTOFEST

Producer Ray Stark and Barbra Streisand on the set of Funny Girl. *Their working relationship was one of mutual admiration—and aggravation.* COLUMBIA PICTURES/PHOTOFEST ©COLUMBIA PICTURES

Before Katie and Hubbell, a meeting of Streisand and Redford (with Jack Valenti) at the 1969 premiere of Butch Cassidy and the Sundance Kid. PHOTOFEST

Hubbell Gardiner and Katie Morosky at El Morocco: the first time audiences see them together. COLUMBIA PICTURES/PHOTO 12/ALAMY STOCK PHOTO ©COLUMBIA PICTURES

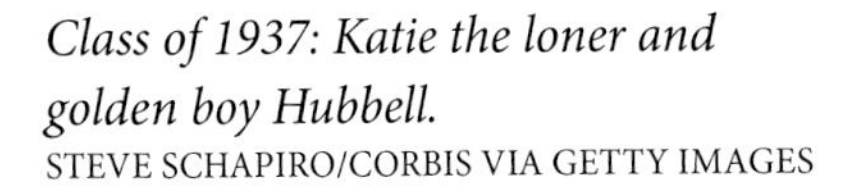

Class of 1937: Katie the loner and golden boy Hubbell.
STEVE SCHAPIRO/CORBIS VIA GETTY IMAGES

Hubbell and Carol Ann (Lois Chiles). Katie's sarcastic jibe: "Look who's here—America the Beautiful."
COLUMBIA PICTURES/PHOTO 12/ALAMY STOCK PHOTO ©COLUMBIA PICTURES

Katie the waitress: "Onions?" Hubbell: "In the Cokes."
MOVIESTORE COLLECTION LTD./ALAMY STOCK PHOTO

Katie's public humiliation. Barbra said of the scene, "I felt like I used to feel a lot, an outcast, people laughing at me. It felt natural."
MOVIESTORE COLLECTION LTD./ALAMY STOCK PHOTO

Hubbell's mixture of pride and embarrassment as his story is read aloud—an incident taken from Laurents's own life. ARCHIVE PHOTOS/STRINGER/GETTY IMAGES

Looking great in period clothes, with no detail too small for consideration: "What am I wearing? The blue? With the white and hat? Could I have changed? Should I . . ."
AF ARCHIVE/ALAMY STOCK PHOTO

Bêtes noires of Arthur Laurents: producer Stark and director Pollack on the set.
COLUMBIA PICTURES/PHOTOFEST ©COLUMBIA PICTURES

Katie and Barbra: vulnerability beneath the bluster.
MOVIESTORE COLLECTION LTD./ALAMY STOCK PHOTO

The senior prom and an intimate, erotic "Wrap Your Troubles in Dreams."
COLUMBIA PICTURES/PHOTOFEST ©COLUMBIA PICTURES

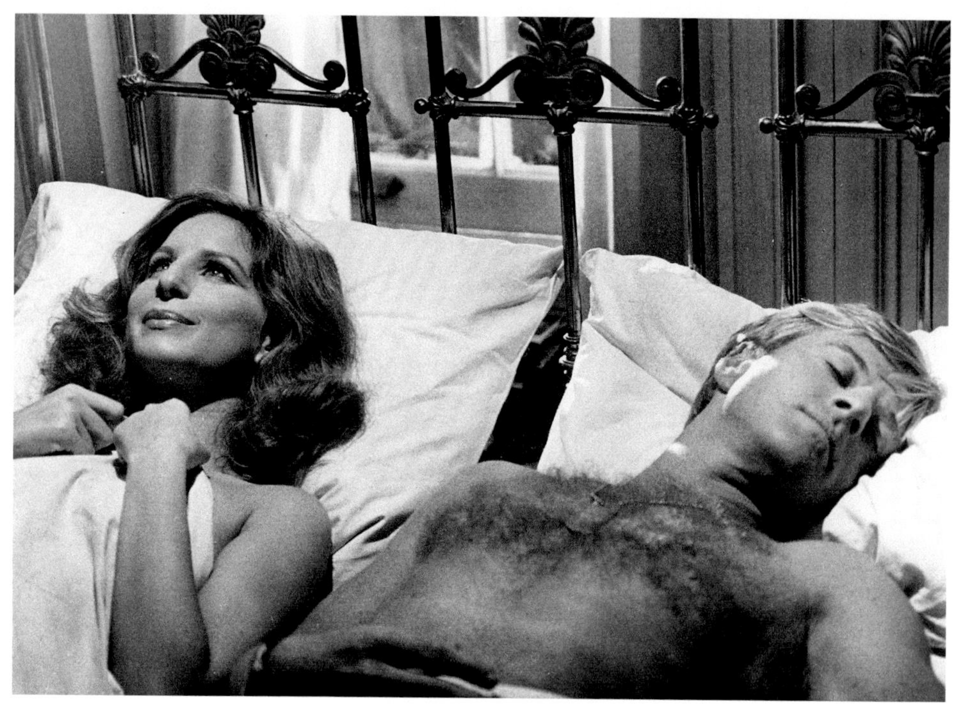

"Hubbell, it's Katie. You did know it was Katie?"
COLUMBIA PICTURES/PHOTOFEST ©COLUMBIA PICTURES

Role reversal: Katie insistently gives her number to Hubbell. ALBUM/ALAMY STOCK PHOTO

Star-driven glamour and a throwback to Hollywood's golden age.
COLUMBIA PICTURES/PHOTOFEST ©COLUMBIA PICTURES

Star power, part two—and a rare shot of Barbra's right profile.
COLUMBIA PICTURES/PHOTOFEST ©COLUMBIA PICTURES

1940s New York City. Thirteen takes, thirteen hot dogs . . . PICTURELUX/THE HOLLYWOOD ARCHIVE/ALAMY STOCK PHOTO

Thirteen hot dogs later, Katie is left holding the umbrella. COLUMBIA PICTURES/PHOTOFEST ©COLUMBIA PICTURES

Happy in New York before the political storms hit.
COLUMBIA PICTURES/PHOTOFEST ©COLUMBIA PICTURES

A Central Park idyll with, no surprise, Katie manning the oars. AP IMAGES

How to direct two superstars: carefully. BETTMANN/GETTY IMAGES

Just before the explosion at J.J.'s party. The staging of this scene infuriated Laurents. KPA PUBLICITY STILLS/UNITED ARCHIVESGMBH/ALAMY STOCK PHOTO

Katie and Hubbell in California. Barbra said in later years, "I did feel safe with him, perfectly safe . . . every day on set." KPA PUBLICITY STILLS/UNITED ARCHIVESGMBH/ALAMY STOCK PHOTO

A Marx Brothers party in Hollywood. Shoehorned in for a change of pace, it didn't really work, but Groucho himself came to the set.
KPA PUBLICITY STILLS/UNITED ARCHIVESGMBH/ALAMY STOCK PHOTO

Katie returns from Washington, Hubbell swings into action—and Arthur Laurents fumed.
STEVE SCHAPIRO/CORBIS VIA GETTY IMAGES

Joint reaction to the possibility of naming their daughter Rakhael Gardiner.
STEVE SCHAPIRO/CORBIS VIA GETTY IMAGES

Just four words—"Streisand and Redford together"—and the audience was hooked.
COLUMBIA PICTURES/PHOTOFEST
©COLUMBIA PICTURES

An international phenomenon.
COLUMBIA PICTURES/ALAMY STOCK PHOTOS ©COLUMBIA PICTURES

"Your girl is lovely, Hubbell." COURTESY OF PHOTOFEST

One last touch. COURTESY OF PHOTOFEST

Goodbye—forever. COURTESY OF PHOTOFEST

The 2002 Academy Awards: "I guess this is the sequel, huh, Babs?" Still friends, still Katie and Hubbell. MIKE NELSON/AFP VIA GETTY IMAGES

Love Letters, Brickbats, and an Adoring Public

> *"We lost a lot of innocence in the dark movie palace of our youth.* The Way We Were *reclaims it for us. Years from now, in some futuristic movie museum, it just might be one of the movies we'll be looking at and remembering with fondness."* —Critic Rex Reed

On October 16, 1973, the night before *The Way We Were* officially opened to the public, a black-tie gala benefit screening on behalf of the Just One Break charity was held in New York City. Barbra Streisand and Robert Redford were nowhere in sight, although Streisand did attend the October 23 West Coast premiere at the ABC Entertainment Center in Century City, a benefit for Cedars-Sinai co-chaired by Ray Stark's wife Fran; according to *Women's Wear Daily*, the turbaned star, escorted by Herb Allen, who had recently purchased a controlling interest in Columbia Pictures, made her entrance an hour late.

It was Ray Stark and Sydney Pollack who represented Columbia Pictures at the New York premiere, mingling with Governor Nelson Rockefeller and Mayor John Lindsay, Barbra's mother Diana Kind, and celebrities ranging from Tony Bennett and Ken Howard to Alice Faye, Lorna Luft, and Joan Fontaine. The Fifty-Eighth Street side of Bergdorf Goodman's department store, located directly opposite the Plaza Hotel, was decorated in the style of the 1940s, with vintage autos lining the street and Harry James's orchestra providing songs from the big-band era. Said James Woods, "I heard about the premiere—I wasn't invited—but I got myself in. Seeing myself on screen as a young actor was surreal because I love movies and I never thought of myself in terms of these big glamorous Hollywood movies. It was almost unbelievable to me. When there was a closeup of me on screen I remember thinking, "Oh, shit! I'm in this movie with Barbra Streisand and Robert Redford—that's very cool. I remember one other thing very clearly from the premiere: when Katie slid into bed with Hubbell, it was like the entire audience was cheering!"

Rapt audience or not, Stark and Pollack had their minds on exactly one item: the reviews appearing in newspapers the next morning. Would there be triumphant lines outside the three theaters showing the film in Manhattan, Long Island, and New Jersey, or were they about to become grist for the schadenfreude mills always running rampant in top-tier Hollywood circles?

The advance review in *Variety* had proved mixed at best, predicting that a big opening would be followed by a sharp drop-off: the film, *Variety* sniffed, was "a distended, talky, redundant, and moody melodrama," before adding that "Robert Redford has too little to work with in the script." The newspaper's heaviest artillery was reserved for Streisand, noting that "[t]he overemphasis on Streisand makes the film just another one of those Streisand vehicles where no other elements ever get a chance."

Variety, however, was an industry publication, not much read by the general public. What of the *New York Times*? Taking a momentary break from the party, Pollack and Stark opened up an advance copy of the next day's *Times* and breathed a sigh of relief: "Streisand is still too shrill at moments; but this is the most forceful, controlled acting she's ever done. Redford is superb."

Scanning other papers, they found a critical reaction that seemed to find a well-acted film featuring two genuine stars almost, but not quite, done in by heavy-handed political storytelling. On the plus side of the ledger, Roger Ebert of the *Chicago Sun-Times* gave the film three stars out of four, and in prose sure to gladden at least one of the film's stars, he then added, "It's easy to forgive the movie a lot because of Streisand. She's fantastic. She's the brightest, quickest female in movies today, inhabiting her characters with a fierce energy and yet able to be touchingly vulnerable." Even in his essentially positive review, however, Ebert was the first to single out the plot holes caused by the excision of so much political material: "[I]nexplicably, the movie suddenly and implausibly has them fall out of love—and they split up without resolving anything, particularly the plot."

Led by *Time* and the *New Yorker*, however, negative word seemed to leak in from the weekly magazines. Carped *Time*, "an ill-written, wretchedly performed and tediously directed film." For her part, the *Village Voice*'s Molly Haskell found the film's plot holes bewildering, writing of Hubbell's decision to leave Katie after she has given birth to their daughter, "She seems to know all about it, but it came as a complete shock to me." *The New Yorker*'s Pauline Kael wrote the most equivocal review among the weeklies, first noting the gaps in the film's plot: "The decisive change in the characters' lives which the story hinges on takes place suddenly and hardly makes sense." She then pronounced the cinematography "ugly"; stated that the film had every reason to end up a disaster; and most amusingly, provided proof that she did not have much of a future as a popular music critic, calling the soon-to-be Grammy Award–winning Song of the Year "a whining title-tune ballad which embarrasses the picture in advance." She concluded her musical criticism by deeming Hamlisch's score "excruciating" and reminiscent of a bad movie from the 1940s.

And yet, after all of those barbs, she admitted that Streisand and Redford turned in first-rate performances and that the film contained some well-written and well-directed sequences before finding "the damned thing enjoyable." The movie, she concluded, actually constituted "hit entertainment and maybe even memorable entertainment."

Unsurprisingly, the most vicious review came from the vitriolic and often-condescending Stanley Kauffman in the *New Republic*. Reliably acerbic (he had thoroughly panned *The Godfather*) Kauffman lit into the film, calling it "glittery trash—a category that to me means New Truth pasted on Old Cardboard. The script is fake-daring. . . . Not one moment in the picture is anything but garbage under the gravy of false honesty. Only the music is frankly awful." Kauffman reserved particular disgust for Sydney Pollack and Barbra Streisand: "The director, Sidney Pollack, makes sure that everything is worse than it has to be. . . . The girl is Barbra Streisand, who is still a monster."

Those who read the *New Republic* did not, it was safe to say, represent the film's target audience, which meant that Pollack and Stark were particularly cheered by positive reviews in mainstream publications whose readers did; wrote Howard Kissel in the second review to run in *Women's Wear Daily*, "It is hard not to be carried away by the film's lush romanticism. *The Way We Were* is the sort of film that makes you wish Hollywood were thriving again." Pollack and Stark cared little for the *New Republic*'s intellectual theorizing in the face of strongly positive mainstream reviews that urged the film's middle-of-the-road target audience to immediately spend their money at a local movie theater. In the words of *The Christian Science Monitor*, "What really makes the film such a gripper is two-fold. First, the really lustrous performances of its two superstars, Streisand and Redford. They are perfect foils for each other in romantic comedy, the way that Katharine Hepburn and Cary Grant were. It is her funny, pummeling energy and style versus his effortless charm, cool, and beauty." Raved Gene Shalit about Streisand, "She acts her head off!" while the *New York Daily News* echoed with a backhanded compliment: "Barbra Streisand does something quite remarkable in *The Way We Were*—she acts." In the words of *Films Illustrated*'s Douglas Slater, "They don't live *for* love, they live in *spite* of it, and that's good drama."

This mixed critical reception was repeated when the film opened overseas in February 1974. In a perceptive review written for *Punch*, critic Benny Green instantly grasped that at heart, *The Way We Were* remained a romance of illusion, and he singled out the bittersweet dialogue near the film's end as symbolic of its missed connections; if Katie, in Hubbell's perceptive gaze, has always remained a nice Jewish girl, then the logical next question remains whether or not Hubbell has remained a nice gentile boy. Asked that very question by Katie, Hubbell delivers the clearest of answers: "I never was—you only imagined it." That contradiction, wrote Green, might make the film itself a bundle of missed opportunities but one that remained worth a viewer's time: "But if *The Way We Were* is a premeditated tearjerker, if its grasp of period, of moral responsibility, and of literary integrity, is so uncertain, why bother to see it? The answer is: Streisand, and I suspect that Robert Redford, who conveys to perfection Gardiner's beautiful, irresistible, fatal weaknesses, will forgive me for saying so."

Ultimately, however, it was Molly Haskell's essentially negative review that actually pointed the way toward an understanding of the film's immediate and enduring appeal: the ending. After two hours spent watching mismatched lovers who can live neither with nor without each other, and after all of the hills and valleys caused by holes in the plot, came a final scene in blazing technicolor for everyone who had ever pined for the wrong person. In uncharacteristically free-swinging prose, Haskell enthused,

> I would trade many an art film classic for the final exchange between Redford and Streisand in the front of the Plaza. As the lovers take their last leave charged with unspoken emotion and

> unslaked desire, we enjoy not just the double vision of Redford as the spoiled and unfulfilled Wasp hero and Redford as Redford who belongs to us all, but the third dimension of Redford as the stand-in for every lover male or female, we've had and lost, lost too soon before we'd had a chance to grow tired of him. Redford becomes the all-purpose lover, the weak drifter, the security minded woman, the married man who doesn't want to get involved. . . . Perhaps the scene derives extra power and sadness because Katie Morosky is saying, along with a number of women, good-bye to irrational love, to love's tyranny over a woman and to reverence for a certain kind of man cast falsely in the image of God. Whatever its appeal it is a thrilling moment, the kind that is usually dismissed as "sentimental" by serious critics because its sources and wellsprings are emotional.

What remained unstated in Haskell's piece was that the power of Redford's image depended on the strength and sensuality of Streisand's own persona; never again, in any of his pairings with Jane Fonda or Meryl Streep, would he generate such heat on-screen, a fact due in large part to Streisand. A feminist in her own life, Streisand simultaneously also served as the one genuine inheritor of the old-school Hollywood dream factory ethos, a woman who had, as a young girl, inhaled larger-than-life fantasies while dreaming of a better life from the balcony of Brooklyn's Loew's King Theatre. Just as with her musical status as the last true believer in Tin Pan Alley sentiment, the on-screen Streisand presented the image of a modern woman still searching for romance even while forging her own singular path through the male-dominated world of show business. She spoke to women caught up in the burgeoning women's movement who nonetheless still believed in the romantic traditions of the past, the ugly duckling turned swan who tries to land the prince, sometimes successfully, sometimes not, but always on her own terms.

As evidenced by the very mixed critical reception that *The Way We Were* received, critics, it seems, don't much like movies that exhibit a direct heart-on-the-sleeve emotionalism. They remain, generally speaking, suspicious of a popular success, especially one that lands squarely in the vein of *Casablanca*, *An Affair to Remember*, and the Frank Capra classics. It was, after all, the openly emotional qualities evident in Capra's *Mr. Smith Goes to Washington* (1939) and *Meet John Doe* (1941) that led critics to derisively dub the films "Capra-corn." That dichotomy between critics and audiences was in fact best summed up by Robert Redford himself: "Critics had trouble with *The Way We Were* because they won't own up to their own emotions. They figure that it's got to be off center or bold before they can accept it. . . . Intellectually you know Katie and Hubbell shouldn't be together, but on a gut level you want them to make it because you like them and because they like each other. That's a fair emotion."

As the film opened around the country, one question loomed: just who would be proven right, Robert Redford or the critics? The answer came as audiences throughout the United States flooded the box office with millions of dollars that caused a palpable sense of relief at severely cash-strapped Columbia Pictures. In *The Way We Were*'s ode to heartbreak, audiences had found a romance to embrace, and as the box-office grosses continued to grow and with the title song climbing to the top of the charts, murmurs of possible recognition in Hollywood's ultimate popularity contest, the Academy Awards, began to grow into a chorus. Would there be nominations for Hamlisch and the Bergmans? For Harry Stradling Jr.? What of the thus far Oscar-less Sydney Pollack and Robert Redford? In fact, was the film's popularity so strong that even the perennially unpopular-with-the-voters Streisand might be rewarded with the town's ultimate status symbol, an Oscar?

As it turned out, no one, not even the most veteran Oscar prognosticators, could have predicted the surprising outcome.

The Academy Awards

> *"Most awards, you know, they don't give you unless you go and get them—did you know that? Terribly discouraging."* —Barbra Streisand

Riding a wave of box-office success throughout the fall of 1973 and into the new year, *The Way We Were* began garnering award recognition even before the Academy Award nominations were announced: Streisand, Hamlisch, and the Bergmans nabbed Golden Globe nominations for Best Actress and Best Song, and after all of the Sturm und Drang over the film's screenplay, Arthur Laurents received a Writer Guild's nomination in the category of Best Drama Written for the Screen. A British Academy of Film and Television Arts (BAFTA) nomination for Barbra as Best Actress proved another welcome bit of recognition from the industry, but the best news of all came when the Academy Award nominations were announced on February 19, 1974: the alternately adored and dismissed *The Way We Were* scored no fewer than six Academy Award nominations: Best Actress (Streisand), Cinematography (Harry Stradling Jr.), Production Design (Stephen B. Grimes and posthumously, William Kiernan), Costume Design (Dorothy Jeakins and Moss Mabry), Dramatic Score (Marvin Hamlisch), and Original Song (Hamlisch with Marilyn and Alan Bergman). There may not have been any *The Way We Were* nomination for Robert Redford, but he was, in fact, nominated as Best Actor that year for his performance in the Best Picture favorite, *The Sting* (in the end, he lost to Jack Lemmon's emotional turn in *Save the Tiger*).

With the ceremony scheduled for Tuesday April 2, 1974, much of the talk centered not on Streisand's nomination but on whether or not she would perform her hugely popular rendition of the title song during the telecast. By this point, Streisand had stopped performing live; forgetting the lyrics to "Lover, Come Back to Me" at her 1967 Central Park concert in front of 135,000 people had frightened her to the point where she confined her singing to the recording studio, a safe, controlled environment where her perfectionist instincts could be granted free rein. Snagging the elusive Streisand, then the world's most popular female vocalist, would prove a coup for the telecast, leading the show's producer, Jack Haley Jr., to pull out all the stops. Please, the Academy asked, would Barbra sing her worldwide number-one hit—for a global television audience in excess of one hundred million?

Haley waited—and then waited some more. Finally, the answer came back from the Streisand camp: no. Barbra Streisand simply would not sing live. Haley accepted the verdict and asked Peggy Lee to sing the song. Lee agreed and cancelled a scheduled appearance in Canada for that same night. Announcements were made, orchestrations prepared—at which point, Streisand changed her mind and said yes, she would in fact sing the song live. Haley, reluctantly but firmly, declined the offer. Peggy Lee had changed her concert schedule to accommodate his request, and he would not rescind the invitation. Peggy Lee, after all, was a proven star; Barbra Streisand, seated in the audience, would hear the song at the same time as the rest of the world.

Streisand rushed to the ceremony from a first day of shooting on *Funny Lady*, but too nervous to sit in the audience, she remained backstage as she watched her friend Marvin Hamlisch (sitting alongside date Liza Minnelli) run to the stage to accept the Best Adapted Score Oscar for his work on *The Sting*. After losses in the categories of production design, costume design, and cinematography, *The Way We Were* team was relieved when Hamlisch followed up his first win with a Best Score Oscar for *The Way We Were*. When Hamlisch won that second Oscar, he joked, "What can I tell ya? I'd like to thank the makers of Maalox for making all this possible!"

As the evening progressed, Peggy Lee turned in a strange if somewhat haunting performance of *The Way We Were*, taking the song at an extremely slow tempo while mixing up two of the stanzas. What Streisand thought of the performance remained unknown, but she was unquestionably pleased when Hamlisch returned to the stage yet again, this time alongside Marilyn and Alan Bergman as the joint winners of the Academy Award for Best Song. Accepting his award from a semi-naked Cher, who mangled his name as "Marvin Hamilschmidt," the composer immediately returned the favor by thanking "Chair" for presenting him with the Oscar. After weeks of abandoned melodies, two completely different songs, and three different orchestrations, "The Way We Were" had triumphed.

A poll of the public, conducted the night before the ceremonies by Channel 5 television's "Your Choice for the Oscar," had found Streisand to be the odds-on favorite to win Best Actress, and yet her win at the Oscars remained far from certain for one reason: the hunt for Academy Awards often devolved into a popularity contest, and Barbra Streisand remained unpopular in Hollywood for not playing by the normal rules. Refusing interviews, she kept to herself and in the process committed the worst Hollywood sin of all: she remained successful even while charting her own, nontraditional path. Hollywood held a grudging acceptance of her enormous talent, but it was far from guaranteed that such acceptance would translate into a second Oscar for the diva.

Among the other four nominees—Ellen Burstyn for *The Exorcist*, Glenda Jackson in *A Touch of Class*, Marsha Mason for *Cinderella Liberty*, and Joanne Woodward in *Summer Wishes, Winter Dreams*—it was Woodward who was perceived as Streisand's chief competition. Yet Woodward, too, was viewed with suspicion as someone who eschewed the Hollywood lifestyle in favor of a quiet life in Westport, Connecticut, with husband, Paul Newman. She had won the New York Film Critics Award as Best Actress but had not endeared herself to the Hollywood-based contingent with her blunt statement that "[t]he Oscar has become a political gesture, or a business gesture."

As the show passed the three-hour mark, the names of the Best Actress nominees were finally read by Charlton Heston and a very ill but still beautiful Susan Hayward (making what was to be her last public appearance). The winner—in an upset—Glenda Jackson. If Streisand and Woodward were not particularly popular, then Jackson, it appeared, had squeaked in as a more palatable substitute. Jackson was not present, and Streisand was not in the audience, but Burstyn appeared displeased by the outcome, and a palpable sense of surprise ran through the audience.

The absent Jackson's award was accepted by *A Touch of Class* producer Melvin Frank, but when queried by the press, Streisand did not hesitate to tell Lawrence Grobel that she felt a bit cheated: "Unlike the year I was up for *Funny Girl* and there were five strong performances, this time I felt [my performance] was the best performance of the year." There was consolation in the form of a David di Donatello Award as Best Foreign Actress (her second) and a Golden Globe as "World Film Favorite," but neither held the prestige of the Oscar.

It was a loss that Barbra did not forget, and the extent of the disappointment was revealed nearly two years later when she saw her makeup artist Don Cash Jr. and quipped, "I thought you said I was going to win the Oscar."

Streisand may have lost, but *The Way We Were* was now acknowledged as a winner. Resolutely old fashioned in its narrative continuity and open-hearted emotional declarations, it had set box-office records and inspired devotion and critical disdain in equal measures. With the passage of time, its success had led to one overarching question: given all of its shortcomings, why did the film pack such an emotional wallop?

The Good, the Great, and the What-Were-They-Thinking: Scene by Scene with Katie and Hubbell

> *"Like anything that's delicate, where something you've wanted for so long is happening, there is this sense that, if you breathe, it will go away."* —Sydney Pollack

To Robert Redford, who never saw the final cut of *The Way We Were* at the time of its initial release ("I was in another country when the film came out"), *The Way We Were* continues to succeed because of the very dichotomy built into its tale of mismatched lovers: "Call it a Jewish *Love Story* or a WASP dilemma. . . . Politics was the only area in which she could find an identity. She is drawn to an All-American boy, a kind of Prince Charming, who apparently has everything she could never have and has always been considered wonderful. He is attracted to her because she represents a commitment and a passion, something he doesn't have in his life." To Barbra Streisand, it was the mysterious attraction between radically different personalities: "We are naturally opposites. There's the mystery of who that person is."

Lois Chiles herself may have been playing the beautiful Carol Ann, yet it was the hard-charging Katie who struck a chord with her: "No question—I identified with Barbra's character. I understood Katie's passion and her political point of view. I actually felt compassion for both Hubbell and Katie—so loving, so mismatched. I understood who those people were."

Neal Gabler, in his idiosyncratic Yale University Press analysis of Streisand, takes a more academic approach, positing that *The Way We Were* represents the "tension between morality and aesthetics"; Katie, in Gabler's view, personifies the moral force and Hubbell, the aesthetic. That dichotomy, he reasons, plays out as an offshoot of the conflicting ideologies between America and Europe, themes most notably explored in the novels of Henry James.

It's an interesting and well-reasoned theory, but it is also doubtful that many fans of *The Way We Were* reach for Henry James when caught up in the technicolor wash of the movie's ill-fated romance. That sun dappled glamor matters, because even before becoming caught up in the star power of Streisand and Redford, audiences respond to the very look of the film. At the time of the film's original release, their response seemed suffused with a near palpable longing for a supposedly more innocent "misty watercolor" era. Filled as they were with economic uncertainty, an unpopular war in Vietnam, and Watergate, the 1970s were making nostalgia for a simpler time into a big business, and Hollywood took note.

Audiences, however, continued to embrace the beautifully designed world of the film well beyond the time of the original release, and as one commentator analyzed, "There is a sense of innocence to that love, and a sense of innocence to America at that time, that feels unforgettable. . . . It feels resonant in any era that you watch." The highly effective period look, of course, was a product of production design, set decoration, cinematography, and costuming. Says film scholar Jeanine Basinger, "When you have the top level of craft in every department—in costuming, design, cinematography, music—people respond to the sheer craft and professionalism. This is what happened with *Casablanca, The Wizard of Oz, The Sound of Music*—every one of those movies featured top pros at the peak of their considerable talents."

Particular credit, then, should be granted to Harry Stradling Jr. for a golden-hued cinematography that presented a Barbra Streisand who looks more beautiful, romantic, and desirable than ever before or since. The cinematography captures a star who appears at home throughout the film's decade-spanning plot, the romance of it all evident right from the film's opening scenes in World War II–era New York City. Streisand looks great in the period clothes—she has always worn clothes with great flair—and she is helped in that regard by the purposefully romanticized look of the film.

Even the opening titles, designed by Phill Norman with a slightly art deco feel, proved to be important in that regard, sending a subliminal message of times gone by. Coming as they did after the film had jumped from the 1940s back to the 1930s, the titles' nonlinear placement, appearing on-screen just as Barbra begins humming the title song, granted Pollack a big advantage: "You can play around with time, go anywhere you want to go. What was important to see here was the contrast in their two lifestyles. His mainstream All-American hero along with Katie being the very serious political student, one who types under a picture of Lenin."

It's a relatively rare Hollywood film that is circular in nature, but this one is. That very structure helps engender an emotional response from the viewer because the ending of the film is actually present in the beginning: Katie Morosky begins in the 1930s as a curly-haired college radical urging students to strike for peace and ends the film as a curly-haired 1950s political activist protesting against the bomb. Hubbell starts the movie as the golden-haired campus jock surrounded by adoring WASPy friends and is last glimpsed in front of the Plaza Hotel in the company of another, much younger WASP beauty. Katie and Hubbell are, in their own ways, the epitome of F. Scott Fitzgerald's famous closing lines from *The Great Gatsby*: "So we beat on, boats against the current, borne ceaselessly into the past."

In Streisand's case, she had thirty-plus outfits to help complete that journey, but Stradling took as much care in lighting Redford as he did Barbra, presenting the handsome star with a sustained power that began with his opening close-up. First glimpsed drunkenly asleep on a barstool in El Morocco, there is such glamour about Redford, such power to his looks when the camera closes in, that if the viewer is reminded of anyone, it is the first sighting of John Wayne in John Ford's *Stagecoach* (1939), in which Wayne nearly jumps off the screen in his masculine beauty and power. There's a reason why, right before Katie leans forward and brushes Hubbell's hair off his forehead, she actually catches her breath at the mere sight of him.

Thanks to Stradling, Pollack, and Redford, the power of Hubbell's image is such that as a bell tolls in the background and Barbra Streisand is heard on the soundtrack beginning to gently hum the introduction to the title song, the film dissolves back to the 1930s in a manner that seems both inevitable and fitting. Who, the audience asks, is this man? What is his story? As Streisand's vocal widens on the words "Mem'ries—light the corners of my mind," the titles flash over silent, brightly lit footage of Redford's athletic prowess (neatly contrasted with the darker-hued images of Katie plodding along at a variety of jobs), and the viewer is seduced. This has all been so skillfully handled that audience members already accept the essential vocabulary of the piece: how time shifts in our memories and how we romanticize the past. In the words of the title song, "Was it all so simple then/Or has time rewritten every line?"

Streisand's humming is essential because if she had instantly begun singing, the entire song would have felt like a full-blown musical number, precisely what Robert Redford did not want to happen in the film. Instead, the humming eases the audience into both the vocal itself and a trip back in time to college. Streisand, age thirty at the time of filming, actually seems a little more believable as a college student than does the thirty-six-year-old Redford, but Hubbell's athletic triumphs seem so complete that as Arthur Laurents aptly pointed out, he does appear to be winning an entire track meet by himself—only the scripted but cut vignette of Hubbell pitching for the baseball team was missing from his seeming ability to dominate world athletics. At the exact same time that Hubbell seems headed for the Olympics, Katie is established as his opposite number, the campus eccentric grimly marching through college life while agitating against the fascists in Spain. Without the use of any dialogue, time, place, and character have all been established within five minutes.

It is clear that Katie is not just a striver but also an underdog and perpetual outsider, which is why Pollack's silent nighttime shot of Streisand walking by a sorority house is so oddly affecting; as rich sorority girls dance and laugh it up, Katie, briefcase in hand, walks by outside, glancing up wistfully but knowing she'll never be invited to join. Katie's habitat, one senses, is her empty room with a poster of Vladimir Lenin for company. For all her disdain of "drippy co-ed humor," she stands with her nose pressed up against the window.

What Laurents's screenplay smartly does is to take its time in showing exactly how Hubbell begins to fall for Katie. Audiences know that with these two big stars front and center, a love story will inevitably ensue, but they don't know how and when it's going to occur. Hubbell does not immediately tumble to Katie's inner beauty, but instead, he is first intrigued by her at the moment of her greatest humiliation: the rally for peace at which she wins over the crowd until pranksters wave signs behind her that collectively read, "Any peace but Katie's piece." Katie's angry knee-jerk response is to brand the students fascists, but as the crowd laughs, Hubbell does not join in. Pollack, in fact, felt that Hubbell was "disturbed when she is humiliated." Hubbell is responding to her intensity and passion, and he silently appraises her—interested but noncommittal. Said Barbra, "I liked that scene. I felt like I used to feel a lot, an outcast, people laughing at me. It felt natural."

It's a beautifully acted scene, which plants the seeds for Hubbell's growing interest in Katie. At the same time, the two characters seem to live at an overwhelming distance from each other, she with the masses, he with the detached elite who stand aside and observe. Indeed, the way Pollack shoots the peace rally further enhances their dissimilarities on a subliminal level: Katie is the speaker, dominant in the frame, while Hubbell, as spectator, stands lower in the frame, distanced from the speaker's stage. Opposites in every way, Katie and Hubbell have still not held a direct conversation, a situation changed by the film's cut to the restaurant where Katie works as a waitress. As Hubbell and gang enter, Katie, in a nice bit of sharp dialogue that keeps any sentimentality at bay, mutters to ever-faithful boyfriend Frankie (James Woods) "Look who's here—America the beautiful."

Intrigued by Katie, Hubbell tries without success to make her laugh while he orders hamburgers and cokes:

Katie: Onions?

Hubbell: In the Coke.

For his troubles, Hubbell receives nothing but a sour look from Katie. They continue to verbally spar:

Hubbell: We weren't making fun of you—

Katie: You make fun of everyone.

The rhythm between Streisand and Redford and their different styles and pace of speech as actors all work to heighten the characters' differences, even while establishing the glimmer of attraction. Streisand thrusts, Redford effortlessly parries, both actors slipping with ease into the rat-a-tat-tat rhythm of the dialogue. Said Pollack, "You couldn't do much improvisation here—the scenes were carefully written—one beat led to another. It was all headed in a very certain direction." James Woods watched both stars carefully, saying of Redford, "He's such a great film actor. Bob slid into that character very well, and make no mistake, he may not have wanted to rehearse as much as Barbra, but he worked very hard on his approach."

Audiences have sensed that underneath her surface disdain, Katie has remained fascinated with Hubbell, and when the film cuts to a nighttime scene in the library, she openly and repeatedly glances at him, even as loyal Frankie McVeigh sits right next to her. (The first part of the scripted scene was cut, a loss because of its delineation of character; when Hubbell temporarily left his seat, Katie slid over to steal a look at his notebook, one filled with drawings and the nicely prescient words "And in the end, would it be worth it?"). Katie simply can't help but stare at Hubbell, and it's no wonder: as romantic music plays on the soundtrack, thanks to the lighting by Stradling, Redford's Hubbell actually seems to glow. Staring at his pencil and oblivious to Katie, his thoughts are a million miles away, while Katie's are all but palpable.

The scene is granted extra texture by the presence of James Woods's Frankie, an outcast who jealously watches Katie eye Hubbell. Woods's presence in the scene was not planned but was cleverly engineered by Woods himself: "I was thinking about how I could be a part of the scene and realized I could be a part of it by being an obstacle. So—I said to Sydney: 'I have a great idea.' Sydney instantly said, 'You're not a part of the scene. We don't need you in there with the two biggest stars in the world.' Then I said to Barbra, 'Let's talk about acting for a minute—the library scene.' Barbra looked at me and kept her reply short: 'The scene is with Bob and me.' I kept going—I told her 'But isn't it more interesting if Frankie is there in the library, looking at Katie while she's looking at Hubbell. Now the scene wouldn't be so simple—it's more interesting.' Barbra took a beat, thought about it, and then said, 'Sydney—the kid is in the scene!'" Such chutzpah came readily to the Utah-born Woods, who in 1970 had snagged a part in the award-winning Broadway play *Borstal Boy* by pretending he was British.

Woods appreciated Pollack's openness to change: "He was open to last minute improvisation. The great directors are because they know you can often get things you wouldn't otherwise. Yes, I was happy to have more screen time, but I wasn't hogging the camera—it was furthering my character as well as Barbra's. Having me in the library added to Katie's emotional confusion about Hubbell. She's so committed to politics yet infatuated with Hubbell even while she has this dorky but devoted boyfriend. It makes audiences wonder 'What's she going to do?'"

Thanks to his own unbridled ambition, James Woods was in the scene, side by side with superstars Streisand and Redford and a presence to be noticed. Said Woods of the experience of filming with the two stars,

> I loved working with both of them. They were so open to discussion. Barbra was great. We talked and she said, "Are you afraid of me?" I said, "No. I can act—it's every man for himself." She wasn't offended—she really laughed.
>
> Redford was terrific as well. He would sometimes come by my trailer, which was, needless to say, a lot smaller than his! We'd talk about acting—at that point I wanted to be a stage actor. I had just won a Theatre World Award, but he's such a

> great film actor I knew I could learn from him. I proudly call myself a character actor, so it's interesting to me that I think Bob and Brad Pitt, two classically handsome leading men, are at their best when they are being character actors.
>
> Having him stop by was a terrific opportunity to talk to this big star. Redford was and is a great underactor—he conveys so much with so little. I was, at that point, an overactor. He talked about how to convey emotion on film. If you look in a mirror and your eyes change focus as you start thinking about a problem, you should think the thought, don't act it. You see the eyes change.
>
> I learned from him and even though I was a complete unknown, both Barbra and Bob were good to me. It's actually hard to explain the level of stardom they held at that time because it just doesn't exist today. They were larger than life stars. The public's fascination with them was extraordinary. That very short sequence at the beginning of the film where Hubbell throws the javelin? Women were standing around all day just to get a glimpse of him!

It is this library scene, in James Woods's view, that helps make the film "a complex Hollywood film," while for director Pollack, it's the scene that anchors the film by serving as "the bridge" to Katie and Hubbell's subsequent relationship. The sequence also held an additional purpose: Hubbell is ostensibly spending his time in the library working on a story for the creative writing class in which both he and Katie are enrolled, and in the next scene, his story is read aloud by a professor who refers to the author as a "surprising new source." Katie bursts into class late, only to be crushed when she learns that it is not her story being read aloud but Hubbell's. Hubbell, who seems nothing so much as embarrassed by the attention, turns out to have genuine literary talent and for the first time, is shown to hold actual substance beneath the golden shell. The sequence works not just because of the unexpected revelation that it is Hubbell, not Katie, who possesses the real literary talent but also because Redford skillfully expresses the appropriate mixture of pride and self-consciousness found in any college student singled out for attention.

Realizing that Hubbell writes with a skill to which she can never lay claim, Katie is intrigued in spite of herself, but the scene is also noteworthy for Laurents's beautifully judged metaphor for Hubbell's own life. Hubbell's short story is titled *The All-American Smile*, and in voiceover, the audience hears the professor reading aloud: "In a way he was like the country he lived in: everything came too easily to him. But at least he knew it. . . . About once a month, he felt he was a fraud, but since most everyone he knew was more fraudulent . . ." (Unfortunately, cut was the character-defining ending to Hubbell's story: "But of course, by then they were too lost or too lazy. It had always been too easy.")

This voiceover helps the depth of Hubbell's writing register with the movie audience, and the scene ends on a finely wrought bit of underscoring as the professor's voice fades away and Katie rushes out to tearfully rip up and throw away her own story. As originally scripted, her rush out of class was to be preceded by a short scene in which the professor gently tries to tell her that he too wanted to be a writer but had to accept the fact that he didn't have any real talent: "Unfortunately, neither commitment nor a first-class mind necessarily makes a first class writer. Of fiction, that is." That scene now exists only as a brief silent shot of Katie nodding her head at the teacher's words of instructions, the dialogue having been cut in order to accelerate the pace at which the audience learns of Katie's dashed dreams.

In an interesting hiccup, Streisand could not at first produce the tears required while tearing up her story. Relayed Pollack, "Howard Koch came up to me and said I just have to warn you she's self-conscious about the crying—about everyone watching. She has a block about it. She thinks she can't cry." Pollack, however, understood that the emotion lay near the surface, just waiting to be unlocked: "No one can sing the way she can sing and not cry. . . . She needs relaxing, in a way, because she's so full of emotion." As Barbra grew increasingly tense and upset, filming halted until Pollack walked to her side and put his arms around her. Whispering words of encouragement, he called "Action!" once again and watched the tears flow precisely on cue.

In that sensitive handling of Streisand lay proof positive of Pollack's reputation as an actor's director. Barbra herself appreciated Pollack's very particular skill set: "Sydney could articulate—could give you that little trigger. He was sensitive to the actor." It's a skill underscored by assistant director Hawk Koch's own on-set observation: "He was a master at casting the right actors for his film, at getting them to say yes. I've worked with Robert Benton, Roman Polanski, and Warren Beatty, but Sydney was the one who really, really knew how to get actors to give their best. He got into an actor's head in a good way. Polanski was the best from a technical standpoint, but Sydney was the best with actors." Pollack, it seemed, knew just when to encourage, when to push, and when to lay back. Echoed James Woods, "Sydney was 100% an actor's director. Ray Stark was on the set all the time because he was a very powerful producer who wanted things his way, yet it remained Sydney's film. He knew exactly when to let the stars work it out."

Even at this early point in production, Streisand and Redford's rapport had grown to the point that their scenes were infused with personal attributes that deepened their characterizations. Redford, in fact, analyzed their multileveled relationship in terms of its growth: "When we started on *The Way We Were*, she wanted me *to be* Hubbell. That was how she conceived me. And then as the shoot went on, she saw I was not that man, not in any way. So she reoriented herself and the professional took over. But afterward I wondered, 'Did she return to that banal concept of me? Was I—am I—a Hubbell figure in her mind?' I had never fully sorted that out, and some of that tension made our chemistry on-screen."

Streisand's attraction to her co-star had by now been supplemented, indeed surpassed, by her appreciation for Redford's personal qualities. He was a man who, for all of his surface dazzle, never skated by on charm alone, instead working hard to investigate every possible layer of his character. Said Barbra in later years, "I just loved working with him. Every day was an exciting adventure. He's a man of depth who has what it takes to be a great movie star: mystery behind the eyes. You wonder, what is he really thinking?"

It is that very sense of mystery that informs the next key scene in the film, a nighttime encounter between Katie and Hubbell at an outdoor café. When Katie spies Hubbell sitting by himself, she is still so uneasy about her attraction to him that she crosses the street in order to avoid him, succumbing only when he calls her over. Hubbell has news, and he wants to share it with Katie.

For all of his status as the big man on campus always surrounded by admirers, there is something about Hubbell that sets him apart from his own crowd, "something soulful" in Pollack's reckoning. Such a personality trait represents a nice blending of actor and role because if, in Redford's own words, "there's a part of me in every part I play," then the silences and distances that inform both Redford and Hubbell are precisely what attract people to actor and character alike. Hubbell has chosen to be by himself at this crucial moment in his life until the one person who can understand what his news means happens to arrive on the scene. Analyzed Pollack, "I felt he was really happy when he saw her and wanted to tell someone he had sold a story. His crowd—it wouldn't matter to them, but it would to her."

Katie is reluctant to join him—even late at night, there are seemingly a dozen places she needs to be—but this time, Hubbell's wondering comment "You never quit, do you?" is said with a smile and admiration. When he insists she drink a beer with him, they clink glasses, and excited by his news, Katie immediately enthuses, "To your first novel." She is already pushing, and he both shies away from the idea and embraces it. Writing is likely the first activity in Hubbell's life that has required actual labor. Will he work at it? Burnish his native talent through the necessary endless revisions? The answer is unknown—the mystery of it all hooks audiences, who begin asking themselves the most elemental question of all: what happens next?

With Hubbell seated behind a low stone wall and Katie continuing to stand, the duo are physically separated until Katie laughs at her own nervousness and begins to relax. Their bond is strengthening, and there is a surprisingly poignant moment when Katie wonders aloud, "Commencement—what a funny word for the end." It's a nicely judged moment, with the value of screenplay tinkering underscored by the smart decision to change exactly one word, jettisoning the original "what a crazy word for the end" and replacing it instead with the more wondering "what a funny word for the end." (It was at this point in the film that Hubbell was to recite the story of teachers loving his smile, but the scene, although filmed, was wisely cut, the point having already been made.)

This nighttime scene resonates precisely because all of the awkward pauses and gestures reveal Katie's essential character. Underneath the bluster, she is shy, vulnerable, and attractive, qualities that help to inform the intimate moment, scripted by Alvin Sargent, in which Hubbell commands Katie, "Put your foot up here"—he is going to tie her shoe. Arthur Laurents objected to the scene as filmed, finding it poorly written and directed, but he was wrong. It is a deeply personal, erotic moment, tender and full of unspoken feeling. Thanks to a beautifully calibrated combination of script, acting, and cinematography, it is at this precise moment that Katie and Hubbell's love affair begins to feel inevitable. Their mutual awareness of both attraction and seemingly irreconcilable differences lends the film an unexpected punch, the deserted nighttime setting underscoring the feeling that the audience is overhearing the most intimate of conversations. It seems as if there is no one else alive in the world at that moment, no one but two college seniors circling each other in mutual desire tinged with just a bit of disapproval.

After exchanging final glances, she takes her leave, their parting marked with the bittersweet emotion that will come full circle in the film's final scene:

> *Go get 'em, Katie.*
>
> *See you, Hubbell.*

The nighttime scene's feeling of near-pulsing desire is deliberately and silently heightened in the final college scene, that of the senior prom. A white tie and formal gown occasion, the prom not only heightens the romantic appeal of the setting but in and of itself, serves as a perfect summary of an entire vanished era. In the twenty-first century, no one in college would don formal wear unless intended as an ironic comment, or as stated in the very first episode of *Sex and the City*, "Welcome to the Age of Un-Innocence."

For a generation of college students raised on rock music, the big-band prom music played by twelve local musicians represented an utterly foreign territory, a fact that resulted in Broadway dancer (*West Side Story*) and choreographer Grover Dale being hired to teach the hundreds of period-clad extras the Lindy and Big Apple dances popular in the 1930s. As it turned out, it was that very dancing that led to an unexpectedly sweet moment during rehearsals. Redford, who enjoyed tweaking the all-business approach of assistant director Jerry Ziesmer, was scheduled to begin the prom sequence by dancing with one female extra before walking over to cut in on Barbra as she danced with James Woods. Sensing a chance for good-natured revenge on Redford, Ziesmer told the star that he would have to dance with twelve different extras for Pollack to choose the right one. Redford hesitated but played along and danced with at least six girls. By this point, the mood proved contagious, and cast and crew began dancing with the other female extras. Wrote Ziesmer, "James Woods danced. Brad Dillman danced. Then there was a bit of excitement on the edge of the circle, and Barbra came onto the set and watched the dancing," at which point, related Ziesmer, "One brave tuxedoed extra, a lot braver than I could ever be, asked Barbra Streisand to dance. I held my breath as I watched her. She hesitated a second, then smiled and began dancing with him. It was a magical moment."

Choreographer Dale quickly began working with his soon-to-be-wife, Anita Morris, to teach the nearly three hundred extras how to fox trot, but he also spent particular time staging a sixteen-bar Lindy for Streisand to dance with James Woods. It was another small opportunity for Woods to register on film, and he was more than ready: "I went to public school in Rhode Island and at the grade school I attended we had two out-of-the-norm activities: we went to the police range to learn how to use weapons safely, and we had ballroom dancing with Mr. and Mrs. Basso. This was just about the time rock and roll was coming in but we had learned to jitterbug, so I was definitely ready for this bit on film. In fact, when I was twelve years old I was in a mother-son dancing competition and we won the cha-cha competition!"

After choreographing the dance on Woods and Anita Morris, Dale, in his own laughing explanation, recalled that he and Morris "ended up following Barbra Streisand around in hopes she'd look at what we'd choreographed. I was nervous—during all of that time, part of your brain is convinced she'll hate it." Finally, after three days of waiting and wondering, Dale and Morris received their audience with Streisand, who, true to form, cut to the chase: "Let me see what you've got."

Even for the veteran Dale, it was more than a bit intimidating. "I remembered that when I was dancing on Broadway I went to see Barbra in the Village in a little club. She was so fantastic—I decided I couldn't go meet her. I was that overwhelmed by her talent." Now, faced with Streisand's scrutiny of his work, Dale asked Morris and Woods to dance the routine he had choreographed for Katie and Frankie McVeigh: "They danced, everyone applauded, and Barbra said, 'OK—teach it to me.'" Said Woods, "With her musicianship, Barbra learned the dance right away. I grabbed her—the music was playing—and that was that."

In Dale's recall, "They brought over the camera and lights and shot it right on the spot. That was it—we were done and said goodbye. It was all so fast that Anita and I were given our contracts after the fact! We took our paychecks, hopped into a limo to go back to the city, and poured champagne. I was relieved—I had passed the test of having all of the dances approved. We had survived *The Way We Were*!"

Arthur Laurents was right when he complained in a memo to Stark that more of the jitterbug was needed, but the key musical moment at the prom came not with the Lindy but instead with a ballad; as standards from the era, including the languid "Red Sails in the Sunset," play in the background, Hubbell deliberately walks over to Katie and cuts in on Frankie. In Woods's recollection, "These were the last shots in Schenectady. Sydney said to me, 'We're rotating the camera around. Hubbell taps in on you, you take a beat, and then get out of there.' I promised Sydney I wouldn't screw up, so he gave me a close-up for my reaction after Hubbell cuts in."

After cutting in on Frankie, Hubbell takes Katie in his arms, and they dance oh so slowly to the gossamer-like "Wrap Your Troubles in Dreams." Not a word of dialogue is spoken, the eroticism underscored by deliberate restraint as Pollack heightens the sensual atmosphere with close-ups courtesy of one of the then new, lightweight handheld cameras: "The cameraman was in his socks trying to dance with them—so close that it makes the focus rocky, but it doesn't matter because I had the shot." Katie and Hubbell, or is it Barbra Streisand and Robert Redford, their faces mere inches apart, gaze at each other the whole time, the erotic heat in full force until dance over, he walks away into the crowd, slowly disappearing as ringing bells bring characters and audience alike back to El Morocco in the 1940s.

As originally scripted, when Streisand and Redford finished dancing, a silent montage of the deserted campus at night—all stillness, shadowy trees, and empty buildings—was to glide by until the chimes heard at the beginning of the college sequence would quietly toll once again and bring the viewer back to New York City in the 1940s. It was an evocative notion, but the cut from the slowly disappearing Redford back to El Morocco accomplished the same task just as effectively and in less time.

Fortunately, the creative powers decided to cut the dialogue that had been written for this return to El Morocco, all of which featured a rather labored metaphor of Hubbell disclosing that he had drawn Katie's face in the sand. That heavy-handed bit of dialogue was to be repeated at two other points in the film and fortunately, never saw the light of day in any of the scenes. Instead, with the sexual heat mounting from a combination of the intimate college dance and the reunion at El Morocco, audiences were now primed for a consummation of that desire. The film delivers—but with a surprise.

After leaving El Morocco and returning to Katie's apartment, a naked Hubbell passes out in Katie's bed, but in a reversal of normal expectations, it is his body the camera lingers over, not hers. As Katie undresses and slips into bed beside him, she softly murmurs, "Hubbell—it's Katie. You did know it was Katie?" In just that one line, Laurents has summed up Katie's extreme vulnerability, asking a question Pollack termed "heartbreaking—heartbreaking because she doesn't know if he really knows it's her or not." If, in his drunken stupor, Hubbell greeted her at El Morocco with a quizzical "Hey—What do you know," audiences are now left wondering if he may have just slept with Katie while still not knowing who she is.

The scene unfolds with such startling intimacy that Pollack filmed it on a closed set, the bed surrounded by long black cloths meant to block the view of any person attempting to catch a glimpse of the stars. He filmed the sequence in an almost entirely silent fashion, shooting the scene from overhead while Katie appears alternately nervous and thrilled, gently touching Hubbell's hair as he rolls on top of her and briefly makes love.

Given the intimacy of the scene, Pollack admitted to worrying a great deal about the staging: "The scene has comedy in it but it has a sweet touching comedy; I wanted it to be touching and sexy and if you look at it, the solution was simplicity. No tricks. I stuck a camera above the bed and shot straight down on them. . . . it's really all lighting and the two of them. Didn't want to get graphic or make you embarrassed or make you laugh. The scene worked because of the two of them."

Hubbell and Katie as well as Redford and Streisand were poised on a precipice here, which is why Pollack felt the scene had to be shot from Katie's point of view. In a beautifully judged analogy, Pollack explained, "Like anything that's delicate, where something you've wanted for so long is happening, there is this sense that, if you breathe, it will go away." Having employed a handheld camera to increase the sensuality of Katie and Hubbell's dance at the prom, in this scene Pollack decided to utilize a slowly tightening zoom lens in order to arrive at the same effect: "I actually had a zoom lens on the camera, and very imperceptibly kept tightening during the whole scene." It's a scene both erotic and unsettling but one with an illusion of nudity so convincing that even without any actual on-screen nudity, Redford's then-wife Lola commented, "You looked stark-raving naked in that bed scene with Barbra! What on earth were you wearing?" His answer, "Aramis."

The sensuality of the scene is startling because of the chemistry between the two stars, their unusually strong connection made even clearer when compared to love scenes in their other films. Streisand never displayed this level of connection in movies with Ryan O'Neal, Kris Kristofferson, or Nick Nolte, and while Redford has made three movies with Jane Fonda, their most explicit bedroom scene, in *The Electric Horseman*, displays little of Hubbell and Katie's eroticism. That lack is partially because Fonda's character is much more sophisticated and sure of herself than is Katie Morosky and partly because of Fonda's on-screen persona: no matter the scene, her own vulnerability was often hidden underneath a steely façade.

At this point, the movie is still unspooling at a nicely measured and bump-free pace, and even when Katie and Hubbell have a brief, free-flowing political discussion about Communism and FDR, Laurents's talent for the character-defining one-line zinger shines through:

Katie: How do you know what the Party says?

Hubbell: You still think a varsity letter stands for Moron.

It's a welcome surprise for audiences that Hubbell is now seen sparring intellectually with Katie, the scene playing out as if one of Pollack's points in his preproduction memo had indeed been heeded—that by the 1940s Hubbell had matured into a different and more serious person than the college senior last glimpsed at the prom. Audiences root for Hubbell and Katie because they make each other better, a point made crystal clear when they begin discussing Hubbell's writing. Katie, it turns out, has read Hubbell's novel—twice—and when he asks her which parts she didn't like, she delivers incisive criticism that allows us to see why she is the one critic he will trust, and trust in a way he never would his Beekman Place crowd.

Katie: Your style is gorgeous—but you stand back. You watch the people from a distance.

Hubbell: Where?

Katie: All through it.

Hubbell the writer mirrors Hubbell the man; even in his role as novelist, he remains reluctant to dive in and wrap himself in the messiness of everyday life. Since it all does come too easily for him, why fuss? Which is precisely why Katie pointedly asks him, "What doesn't come easy now?," and while Hubbell may jokingly answer, "Hotel rooms," he doesn't speak further because at this point, everything in America really did still prove easy for a golden boy.

When they are glimpsed drinking wine in front of a fire, lit to a fare-thee-well in profile, it is clear that Katie and Hubbell have fallen into a love that they will never find with anyone else, no matter how much easier such a love might prove to be. Commented Pollack about his stylistic choices in the scene, "The first time they really are consciously together is the firelit scene discussing his book. Like all love scenes you try to find a way to make it romantic without being sappy and sentimental about it. I worried about the fire but I went for broke."

By the 1970s, the subject matter of films had begun to matter more than did the stars themselves, and the combination of a growing sophistication among audiences, the intrusion of television, and the proliferation of alternative ways of spending leisure time had all led to a diminution in the importance of stars. All of this meant that Pollack could have fallen on his face with the overt romanticism of the fireside scene, but it worked for exactly one reason: a pairing of Barbra Streisand and Robert Redford that proved star power still existed—in spades. Here was a chance for audiences to wallow in the sight of two hugely popular movie stars at the peak of their appeal, and as "The Way We Were" theme played softly underneath the dialogue, it was clear that the filmmakers had deliberately traveled back to the ultra-romantic style of filmmaking prevalent in 1940s Hollywood before the breakup of the studio system dismantled the publicity machinery that so carefully cultivated the aura of larger-than-life stars.

At this point in the film, Hubbell and Katie return to the monied world of J.J. and Carol Ann for a cocktail party, with Katie still reacting to that group as if they are the "in" crowd at school and she the outsider. Speaking with the coolly beautiful Carol Ann (Lois Chiles), Katie finds the distance between them still unbridgeable:

Katie: You haven't changed at all—

Carol Ann: Neither have you.

Those two lines speak volumes about the different universes in which these two women live, and not only because Chiles's deliberately laconic manner of speech lies light years away from Streisand's charged delivery.

By now Chiles had played scenes with both Redford and Streisand and did not actually find their styles to be the polar opposites of legend: "I think the talk of their very different styles has probably been somewhat exaggerated. I liked both of their styles. Bob Redford and I developed a real friendship—it was like he became a big brother in a way. I actually didn't rehearse this scene in the apartment with Barbra very much—I remember being very struck by her vulnerability. I was happy with both of the apartment scenes we had, the first when we speak one-on-one and then when Katie explodes after the death of Roosevelt."

It is in that second scene, when Hubbell and Katie return to J.J.'s apartment immediately after the death of President Roosevelt, that Katie blows up over the Eleanor Roosevelt jokes: "Her husband is dead! Yes, Mrs. Roosevelt went down into the mines! When they asked her why, she said, 'I am my husband's legs.' Did you tell the cripple jokes, too? Is there anything that isn't a joke to you people?!" Breaking the very uncomfortable silence that follows her lecture, Katie ups the stakes by lashing out at all of Hubbell's friends. She insults J.J. and causes Hubbell to draw a line in the sand—he doesn't want to be anywhere sad right now, and he displaces all of his anger onto Katie: "Everything in the world does not happen to you personally! Behave yourself!" The fact that Katie takes everything personally is precisely what makes her both so effective and so frustrating: she is the center of her own moral universe. Isolated in J.J.'s apartment with all eyes upon her, she storms out.

The scene is dramatic, well acted by all involved, highly interesting—and yet still detrimental to the film, sending the heretofore smoothly unfolding love story spinning off the tracks and jolting the audience out of its willful disbelief. What Laurents had written as a private disagreement had now been rewritten and staged by Pollack so that Katie and Hubbell's argument detonates directly in front of the entire Beekman Place gang. The emphasis of the scene had now changed, and as a frustrated Laurents pointed out, the claustrophobic public staging of the argument has made Katie into an unreasonable humorless shrew, while Hubbell remains a strong, stoic leader of men. Why, in fact, would Hubbell stay with someone so aggressive in her anger? Coming as the second of two consecutive arguments between Katie and Hubbell, it's a scene that causes an imbalance in the film's structure: they have tangled at J.J.'s cocktail party with Katie barking, "You're too good for Hollywood!," and they are now quickly fighting again after the death of FDR. The audience's goodwill has been damaged.

There is, however, one element that partially—but only partially—redeems the scene: for the first time ever, Hubbell has taken a strong position of his own. Katie, he witheringly points out, does not hold a monopoly on the world's pain. Hubbell finally has some guts: he has acquired the substance Redford so desired, but it has been achieved at a cost to the overall effectiveness of the film.

And what exactly was that cost? The fault does not lie with Streisand's performance but instead with how Pollack stages the scene; Katie may be exciting, but she now also seems exhausting—and to the audience, somehow too exhausting. She's a woman of substance but also one who uses up all the oxygen in the room. At the same time, while Hubbell remains the essence of charm, he still registers as aimless, and if the scene after FDR's death had lingered for any more time, the audience's goodwill would have been permanently damaged. The movie is here teetering on the edge of bursting the bubble built so carefully over its first hour. The question remained: could it be stitched back together?

The short answer is yes, with the film pulling back from off-putting personality traits until the viewer realizes that those flaws are precisely why Hubbell and Katie fall in love and audiences root for them. They complete each other. Analyzed Pollack, "The first rule of any love story is you don't make one character attractive at the expense of the other. Then you're canceling any move forward. The object of love stories is to make audiences care about both people. You have to see the downside, the weakness of both characters. You have to see him unfaithful, see her not hold her anger in one too many times."

After the fight at J.J.'s apartment, Hubbell comes to the radio station to break up with Katie because their differences now seem insurmountable. In a nicely judged bit of direction, Pollack separates the lovers spatially in the frame: Katie, aptly, is in the control room, while Hubbell paces in the studio itself. They may be speaking directly to each other, but they never touch. At first, Katie begins to repair the damage she has caused to Hubbell (and the audience) in a frank and welcome bit of self-awareness, admitting, "I'm a pain in the ass." It's a throwaway line—Katie can now actually swear!—but a crucial one in context because it allows the audience to forgive her.

Charging ahead as always, she asks why Hubbell insists that they're not going to make it, but before he can utter a syllable, she proceeds to answer her own question: "I was too easy for you." Retorts Hubbell, "You really think you're easy? Compared to what—the 100 Years War?!" It's throwaway line number two—and now the audience is back on both of their sides, rooting interest in the love story fully restored.

Fortunately cut was some rather turgid quasi political dialogue that found Hubbell intoning that he didn't believe in any theory, whether Marxist, Freudian, or Christian. All of them, he pontificated, were pointless. Right then, audiences didn't care about Hubbell's philosophical world view—they just wanted to know if he and Katie could get back together. What makes the attempted reconciliation work and allows the audience to regain a personal investment in the outcome is the moment being heightened not just by the characters but by the personalities of the two stars as well. Observed Pollack of the scene, "[Bob and Barbra] were really right for these roles. They brought themselves in a way to it. Bob was slightly more improvisational—he didn't have a laundry list of answers during the argument. He did that very well. There were a lot of takes—it was a tough scene and she also did it great."

When Hubbell walks out of the radio station, leaving behind his key to her apartment, the film has arrived at a turning point, the scene that caused Sydney Pollack to say yes when asked to direct the movie. Alone in her apartment and staring at the phone, a vulnerable Katie finally gives in and calls Hubbell, begging him to come over and stay with her until she falls asleep. This is the scene that made Pollack cry when he first read Laurents's initial treatment: "That speech verbatim was in the treatment. There's something so appealing about her as a character and the intensity of their feelings for one another. That's when I knew I wanted to do the picture."

Pollack here gives Streisand a moment reminiscent of tearful Luise Rainer's Oscar-winning telephone scene in 1936's *The Great Ziegfeld*. Sobs Streisand as she sheds her own Oscar-worthy tears, "I can't sleep, Hubbell. It would help me so much if you could—well if I had someone to talk to—a best friend and you're my best friend. Isn't that dumb? So dumb. You're the best friend I've ever had. I promise I won't touch you."

When it came time to shoot that tearful phone call, relates Hawk Koch, Pollack asked him to clear the set of everyone but Harry Stradling Jr., the camera operator, and the sound man, with Pollack taking Barbra off to the side and talking to her for a long time. Relayed Pollack, "That scene was done in one take and she was really crying. Her eyes were plenty red. . . .I set it up in one shot so that I wouldn't have to cut because of the emotional line of it. I didn't want to have to stop in the middle and then crank it up again."

Pollack was thrilled with the result: "Barbra knocked it out of the ballpark—she did it on the first take. There were only two takes total. I found it hard to watch on the set—it was very, very moving." Just as important, the ever self-critical Barbra was happy: "I didn't have to prepare for that scene because you read it and you cry. It always moved me to read it. I had to improvise during the scene because my nose was running from crying. I had to ad-lib—'I have to get a tissue.'"

Pollack was happy, Barbra was happy—but the list ended there because when Arthur Laurents viewed that very scene, he was decidedly not returning the compliment to either his star or director. Never one to shy away from controversy, Laurents seemed to blame Barbra and Pollack in equal measure for shortchanging his script. To his eye, instead of earning sympathy for Katie, the tearful scene he had so carefully constructed for his star played on-screen as nothing short of phony: "Her concentration seemed to be on producing tears. . . . [H]er discomfort was too evident in the way she kept hiding, covering her face again and again with her hand which inevitably drew the eye to those unreal fingernails." Laurents is only half right here; contrary to his claim, Katie's inherent fragility shines through in a genuine manner because Streisand succeeds beautifully in showing that for all of her tough-girl persona, Katie Morosky is one emotionally fragile woman. Where he may be right, however, is about the fingernails; they draw the focus away from Barbra's face and in the process, shortchange the drama. Would hard-working Katie Morosky, she of the ten different jobs during the war, really sport such long nails?

To Laurents, that misplayed and misdirected tearful phone call to Hubbell actually cost Barbra the Oscar. The scene's combination of vulnerability and desperation, always catnip to Academy voters, should have won Barbra the Oscar, but instead, by his reckoning she lost the Oscar because she had been more concerned with her looks than with her performance: "They would never have denied her the Oscar if she really had let go in that scene. It was a set piece for her, from the very first draft of the screenplay. She did not grab the chance and it was her loss. She was just worrying about her looks." By keeping her hand in front of her face, "it looked like she was trying to hide the fact that she wasn't acting very well. She was acting beautifully but you couldn't tell it." After his first viewing of the scene, in fact, Laurents had immediately suggested that it be reshot, but in his telling, Barbra's response to the mere idea was to exclaim, "But I look so beautiful in that scene." A reshoot, he remained convinced, would have given Streisand the Oscar, no matter how unpopular she remained in Hollywood.

Does that tearful phone call mark the end of the love affair? Not in the face of Katie's insistence because after Hubbell arrives with a sleeping pill and admits that she does not, in fact, have the right style for him, she instantly insists that she'll change. As the charged dialogue escalates the stakes, Katie's urgency begins to wear down Hubbell's crumbling reservations:

> *Katie: I'll change.*
>
> *Hubbell: Don't change. . . . You push too hard—every minute.*
>
> *Katie: If I push too hard it's that I want things to be better. I'll keep making waves until you're every wonderful thing you should be.*
>
> *Hubbell: Katie, you expect so much.*
>
> *Katie: Oh—but look what I've got!*

For any audience member who has ever loved the wrong person, who has followed heart rather than head, here is the big-screen, swoon-inducing romantic incarnation of it all: Katie's belief in Hubbell's talent, a belief deeper than his own, is what has brought them together and provided the glue in their relationship. What, the film asks, could be more seductive than a partner's unfettered belief in your talents? Faced with the sheer force of Katie's love, Hubbell has fully surrendered, the reconciliation working for the audience because it had been earned, for reasons both dramatic and romantic.

As originally written, a montage of V-E Day celebrations was to follow, followed by Hubbell and Katie's wedding and around-the-world honeymoon. None of that international travelogue ever saw the light of day, although the one part that would be missed was a nicely judged cut from a European medieval castle to an African jungle, with the jungle turning out to be the setting for a movie being filmed on a Hollywood back lot.

Pollack does, however, utilize a montage after Katie and Hubbell marry and move to California, the effectiveness of the entire sequence greatly aided by Hamlisch's score. Yes, he uses the melody of the title song repeatedly throughout the film, but he judges those moments with great skill: when a jump cut to California finds Katie and Hubbell on a sailboat, with gentle waves smoothly charting their course, the musical theme swells up until the fifty-five-piece orchestra seems to propel the boat all on its own. It is lush musical romanticism at its best.

The montage is effective because in Pollack's words, "the audience is anchored," but as soon as it ends, problems in the film's narrative begin with the full-blown intrusion of politics upon the story. For every effective scene of Hubbell typing a third draft of his script—the writing is not so easy this time around because golden-boy credentials don't count for much in Hollywood—there is a clunky scene about political blacklisting. Hubbell and Katie's beach party is interrupted by radio reports of the blacklisting, and although Katie and Rhea talk in the kitchen about the evils of the witch hunt, the scene is so truncated that it's hard to differentiate Rhea from Paula (Viveca Lindfors), a political émigré who shortly thereafter shares the kitchen with Katie for their own chopped-up political discussion. So severe are the cuts that the audience is left in exactly the same place as they were before the scenes began: all three women are upset by the current political scene. Nothing has been learned, nothing has changed, and disjointed speeches about blacklisting begin to appear and disappear in fits and starts for the remainder of the movie.

It's not that the emphasis on politics is completely misplaced because the theme of politics as reflective of character has been established since the opening scenes, but the manner in which it rises to the forefront remains forced and confusing. Little action remains, only talk. Even Lindfors herself found the wholesale editing to be jarring, which led her to deliver her own equivocal review of the film: "The viciousness of the McCarthy period was easier to handle in retrospect. Yes, I guess I would have to say *The Way We*

Were was 'Hollywood schlock' all right, although it did do a service in re-introducing a difficult period of American history to the public at large."

By now, the tone of the movie has switched: out with the romance and glamour, in with political lectures. The atmosphere is heavy, too heavy, and even the attempts to lighten the mood backfire. Why is a Marx Brothers–themed costume party, supposedly held in honor of J.J.'s birthday, plopped into the middle of the movie? The sequence seems so extraneous that one idly wonders if Groucho Marx was a cousin of Katie's beloved Karl. The party itself, based on a 1949 photograph in *Life* magazine, came about because, Pollack explained, "I was looking for a lighter scene in Hollywood. Ray started talking about a Groucho party. I thought it was nuts, but I couldn't think of a better idea. It was an attempt to find some fun in Hollywood before things go bad."

The eighty-two-year-old Groucho himself had shown up for the filming of the party, and in Jerry Ziesmer's approving recall, "for the time that Groucho Marx was on our stage, Barbra and Redford were just two more excited fans like all the rest of us." Laurents, however, found the scene too cute by half, and he proved right in one key regard: the one-joke nature of the sequence only served to make the movie feel long.

What does work very well, however, and brings the audience right back into the center of the action is a party sequence at Bissinger's home (one of the briefly glimpsed party guests is played by Marvin Hamlisch), in which Laurents cleverly creates a mash-up of Irene Selznick's private after-dinner screening with the bugging of Clifford Odets's party. The scene begins with a wonderfully evocative shot of Hubbell and Katie dancing alone in the corridor as Hamlisch's romantic "Like Pretty" swells in the background. It's a period-accurate reminder of a vanished era in which guests dressed up, not down, for a gathering among friends and a chance to see that costume designer Moss Mabry had in fact collaborated successfully with Barbra: if star and designer alike felt that her best physical attributes lay in her shoulders and bust, then here was the pewter-colored satin halter-style dress to prove it. Carefully lit by Harry Stradling Jr., the sight of Streisand and Redford dancing alone for thirty seconds sums up an entire universe of movie-star glamour.

But it's the lowering of a movie screen and the sight of a listening bug ripping through a valuable painting that constitute the main event. Here, at last, is a political sequence that unfolds as a scene of action and atmosphere, not speechifying; in short order, the bug is discovered, a valuable painting is ruined, no one pays attention to the movie being screened (*The Last of the Apaches*—"the Indians are the good guys"), and Katie begins demanding action in Washington. In Pollack's terms, it is show, not tell ("Try to show always—if you can't, you tell. Try desperately not to do both"), and in contrast to the meandering Marx Brothers party scene, it allows the movie to leap forward with momentum.

After Katie and the Hollywood Ten return to Hollywood from Washington, the fabric of her marriage begins to unravel. She is attacked by an angry crowd, and Hubbell punches a man who calls his wife a "Commie bitch." Hubbell has finally taken action, gets bloodied for his troubles, and explodes at Katie, delivering the impassioned speech Redford had long insisted be included. It's a speech that works not only for what it says about politics and human nature but also for its effect on an audience; reflective of 1950s Hollywood and yet at the same time capable of speaking to twenty-first century America, it strikes world-weary audience members as a cynical voice of experience responding to every real-life political or Hollywood "comeback" fueled by money and foisted upon the public:

> *Nothing will change, because after jail, after five years, when it's practical and fashionable for a producer to hire a Commie writer*

> *to save his ass because his hit movie is in trouble, he'll do it, they'll both do it. They'll make movies, have dinner, make passes at each other's wife, and what the hell did anyone ever go to jail for? I'm telling you that people are more important than any goddamn witch hunt. We're more important than any principles.*

Katie's withering reply is exactly one fully weighted sentence: "Hubbell, people are their principles." This pronouncement, the line Streisand fought desperately to have included, so infuriates Hubbell that it causes him to smash things off a table, a man of action at last. Streisand and Laurents were right: Katie's one-line reply helps to explain why Katie and Hubbell ultimately must face the reality that they are finished.

Hubbell's soliloquy is a remarkable speech, full of passion and common sense and clearly the work of someone who understood the innermost workings of a Hollywood film industry in which money and expediency trump all. It also fulfills the important function of contrasting Katie's rush from cause to cause with Hubbell's more long-range, practical view. To Pollack, "She's wonderful and committed, but it's this cause today, and tomorrow another one. Hubbell takes the more existential view of things. There's bad and good in both. But it was easier to articulate what's good in her point of view than to articulate what's good in his point of view."

Hubbell's view that political action will likely end in a feeling of utter futility rather remarkably seems to foreshadow a speech ten years later from Streisand's very personal screenwriting and directorial debut, *Yentl*. Says Yentl's father of his daughter's determination to upend centuries of Jewish tradition by entering the men's world of scholarly learning, "Go on, turn the world upside down and inside out; you won't have a moment's peace." At heart, this fatherly warning registers as nothing so much as a nineteenth-century European iteration of what is essentially Hubbell's ethos: "Play the game. Don't make waves because nothing will change. All it will bring you are problems—and unnecessary problems at that."

One of the better scenes to emerge in rewrites follows, one in which Hubbell begs Bissinger to keep his job as screenwriter: "No one else knows this story the way I do. I can fix the dialogue. I learn fast—I always have. Things come . . . ," and it is here that Hubbell stops dead in his tracks because he leaves out the word "easily." There is little about Hubbell's life now, as writer, husband, or soon-to-be father, that comes easily. He hurries on: "I know what your concept is. I'll make your changes. Let me."

Laurents, unsurprisingly, didn't like the scene, bluntly stating that it failed to further the story and should be cut. In reality, the scene actually contributes to an understanding of how far Hubbell has traveled and yet how little he has gained. Far from being in charge, the golden boy is begging for his professional life, and when Bissinger asks if he'll make the necessary changes "without resistance," Hubbell caves completely, agreeing to comply wholeheartedly. It's an interesting take on Hubbell's eagerness to always follow the path of least resistance, but contrary to Laurents's belief, the cumulative effect of Hubbell's fight at the train station followed by this scene of begging for his job is to haul the movie back on course.

The movie veers away from the political and back to the personal with a screening of Hubbell's film; in a slick piece of shorthand, all we see of Hubbell's film is a clichéd final image of a woman kicking off her shoes as she is lifted up and embraced by a man. We don't even see the actor's faces and don't need to. This is 1950s Hollywood filmmaking at its most awkward, and silence among the spectators in the private screening room proves the order of the day. Left alone at the end of the film, Katie and Hubbell's differences are laid bare in a nicely scripted exchange bearing the hallmark of Laurents's sensibility:

Hubbell: Katie, the day you die you'll still be a nice Jewish girl.

Katie: Are you still a nice gentile boy?

Hubbell: I never was—I only looked it to you.

This is the personal story that hooked audiences to begin with, and for the first time, Hubbell's affair is acknowledged:

Katie: Why did you have to go with her? Tell me I'm not good enough . . . but for God's sake you didn't have to go back to Beekman Place, did you?

Hubbell: What's wrong with us has nothing to do with another girl. Give up. Please.

Katie: I can't.

Because of the wholesale cutting of sequences, the audience is confused—Hubbell had an affair? Because he talked to Carol Ann for two seconds on the studio lot?! Yet at the same time, Laurents's pungent dialogue somehow still manages to depict the unraveling of a marriage in a very adult manner, the blending of love story, nostalgia, and politics making it clear that the foundation of Katie and Hubbell's union has crumbled. *The Way We Were*, it turns out, has more than surface prettiness on its mind, and that's one big reason why the film continues to resonate.

Hubbell may be frustrating and indolent yet in some ways, always clearer eyed than Katie, who can still wonder aloud:

Wouldn't it be lovely if we were old—we would have survived all this and everything would be easy and uncomplicated like it was when we were young.

Katie, like Gatsby, wants to recapture the past, an attempt doomed to failure, but Hubbell, aware of his own failings, rips off her blinders:

> *Hubbell: Katie, it was never uncomplicated.*
>
> *Katie: But it was lovely, wasn't it?*
>
> *Hubbell: Yes, it was lovely.*

Or as Ernest Hemingway wrote in the famous last line of *The Sun Also Rises*, "Isn't it pretty to think so?"

The irreconcilable differences between Hubbell and Katie, present from the very first scenes of the film, now register as insurmountable. Katie seems unable to step back from carrying the weight of the world on her shoulders, and Hubbell's dilemma, the reason they can't succeed as a couple, is that underneath the surface assurance, he is still trying to believe in himself. In James Woods's perceptive analysis, "The reason they don't work—his dilemma—is about whether his actual being is how he's perceived or how he actually truly is. A part of him wants to be the writer she wants him to be but he just can't believe it's true." The film presents Hubbell as selling out to Bissinger, but in reality, he just does not believe in his talent in the same way as does Katie.

Lost in the wholesale cutting that took place was another nicely scripted scene that at this point, would have laid more groundwork for the divorce. With Hubbell smoking in bed while a pregnant Katie drinks warm milk, she sadly asks him, "You don't really want to go to Europe, do you?" and he laconically answers "someday." To her fading hope that he'll write his book in Europe, he indifferently replies, "Wherever we go the same baby gets born . . . the same book gets written . . . or not." Here lay a deeper, truer explanation of Hubbell's near-existential philosophy than the line that did make the final cut: "I guess I really never thought there was much point."

Because of the blunt-edged, wholesale cuts in the political sequences, by this point, the overall effect for the audience is one of puzzlement. Admitted Pollack in later years, "[T]here's a disjointed feeling in the third act of the picture—where you can see the surgery. This film has been successful from a commercial point of view, extremely successful—but it never has been an ultimately satisfying picture in terms of what it set out to do."

In fact, asked point blank how he felt about the finished film, Pollack admitted to decided feelings of ambivalence: "My strongest feelings in favor of it are the two performances, which I think are wonderful. But the picture is very unfinished in many areas. . . . [A]mong the many failures of the picture, the two that stand out the strongest are its failure to deal satisfactorily with the political issue it raises, and perhaps its failure to present a fair, honest contest between these two opposing philosophic approaches to life." And yet even twenty-five years after the film's release, Pollack still felt he had made the right cuts to the political sequences: "I think there is real value to a lot of these scenes. But I made the decision at the time that I was going to sacrifice some of those little moments both for an overall shape that felt right and for a certain amount of pace. I don't say to this day that I was right—but they seemed like the right decision after I looked at them again, even now. I don't say that including the scenes would have destroyed the picture if they were in, but I think there's a cleaner emotional line now."

As the end of the film approaches, the audience senses that Katie and Hubbell will have to see each other one more time, and as the screen fills with the same shots of Central Park that began the film, Hubbell and Katie run into each other outside of the Plaza Hotel. They are clearly still in love, even while Hubbell stands with his latest and ever-younger version of Carol Ann. Looking like an aging golden boy, Hubbell smilingly exchanges information with Katie, who is once again sporting her naturally curly hair. Hubbell is in

New York writing for television, a piece of news, to which Katie replies, "Really?" with a genuine smile that nonetheless speaks volumes about all he has failed to accomplish as a writer.

It is Hubbell who now seems the sadder of the two characters. In writing for television and never having completed the novel worthy of his talent, he has taken the easy route, both professionally and personally. In Pollack's memorable phrase, Hubbell has drifted back "into another interchangeable beige girl—pretty but not much beyond that." It's Katie who has triumphed, raising their daughter, happily married to "Dr. David X. Cohen—the only one in the book!," and still filled with a political passion that runs stronger than ever. Jeanine Basinger posits, in fact, that Katie's marriage to "Dr. David X. Cohen" perfectly fits the tenor of those times: "The romantic movie of those particular years is a divorce story—the marriage of passion doesn't have to get fixed for a happily ever after. People understood that you don't necessarily marry or stay married to the person you were most in love with—you are marrying the right person to be your partner at that point in your life."

Ironically, Pollack, who alienated his own screenwriter in his relentless advocacy for making Hubbell into a stronger personality, pronounced himself satisfied with the fact that Hubbell has ended up the more somber, even wistful, character at the end of the movie: "If that feeling is pervasive all throughout the picture, then I don't think you have a picture. So the biggest battle was trying to give Hubbell enough strength so that there was a balanced argument at least until the end—at the end it's unbalanced—it's in her favor." At the conclusion of the movie, Katie knows exactly who she is. Hubbell, however, remains a bit of a mystery: has he learned anything about himself?

What makes this Plaza Hotel ending so memorable that audiences viewing the film fifty years later still respond viscerally are the small gestures and stutter steps that build to Katie and Hubbell's final emotional embrace. Katie invites Hubbell to come visit his daughter, and then taking her leave, she crosses the street to hand out "Ban the Bomb" leaflets. They are now quite literally standing on opposite sides of the street, leaving audiences to ask, "Is that the end?" It isn't, of course, because Hubbell can't quite leave—can't leave, that is, before raising audience hopes by crossing through traffic for one final admiring but clear-eyed word with the love of his life:

Hubbell: You never give up—do you?

Katie: Only when I'm absolutely forced to. But I'm a very good loser.

Hubbell: Better than I am.

Katie: I've had more practice.

It is only now that Hubbell delivers the coup de grâce, the final words that the entire audience has known were coming yet doesn't want to hear:

Hubbell: I can't come—I can't.

Katie: I know.

Volumes are spoken in those seven words, with just as much left unspoken as actually stated—Katie is now accepting Hubbell's shortcomings, and the audience feels the pain of both characters. In an echo of her signature gesture, Katie touches his hair one last time, and as the theme music drifts in, there is a final hug and the last words Katie and Hubbell will ever exchange:

Hubbell: See you, Katie.

Katie: See you, Hubbell.

The soundtrack swells as Katie resumes urging the busy Fifth Avenue bystanders to "Ban the Bomb," and as the music flows into Streisand's quietly murmured rendition of the title song, the credits roll. A minor, bittersweet chord floats by, and the film is over.

Over—yes. But the impact of the movie on audiences and the stars alike was only beginning. It proved to be, for all concerned, a genuine game changer.

Katie and Hubbell/ Barbra and Bob

"Audiences got this story—the not so attractive girl in love with the campus heartthrob. It wasn't just women—men had experienced that feeling of longing too. Everyone can relate to that feeling of misguided but passionate love—except maybe ten people, and who wants to know them?!" —Jeanine Basinger, film historian

Mention *The Way We Were* to any fan of romantic movies, and the ending is the one scene always mentioned: one final hug in front of the Plaza and a gentle tousling of Hubbell's hair before Katie and Hubbell part forever. There are no heaving sobs, no cries of "I'll always love you." Instead, there is a quiet acceptance of life's vicissitudes and a rueful adult acceptance that life often doesn't contain happy endings. It remains a sequence that resonates for anyone who has ever loved the wrong person and clung too long to an erroneous belief that they have found their soul mate.

It's the sheer bittersweet "if-only" atmosphere pervading the film that heightens the impact, and in some ways the sorry–grateful ending echoes that found in William Inge's Oscar-winning screenplay for 1961's *Splendor in the Grass*; in that film, soul mates Deanie (Natalie Wood) and Bud (Warren Beatty) briefly reunite at the very end of the film, with Bud, just like Katie Morosky, now married to someone else. It is clear not just to Bud's jealous wife, Angelina (Zohra

Lampert), but to the entire viewing audience that strong feelings remain between Deanie and Bud, and when asked by her friends if she is still in love with Bud, Deanie does not answer. Instead, in the same echo of bittersweet emotion that runs between Katie and Hubbell, Deanie's voice is simply heard reciting the last four lines of Wordsworth's "Ode: Intimations of Immortality":

> *Though nothing can bring back the hour*
> *Of splendor in the grass, glory in the flower*
> *We will grieve not; rather find*
> *Strength in what remains behind.*

In *The Way We Were*, that Wordsworthian ache, the impossibility of such a fairy tale love, was now, in the larger-than-life personae of Robert Redford and Barbra Streisand, preserved forever on-screen.

And that leads to one essential question: both Streisand and Redford had starred in major hits before *The Way We Were*, so what was it about their pairing that not only turned the film into a box-office success but also forever sealed them together in the minds of the public? Why is it a pairing that is still referenced in popular culture some fifty years after the film's release, long after other popular films of the day have faded from public memory?

For starters, that brief but emotionally weighty farewell was so well acted and underplayed by Streisand and Redford that it makes for one of the most memorable endings in the history of Hollywood romances. Its "oh-what-might-have-been" tone lent an extra layer of resonance because of how snugly it fit in with the cinematic Streisand template: she has loved and lost Prince Charming, but in the process, gained strength and wisdom. It is that essential aspect of her persona that has always been embraced by her most devoted fans because the happiness of her characters comes only after each woman pursues her own vision of how to live an authentic life: frizzy-haired, politically active, married, and raising a daughter, Katie Morosky is her own true self, even while knowing that she'll never again love anyone as she has Hubbell.

In her very best films—*Funny Girl*, *Yentl*, *The Prince of Tides*, and *The Way We Were*—the unapologetically Jewish Barbra/Fanny/Yentl/Lowenstein/Morosky, conquers her leading man, even while suffering through a bittersweet ending that is, in the Streisand universe, best expressed in song. Here, in front of the Plaza, it plays out very effectively, as if the socko "My Man" ending to *Funny Girl* is hovering over the entire proceedings, only this time in the form of one of the most beloved title songs in Hollywood history.

Awkward Katie had, at least temporarily, landed her Prince Charming, a fact that represented a form of wish fulfillment that made Barbra's core audience of outsiders think, "If she can do it, so can I." Through sheer force of personality, she had succeeded in romance, proof positive of Pauline Kael's early aphorism on the subject of Barbra: "Talent is beauty." Wrap up that message in gorgeous technicolor photography and a romantic score highlighted by a wildly popular title tune, and *The Way We Were* had found its audience.

In fact, throughout her career, Streisand's key gifts have been anchored by her extraordinary willpower and fortitude, a refusal to give up that informed both her singing and acting. The unspoken, not-so-sub-text of her determination lay in vocal and acting displays of "I'll show them. They're going to end up playing by my rules." Katie Morosky may be ridiculed at a college peace rally, but disdain won't stop her as she charges through life. And her strong self-belief, layered directly alongside that palpable vulnerability, played into the public perception of Barbra Streisand herself. The result proved irresistible to millions of moviegoers.

Fit the Streisand archetype it does, but *The Way We Were* also represents a pairing of equals, a rarity in male-driven Hollywood and one still rather uncommon fifty years after the film's initial release.

Streisand and Redford informed Katie and Hubbell with their own disparate personalities: hot and cool, relentless and laid back, vulnerable and diffident, until the actors and their characters began to seem inseparable. The yin/yang differences between the two stars in looks, acting style, and personality were even appreciated by Redford himself: "Barbra's femininity brings out the masculinity in a man, and her masculinity brings out a man's femininity, vulnerability, romanticism, whatever you want to call it." This dichotomy worked to the film's advantage, underscoring the fact that both Hubbell and Katie are deeply attracted to their polar opposite. For Pollack, that is why the pairing remained not only exciting but also "stimulating, intellectually and sexually."

Films exploring romantic tension between mismatched lovers had been a staple of Hollywood since the first days of the film industry, but seldom had the differences been laid out in terms so starkly encompassing of not only physical desire but also intellect and morality. Katie's belief in Hubbell causes her to push him, which would be fine if only she knew when to stop. While admirable in many ways, Katie's relentlessness can be suffocating; she's the Eleanor Roosevelt of Hollywood in not knowing when to allow for breathing room, yet in that resultant comingling of the personal and professional, lies the film's romantic tension.

That frisson between Streisand's drive and Redford's laid-back cool helps to offset the fact that Katie in some ways represents the part of Streisand herself that some find most off-putting: she's brash and simultaneously aggressive and defensive. Yet star and character alike hold audience interest and identification because each possesses a vulnerability capable of making an audience root for and want to protect her. Streisand/Katie carries a physical charge that helps explain Hubbell's attraction, but it happens to come in a package completely unknown to Hubbell's circle: never conventionally pretty, she is nonetheless personally and emotionally attractive, a passionate woman who is determined never to give up, no matter how often she may be knocked down. When Hubbell wonderingly murmurs, "You never give up—I don't know how you do it," Katie responds, in words Streisand herself might use, "I don't know how you can't."

In fact, accurately or not, for both Streisand and Redford, the roles of Katie and Hubbell played directly into the audience's idea of who they were as people: their own personae and that of the characters seemed inseparable. Redford struck audiences as so impossibly good looking, such a WASP paragon, that they really did think of him as someone for whom everything came too easily. At the same time, Katie Morosky's unconventional but striking looks, drive, and outspoken liberal political beliefs seemed drawn directly from Barbra herself, a nonmusical iteration of her fervent personal politics and *Funny Girl* persona.

The Way We Were wore its heart on its sleeve, a genuine male–female romance that stood in stark contrast to the male-centric "buddy" films that dominated the 1970s. It was the concept of the unobtainable that resonated with every person who ever felt that their own true, smart, attractive personality remained totally unrecognized. Women understood Katie's love of Hubbell's golden shell. So, too, did gay men, but straight men also accepted the concept of these mismatched lovers, even if on somewhat different terms. They too had experienced overwhelming feelings of longing and, in the words of E. M. Forster, the need to "only connect."

In looking at these different audiences, Jeanine Basinger analyzes the lasting appeal of the film in terms of both timing and star power:

> *The Way We Were* has an incredible following and it took me quite a while to realize what a large one it is. Here you have a very strong story—a mini-history of the 30s, 40s, and 50s, as well as an insight into the era in which the film was made. But when all is said and done, it starts with the fact that the

> film has the two top stars of their era—an audience fantasy in technicolor—and Streisand and Redford are astonishingly good together. This was really la crème de la crème and audiences went to the theatre to see those two together. With particular films—like this one—the impact is such that people remember the act of going to the theatre to see the film as well as remembering the film itself, and it all combines to become part of their memory bank. That's what happened here—the impact gains with time and audiences share these memories while they are sharing the film itself.

Streisand herself held much the same view: "The audience was rooting for Katie and Hubbell because it was clear that they loved each other. That's why I kept telling Ray Stark that he must hire Robert Redford, when he and Sydney Pollack were casting the film. I just knew that the chemistry between us would make the movie work. And it did."

Barbra Streisand and Robert Redford were not only enormously appealing as a team, but each here arguably delivered a career best performance. Redford conveyed so much information through glances and hesitations, through both ease of movement and dawning self-awareness, that contrary to his initial fears, Hubbell Gardiner unquestionably registers as a fully recognizable three-dimensional mid-century American male. For her part, Streisand charted Katie's growth from lovestruck college student to weary yet hopeful wife and activist by eschewing all of the musical comedy mannerisms that had helped make her a star and delivering a first-rate dramatic performance.

As Sydney Pollack pointed out, Streisand's overwhelming persona had proved a simultaneous blessing and curse, just as it usually did for any star of the first rank. Intriguing personalities separated stars from actors more than did any differential in talent, with stars rarely possessing a chameleon-like ability to disappear into a role like a character actor. Instead, they maintain a consistent on-screen presence that keeps the audience collectively asking, "What are they thinking? What's going on beneath the surface?" Stars keep audiences guessing, and thanks to Streisand's finely crafted performance here, audiences genuinely wondered if Katie and Hubbell would end up together. It's a performance that impresses upon the viewer just how much Streisand was capable of as an actress and at the same time, serves the unintended effect of underscoring the waste of her talent inherent in the lightweight nonsense of follow-up films like *For Pete's Sake* (1974) and *The Main Event* (1979). Streisand may impose her will on directors who don't stand up to her, but faced with a strong director like Wyler (*Funny Girl*), Vincente Minnelli (*On a Clear Day*), or in this case, Sydney Pollack, she delivers.

More than any other film in the Streisand oeuvre, *The Way We Were* solidified Barbra's hold on the moviegoing public, resonating with the core audience that had made her the most popular female movie star in the world in the 1970s. In an April 23, 2013, *New York Times* article timed to Streisand receiving the New York Film Society's Lifetime Achievement award, Manohla Dargis theorized that *The Way We Were* played a big role in Streisand's popularity, writing that she herself, "like a lot of women, I suspect, fell in love with her while watching *The Way We Were*."

The famous final scene in front of the Plaza Hotel certainly struck a chord with millions of women like Dargis, but it was an unusual article by Andy Tiemann, titled "The Barbra Streisand Litmus Test," that most tellingly explained the star's hold on her public. Tiemann, a minister's son who grew up in 1970s Texas, explained that any boy who wanted a girlfriend in that bible belt territory required three things: "An all-encompassing knowledge and adoration of the New Testament; membership in good standing with the Fellowship of Christian Athletes; and the ability to converse intelligently about Barbra Streisand."

Why did Southern Baptist girls feel that way? Because, the girls explained to Tiemann, Barbra Streisand was never, ever a doormat—no man would dare try to control her: "If they did, she'd eat them alive and not even burp. Streisand was a real woman because Streisand knew how to take care of herself."

Girls who came from difficult homes or unhappy situations looked to Barbra as a touchstone for an independent life. Continued Tiemann, "[T]hat was her appeal. And that was her gift, her lovely, simple-hearted gift to these broken little girls of the Texas plains who had no choice but to watch their parents enact the same psychodrama night after night after night."

Famed screenwriter Jay Presson Allen (*Marnie*, *Cabaret*, *Funny Lady*) placed Streisand's popularity at the time of *The Way We Were* directly within the context of the late 1960s and early 1970s. The Vietnam War had divided the country more than at any other time since the Civil War, and in Allen's view, "any time there's a war, society concentrates on its masculine qualities. Films have been doing this for the past few years, and I believe that female audiences have been lost because there've been no stars they could identify with in a positive way. In masochistic ways, yes. For some time, Streisand has been the only bankable female because she alone plays gutsy roles, winners. Even when she's getting the hell kicked out of her, you know she's going to get up again."

Attempting to explain the film's overwhelming success, even director Pollack gave top honors to Streisand and Redford before trying to ameliorate the remaining hard feelings with Laurents: "My instinct is to say everyone who worked on this movie was absolutely essential to its success. The two people most responsible to its success are Barbra and Bob—and then Arthur." Given their contentious relationship, it is not surprising that what Pollack gave to Laurents with one hand he took away with the other, adding, "David and Alvin made major contributions to the character of Hubbell." He rated himself somewhere lower on the food chain: "Sometime way after that comes me because I didn't write it and didn't have to do it. I directed it. You also have music that's very important and you can't say that music wasn't a big part of the success of the picture—Marvin, Alan and Marilyn. . . . It all comes together."

In fact, Jeanine Basinger gives much of the credit to Pollack himself:

> Sydney Pollack was enormously skilled at casting and at establishing credibility of performance with his actors. He was a first rate actor himself, very funny in *Tootsie*, so he understood the pressures facing actors, understood their personae. He was the right director to handle both Streisand and Redford at the peak of their careers. The characters of Katie and Hubbell drew on essential parts of Streisand and Redford themselves, but thanks to Pollack's skill, you can get past the star persona and believe in the characters. He was not overtly cinematic in his approach but I really came to appreciate him over time. He may have won the Oscar for *Out of Africa* but it's his work with the stars here that I truly appreciate.

Perhaps still sore from the changes to his script, Laurents professed surprise at the film's success: "I was always surprised that people liked the picture. They keep crying, they sit through it over and over watching on television." At the time of the film's twenty-fifth anniversary in 1998, a smiling Laurents added, "Redford told me rather recently that people come up to him and brush his hair the way she does. He should be very grateful."

To Alan Bergman, the movie's success was a result of the biggest Hollywood talents all working at the top of their game: "You had two big stars, a well-written script, and a top-flight director—one of the very best. The movie was crafted very carefully. It's a very moving film."

For assistant director Hawk Koch, the appeal lies in the very idea of star-crossed lovers: "I was either in the dubbing room with Sydney or else at the first Directors Guild screening when I saw the completed movie for the first time. I knew every shot in the film, but I was still affected emotionally. I think the reason for the movie's staying power is because a lot of people have that one great love in their life that didn't work out, but it's always there inside of you, a feeling of 'I'll always love you.' That was Hubbell and Katie. Add in those two big stars and that terrific score and all these years later, the movie really continues to resonate."

It is one of Koch's subordinates, Art Smith Jr., an East Coast production assistant, who provides an insightful take on why the film continues to fascinate: "I think that the sheer romance of the story hits the target audience, especially women, right in their emotional center. It's an antidote to all the films that say how bad life is. Even with the sad ending, I think people watch it when they're depressed—it makes them feel better because it shows that true soul mates do exist."

That sad ending had been pointed to by Barbra herself as one reason for the film's continuing power and popularity, as she theorized recently: "Everybody loves a good love story. The audience fell in love with Katie and Hubbell. They wanted them to stay together, and were torn apart when that didn't happen.

But it's interesting—in the greatest love stories, the characters don't end up together. So what does that suggest? It seems we all want a happy ending, and yet it's the sadness, the loss, the missed opportunity that really resonates and stays in our minds forever."

Crater-sized political cuts and all, Redford himself lay the ultimate credit for the film's success at Pollack's feet: "I think we'd both have preferred a more political Dalton Trumbo–type script. But finally Sydney came down on the side of the love story. . . . We trusted his instincts, and he was right. *The Way We Were* became a success because Sydney controlled the project with his point of view, which was not easy given Ray's behavior and interference."

Controlling to the end, Stark had withheld monies due Pollack at the completion of shooting. Explained Pollock, "I was overschedule—I always am—and they withheld a sum of money as a penalty for going over budget. Then in the third or fourth week of release, when it was clear the movie was a hit, I got a check with a note from Ray." Ironically, the person who most easily profited from the film's success was Arthur Laurents; his firing and subsequent reinstatement midway through shooting had, thanks to the efforts of his agent Shirley Bernstein (Leonard's sister), ensured that he would receive a piece of what Ray Stark made from the movie. The $90 million worldwide box-office gross (equivalent to $495 million in 2022), which was earned roughly fifty-fifty between the domestic and international markets, granted him a very nice windfall.

With percentages based on the movie's gross, Streisand, Redford, and Pollack were set to share in the profits, but when checks did not prove forthcoming, Redford and Pollack found it necessary to sue Columbia and Ray Stark for their percentage, one they "estimated in 1976, to be $5.3 million," or close to $30 million in today's money. In a suit filed in Los Angeles Superior Court, Pollack and Redford charged Columbia Pictures and Rastar Productions with fraud and breach of contract, alleging that "Columbia Pictures and Rastar charged off against Redford's and Pollack's slices of the pic's proceeds, projects not related to the production." Star and director further claimed that Columbia and Rastar failed to report "substantial amounts of income earned by the film worldwide," and the two men sought general damages of $300,000 as well as punitive damages totaling $5 million.

Screenwriter Laurents questioned the finances as well, and three years after the film's release, in a letter dated October 6, 1976, he received very specific financial information from Attorney Gerald Lipsky regarding distribution statements for the film; when combined, Laurents's pre- and postproduction fees had earned him over $300,000. Along with Pollack and Redford, he had received a lucrative share of the highly profitable film, final proof that for all three men, *The Way We Were* had proved successful right where it counted most in Hollywood—the bank.

And on into the Future

> *"Nothing can explain success.* The Way We Were *works in the sense that it moves the audience. What's the point of anything you do: move the audience, stimulate the imagination and hopefully make them think a little."* —Arthur Laurents

Does *The Way We Were* speak to twenty-first-century audiences some fifty years after its initial release? Does it impact people of different generations, or is it viewed as a curio from the distant past, a film forgotten by most and only trotted out for an occasional showing on Turner Classic Movies?

The answer could hardly have been anticipated by any of the film's creative personnel in 1973 because *The Way We Were* has actually continued to grow in popularity throughout the past half century and now serves as a romantic standard for no fewer than three generations. Embraced, parodied, and above all, instantly recognizable, *The Way We Were* endures.

The bare statistics: 20 million views and counting on YouTube. A number-six ranking on the American Film Institute's (AFI's) "100 Years . . . 100 Passions" survey of the top one hundred love stories in the history of American cinema. A title song that was inducted into the Grammy Hall of Fame in 1998 and finished at number eight on the AFI's 2004 "100 Years . . . 100 Songs" list of the top songs in the history of American cinema. Capping the awards was the song's inclusion in the list of Songs of the Century compiled by the Recording Industry Association of America and the National Endowment for the Arts.

Given the title song's inclusion on all of those "Best Of" AFI lists and the key role it played in expanding the film's popularity, it is, in fact, a valid question to ask whether there has ever been a title song that played such an important role in a film's success. Representing the most lasting composition in the entire impressive catalogues of Hamlisch and the Bergmans, the song endures into the twenty-first century not only because it is a beautifully crafted piece of songwriting but also because, just like the screenplay, it channels an essential part of the Streisand persona. Barbra Streisand had become the world's leading vocal essayer of longing, the last true believer in the Tin Pan Alley ethos of happily ever after. When she sang of unrequited love, every listener understood that she felt those sentiments at the core of her entire being. In song after song throughout her six-decade-and-counting recording career, she explored her essential feelings: Where is my happy ending? I want, I need. In "The Way We Were," Barbra Streisand had found a song that spoke to part of her own persona while exploring a character with whom she identified, and in the process reached the widest audience of her entire recording career.

Billboard called "The Way We Were" the top pop single of the year, and in February 1974, it became the first gold single of Streisand's career as well as her first to reach number one on the charts. That single, recorded in a four-hour session, which reportedly consisted of thirty-three takes, eliminated the tolling bells heard at the start of the song in the movie and ultimately sold two million copies while winning the Grammy Award as Song of the Year. Ironically, while the recording won the Grammy as Song of the Year, Streisand herself was not even nominated as Best Female Vocalist.

When it came to awards, it seemed controversy trailed Streisand wherever she landed.

The song's success was ultimately replicated around the world, yet that extraordinary commercial success was far from preordained. Explained Hamlisch, "I couldn't get anywhere with 'The Way We Were' with disc jockeys before the film came out. Just because it wasn't rock, they didn't want any part of it. Then the movie was released, was an immediate success, and the song took off."

Columbia Records was able to mine no fewer than three successes from that one song: the single itself; the movie soundtrack, which rose to number twenty on the charts and was certified gold; and a hastily assembled Streisand vocal album, titled *The Way We Were*. Filled out with unreleased material from an aborted recording project, titled "The Singer," as well as vocals from the never-released soundtrack from her least-successful television special, *The Belle of 14th Street*, the album rose to the number-one position on the charts, a success that Streisand had last enjoyed ten years earlier with "People." The album featured a memorable cover shot of Streisand in a hooded caftan that had been intended as a costume for the film, the look accessorized with period-appropriate bright red lipstick and nail polish. The caftan, said Streisand, had been ruled out as "too sophisticated for the character I played," and while it did in fact look rather cosmopolitan for the ever-striving Katie Morosky, for anyone browsing in their neighborhood record store, the photo served as an attention-getter.

Interestingly, the quickly assembled Streisand vocal album did not include the same version of "The Way We Were" as that heard on the single. Streisand, who never sang songs the same way twice, changed the vocal line, most notably on the phrase "Smiles we gave to one another." By now the song was proving ubiquitous, recorded by dozens of middle-of-the-road singers ranging from Doris Day to Andy Williams. It was only six years later, during a June 1, 1980, rare live concert appearance, that Barbra publicly sang the discarded version of the song, wittily introducing it as "The Way We Weren't." She delivered a beautiful melody with a poignant lyric—and one that never would have grown into the career-defining hit that the first version became.

Beyond the title song, pop-culture references, parodies, and tributes have abounded on dozens of popular shows ranging from *Gilmore Girls* and *Saturday Night Live* to *Seinfeld*, *Modern Family*, and *Sex and the City*. In Gilda Radner's concert film *Gilda Live*, her nerdy and hopelessly unhip *Saturday Night Live* character Lisa Loopner performs "The Way We Were" on the piano explaining that the movie is "about a Jewish woman with a big nose and her blond boyfriend who move to Hollywood, and it's during the blacklist and it puts a strain on their relationship." Lisa's own idealized dreamboat? Marvin Hamlisch himself. Her biggest wish? That she and Marvin could double date with Marilyn and Alan Bergman. For its part, *The Simpsons* did not even bother to reference the film's story, content instead to merely borrow the title for two episodes, one called "The Way We Was" (1991) and the other, "The Way We Weren't" (2004). In a sure sign that the film had arrived as a cultural touchstone recognizable to all, *Mad Magazine* ran a satire, titled "The Way We Bore," starring, rather hilariously, Sadie Mafoofsky and Hubbard Goyisher.

The *Gilmore Girls* referenced *The Way We Were* in no fewer than three episodes, most notably in season five after Luke and Lorelei have broken up and she reaches back to the telephone scene in *The Way We Were* to explain how badly she is faring: "Hey, Luke, it's me. I know I'm not supposed to be calling, but I am not doing really great right now, and [pause] I was just wondering if you do remember in *The Way We Were* how Katie and Hubbell broke up." On the references run, with Rachel (Jennifer Aniston) on *Friends* citing *The Way We Were* as the most romantic movie of all time, while *That '70s*

Show's Kitty (Debra Jo Rupp) counters Eric's explanation of a scene in *Star Wars* by citing the virtues of *The Way We Were*.

It was, however, an episode in the second season of *Sex and the City* that most thoroughly used *The Way We Were* as a comment on modern relationships. What was most striking about the mention was the assumption on the part of the show's creators that those watching would immediately grasp all of the references: the core audiences for both *Sex and the City* and *The Way We Were* immediately understood what the four best friends in the series meant when they commented that girls are divided into two groups—simple girls and Katie girls. And when journalist Carrie Bradshaw (Sarah Jessica Parker) ran into former boyfriend "Mr. Big" (Chris Noth) outside of the Plaza Hotel after a party celebrating his engagement to another woman, she brushes the hair out of his eyes and murmurs, "Your girl is lovely, Hubbell." That's the farewell that Carrie wants, and when Big replies, "I don't get it," a wised-up Carrie can only regret, "And you never did."

The Way We Were, it seemed, had by now reached the most rarified status of all in pop culture: it had done nothing less than become a prism through which life itself was viewed, a movie that informed and explained the lives and romantic entanglements of fictional and real-life characters alike.

Life after *The Way We Were*

"I'm a work in progress." —Barbra Streisand

So successful was *The Way We Were*, so indelible the images stamped forever on-screen, that for actors, writers, composer, and director alike, their work throughout the next decade often seemed to involve a quest to top their success with *The Way We Were*. Was it even possible? In some cases yes, and in some decidedly not. But the efforts to do so proved consistently interesting.

James Woods parlayed his small role in *The Way We Were* into an extraordinarily prolific and award-winning career. He played Meryl Streep's husband in the Emmy-winning television miniseries *Holocaust* (1978) and the next year, put himself on the map with a Golden Globe–nominated performance in the police drama *The Onion Field*. Continuing to work at a breakneck pace, he appeared in Sergio Leone's epic gangster movie *Once Upon a Time in America* (1984) before nabbing his first Academy Award nomination for 1986's Oliver Stone movie *Salvador*. He worked again with Stone on the director's 1995 political epic *Nixon* before earning a second Academy Award nomination playing a murderous white supremacist in *Ghosts of Mississippi* (1997).

Although he was by now starring in films, if a project intrigued Woods, he was happy to accept supporting roles as long as it meant working with A-list directors he admired: Martin Scorsese–*Casino*

(1995); Robert Zemeckis–*Contact* (1997); a third Oliver Stone film, *Any Given Sunday* (1999); Clint Eastwood–*True Crime* (1999); and Sofia Coppola on her directorial debut *The Virgin Suicides* (1999).

He won an Emmy Award for his portrayal of a disabled man in *Promise* (1987); a second Emmy playing the founder of Alcoholics Anonymous in *My Name Is Bill W* (1989); and then a third for his performance as chairman and CEO of Lehman Brothers, Richard Fuld Jr., in *Too Big to Fail* (2011).

In the twenty-first century, he remained a controversial presence in the public eye for his sharply expressed political views. By the end of 2020, he had appeared in over 130 television series and films and been rewarded with a star on the Hollywood Walk of Fame; yet even fifty years later, *The Way We Were* remained a special memory: "Barbra was so hardworking, such a talented artist, and Sydney was a terrific director. Years later I was in New York and Barbra was on location shooting a film. I went over and we sat and talked for nearly an hour. She couldn't have been nicer."

At the time of the twenty-fifth anniversary of *The Way We Were*, Woods cohosted a screening of the film with Sydney Pollack at the AFI. Laughed the actor as he recalled the evening, "Someone in the audience asked Sydney how he coaxed the performances he wanted from actors—how he controlled them. Sydney responded, 'I'm sitting here with the most uncontrollable pain in the ass actor from my entire career. Everything he did was a burr under my saddle—and I used every idea he had."

After that anniversary screening, Woods did not sit down and watch *The Way We Were* for another twenty years, but after recently screening the movie once again, he found himself feeling rather emotional over the experience.

> It was very moving to me to screen it recently. I felt both a sense of hope and of wonder. It reminded me of what an extraordinary

experience it was, to have been in the film and fifty years later to find it so moving once again. I feel like *The Way We Were* was really the launching pad for my career.

Watching it once more made me think about my career—the decisions I've made and the path I followed, because I felt great sympathy, real empathy, for both of the leading characters. I identified with Katie Morosky and her passionate take on life, and yet I also identified with Hubbell's pain. When you can identify with both leading characters, male and female, that's really something. It just shows you the depth of the film. All in all, it proved to be a truly formative experience for me.

Bradford Dillman hit his feature film high-water mark with *The Way We Were* but in later years worked consistently in television, playing recurring characters on *Barnaby Jones* and *Falcon Crest* as well as numerous roles on such popular television series as *Cannon*, *Dynasty*, and *Murder She Wrote*. He turned author, penning both an autobiography and an acclaimed football fan's book, titled *Inside the New York Giants* (1995). He remained a *Mad Men* Don Draper prototype to the end of his career, smilingly remarking of his own WASPy name, "Bradford Dillman sounded like a distinguished, phony, theatrical name—so I kept it."

Speaking after his death in 2018, Dillman's daughter Pamela explained the importance of *The Way We Were* in his life, citing the beautifully shot sailboat scenes of Dillman and Robert Redford as "perfectly capturing the essence" of her father.

Lois Chiles built on the success of *The Way We Were* by playing the pivotal role of Jordan Baker in the Robert Redford–Mia Farrow version of *The Great Gatsby* (1974). She had strong supporting roles in the popular films *Coma* (1978) and *Death on the Nile* (1978), but her most recognizable role came as the "Bond Girl" Holly Goodhead opposite Roger Moore in 1979's *Moonraker*. Starring in *Moonraker*, she achieved the sort of screen immortality common to all "Bond

Girls," and throughout the following decades made occasional appearances at James Bond film festivals.

In 1982, she landed a starring role on the popular primetime television soap opera *Dallas*, and determined to expand her range as an actor, she studied with directors José Quintero and Sandy Meisner, appearing onstage in *Cat on a Hot Tin Roof* and *The Best Man*, both directed by Jose Ferrer. She embraced the experience of being onstage: "My first play was *Cat on a Hot Tin Roof*, an absolute masterpiece. It's such a rich play—I really feel I would have loved to have played it forever!"

She taught acting at the University of Houston but developed health issues that "put the teaching on pause." Having married wealthy philanthropist Richard Gilder following a long-term relationship with Don Henley of the Eagles, she moved back to New York City and became active in raising money to combat non-Hodgkin lymphoma.

Coming full circle with her acting career, Chiles recently rediscovered her first film, *Together for Days*, the film that had first brought her to Ray Stark's attention: "Michael Schultz, the director, and I located the film and put it together. I'm very proud of my work in that film—and I'm proud of *The Way We Were*."

Herb Edelman followed up *The Way We Were* with extensive work on television shows ranging from *Knots Landing* and *Cagney and Lacey* to *McMillan and Wife*. He had a recurring role on *St. Elsewhere* and earned two Emmy nominations for playing Stanley Zbornak, Bea Arthur's ex-husband, on the wildly popular *Golden Girls* (1985–1992). If not a household name, he had by this time become a recognizable household face, and before he died in 1996 at age sixty-two, had amassed a staggering total of 132 film and television credits.

As proved the case with Herb Edelman, the focus of **Allyn Ann McLerie**'s career after *The Way We Were* switched to television, where she worked consistently in series ranging from *Lou Grant* and *Barney Miller* to *Trapper John*. She landed a supporting role on the highly acclaimed miniseries *The Thorn Birds* as well as recurring roles on *The Tony Randall Show* and *The Days and Nights of Molly Dodd*. She retired in 1993 and died in 2016 at the age of ninety-one.

After landing a small role in Robert Redford's Oscar-winning *The Sting*, **Sally Kirkland** worked once again with Barbra Streisand on *A Star Is Born* (1976). A supporting turn in *Private Benjamin* (1980) was followed by her highly acclaimed performance as a Czech émigré actress in *Anna* (1987), for which she received both Golden Globe and Academy Award nominations. She worked consistently on television (*Three's Company, Murder She Wrote*) and has spent substantial amounts of time as both an acting teacher and an ordained minister of the Movement of Spiritual Inner Awareness.

Although **Patrick O'Neal** continued to work in feature films such as *The Stepford Wives* (1975) and Sydney Lumet's *Q & A* (1990), he spent a great deal of time on television both as a guest star (*Columbo*) and in recurring roles (*The Doris Day Show*). In the process, he amassed 118 credits and like Sally Kirkland, spent time in nonacting pursuits, achieving great success as a restaurateur in New York City with the Landmark Tavern, the Ginger Man, and O'Neals' Saloon. He died at age sixty-six in 1994.

Ray Stark worked with Barbra Streisand two more times after *The Way We Were*, first on 1974's slight but profitable *For Pete's Sake* and then *Funny Lady*, their popular 1975 sequel to *Funny Girl*. He subsequently formed a successful long-term partnership with playwright Neil Simon, and the two men worked together on no fewer than eleven films scripted by Simon, most notably *The Sunshine Boys* (1975) and *The Goodbye Girl* (1977).

Stark had long since been acknowledged as one of the last true Hollywood moguls, and he ultimately received both the 1980 Irving G. Thalberg Memorial Award from the Academy of Motion Picture Arts and Sciences and the 1999 Producers Guild of America's David O. Selznick Achievement Award in Theatrical Motion Pictures.

Although Stark was a renowned art collector, it was his professional standing as a last connection to the golden-era studio moguls that proved most noteworthy upon his death in 2004 at age eighty-eight; with his passing, that autocratic but personalized style of Hollywood leadership seemed to disappear forever. In the words of his friend and fellow producer Don Safran, "Ray used to say that the problem with the new Hollywood is that the creative people on top don't have time to teach the younger people. Louis Mayer and Harry Cohn and Sam Goldwyn all mentored him when he was young. Ray was the last of the great old-world Hollywood producers."

Harry Stradling Jr. followed his Oscar-nominated work on *The Way We Were* with an additional twenty-seven features, in the process forming a partnership with Blake Edwards on four films, most notably the scathing 1981 Hollywood satire *S.O.B.*

Known for his skill at shooting Westerns, he served as cinematographer on the 1975 John Wayne–Katharine Hepburn *Rooster Cogburn*, following that with both the all-star *Midway* (1976) and Billy Wilder's last film, *Buddy Buddy* (1981). He retired in 1988 after serving as cinematographer on *Caddyshack II*, his place in film history secured by his two Oscar nominations for *1776* (1972) and *The Way We Were* and an Emmy nomination for the 1984 television miniseries *George Washington*. He lived until 2017, passing away at the age of ninety-two.

After *The Way We Were*, the indefatigable **Margaret Booth** continued to work on dozens of feature films, often without credit, and in 1978 the Academy of Motion Picture Arts and Sciences acknowledged her groundbreaking career with an Honorary Oscar. In 1983, she received the Women in Film Crystal Award, awarded annually to outstanding women who "through their success, are creating increased opportunities for the advancement of women working throughout the screen industries: in front of and behind the camera."

Her awards and tributes continued to multiply, and in 1990, she was awarded the American Cinema Editors Career Achievement Award. She died in 2002 at age 104, the second-longest lived Oscar recipient in history (only Luise Rainer, who died twelve days shy of her 105th birthday, lived longer). By then, her status as a historical pioneer had long been assured, her obituary in *The Guardian* noting of her career at MGM, "All the filmmakers had to go through her in order to have a final editing of sound and vision approved." It seemed befitting of her pioneer status that obituaries pointedly noted her standing as the first film cutter to have ever been called "film editor." It was a distinction bestowed on Booth by legendary producer Irving Thalberg himself.

In the decades after *The Way We Were*, **Arthur Laurents** spent the majority of his professional life writing and directing for the theater, but he did have one last great triumph in Hollywood with his screenplay for the highly successful *The Turning Point* (1977). For his tale of two aging former ballerinas, Laurents once again wrote juicy female roles, this time for stars Anne Bancroft and Shirley MacLaine, and the film was nominated for eleven Academy Awards, including Best Screenplay. Twenty years later, he had a more indirect piece of Hollywood success through the popular 1997 animated film *Anastasia*, which was based in part on his screenplay for the 1958 film of the same name.

It was theater, however, that claimed the majority of his attention, and he won a 1983 Tony Award for his direction of the Jerry Herman musical *La Cage aux Folles*. He once again explored the blacklisting era in his 1995 play *Jolson Sings Again* (revised in 1999), a tale of four fictional young artists whose lives are upended by the HUAC. He then directed successful revivals of his own shows, most notably *Gypsy* in a 2008 production starring Patti LuPone, and a 2009 bilingual production of *West Side Story*.

He received a great deal of press attention for his 2000 memoir *Original Story By*, a no-holds-barred account of his professional and personal lives in both Hollywood and New York. The recipient of a Career Achievement Award from the National Board of Review, he passed away in 2011 at the age of ninety-three, having been inducted into the Theater Hall of Fame. Said Barbra Streisand at the time of his passing, "He created people you care about because he cared about people. He was lucky to have lived a full and creative life up till the very end."

In the wake of their triumph with *The Way We Were*, **Alan and Marilyn Bergman** reigned as Hollywood's go-to lyricists for movie theme songs, and in 1983, they managed the extraordinary feat of snagging three of the five nominations for Best Original Song, a feat equaled only by legendary composer Harold Arlen in 1943.

Streisand continued to record dozens of Bergman penned songs, most notably the beautiful and underrated 1983 Oscar-winning *Yentl* score, which they wrote with composer Michel Legrand. Their "Ordinary Miracles," written for Streisand's 1994 return to live concerts after a twenty-seven-year hiatus, won them a third Emmy, and they then reunited with Sydney Pollack on his 1995 remake of *Sabrina*, penning the Oscar-nominated song "Moonlight."

In 1999, they teamed once again with Marvin Hamlisch on the song "A Time to Dream," written for the *AFI's 100 Years . . . 100 Movies* special. That song netted them another Emmy Award, but it continued to be their association with Streisand that kept them at or near the top of the pop charts, with their partnership culminating in Barbra's 2011 all-Bergman CD *What Matters Most*.

The duo remained professionally active into their nineties, by which point their awards and honors had proliferated at an extraordinary rate: Honorary Doctorates; a 1980 induction into the Songwriters Hall of Fame; Marilyn's 1994–2009 presidency of ASCAP

(American Society of Composers, Authors and Publishers); Alan's seat on the board of the Johnny Mercer Foundation; Marilyn's Women in Film Crystal Award; the release of Alan's first solo album; and most fitting of all, a joint Lifetime Achievement Award from the National Academy of Songwriters. Marilyn passed away in 2022 at age ninety-three, her legacy secure as one of the most successful and lauded lyricists in Hollywood history.

After winning three Oscars in one night and becoming the hottest composer in Hollywood, **Marvin Hamlisch** proceeded to pick up stakes and return to New York City for a salary of $100 per week as composer of a musical that had no script. That show came to be known as *A Chorus Line*.

After picking up a Tony Award and a Pulitzer Prize for his work on *A Chorus Line*, the peripatetic Hamlisch began to alternate his time between theater and film, writing songs and music for many successful films, including the James Bond epic *The Spy Who Loved Me* (1977). He reunited with Robert Redford when he scored *Ordinary People* in 1980, but all of this overwhelming success did little to quell Hamlisch's self-doubts: "I still need terrific reinforcement. I still go into severe, endless depressions. When I get into one of those things, it can last for weeks, even months; I don't want to talk to anyone, I don't want to see anyone."

He wrote the score for the Academy Award–winning *Sophie's Choice* in 1982 and earned another Oscar nomination for the unsuccessful 1986 film version of *A Chorus Line*. Interspersed with the film scores were additional Broadway musicals, such as 1978's *They're Playing Our Song*, *Smile* (1986), *The Goodbye Girl* (1993), and the first-rate but ultimately unsuccessful 2002 musical *Sweet Smell of Success*.

He continued his association with Barbra Streisand by conducting her triumphant 1994 concert tour, winning two Emmys in the process. Even Hamlisch, it turned out, was not immune to the pressures of working with Streisand, and he frankly admitted, "Now I'm afraid to go near her with a new song. She scares me to death." Even with all the stresses and strains, their friendship remained strong, two hugely talented New Yorkers who had by now known each other for thirty years. Interviewed in the middle of his monthslong stint conducting a sixty-four piece orchestra for Streisand's 1994 concert tour, he assessed the experience as "so far, so terrific." Yes, Barbra could be a demanding perfectionist, "[b]ut that doesn't mean she is a kvetch. Besides, I told her that two perfectionists have gotten together here."

He died unexpectedly in 2012, having just completed the score for the successful television film *Behind the Candelabra*. By this time, he had been inducted into the Theater Hall of Fame and had acquired a staggering roster of awards: three Oscars, plus nine additional nominations; four Grammys (eleven total nominations); four Emmys (seven nominations); and one Tony Award. As news of his death spread, tributes poured in from around the world, and as a measure of his stature, a concert in New York City found the once-in-a-lifetime combination of Liza Minnelli, Aretha Franklin, and Barbra Streisand all paying musical tribute to their friend. Said Barbra, "I'm devastated. He's been in my life ever since the first day I met him in 1963, when he was my rehearsal pianist for *Funny Girl*. He played at my wedding in 1998 . . . and recently for me at a benefit for women's heart disease. When I think of him now, it was his brilliantly quick mind, his generosity, and delicious sense of humor that made him a delight to be around. He was a true musical genius, but above all that, he was a beautiful human being."

Sydney Pollack followed up *The Way We Were* with a series of hit films—*Three Days of the Condor* (1975), *The Electric Horseman* (1979), and *Absence of Malice* (1981)—and in the process, fashioned an enviable track record that was only occasionally interrupted by misfires like *Bobby Deerfield* (1977).

His continuing successful collaboration with Robert Redford on *Condor* and *Horseman* was, he explained, "a question of trust, I think. We trust each other's taste. We usually like and dislike the same things in films. I can't explain it any other way." Theirs proved to be a mutual admiration society that nonetheless did not prevent Pollack from frankly assessing what he regarded as his own hand in Redford's success: "I think his work in the films we've done together is better than a lot of his work in the films that we haven't done together. . . . I always have problems directing him; he's a maniac. He drives me nuts in ways, but that's what happens if you're friendly with somebody for 20 years. You fight and holler and argue with each other. But he's awfully good."

Pollack hit a commercial peak with the wildly popular *Tootsie* in 1982, the filming of which was punctuated by his well-publicized difficulties with Dustin Hoffman. Star and director clashed repeatedly, but that did not prevent Pollack from taking Hoffman's suggestion that he play the role of Hoffman's exasperated agent, and the film, as well as Pollack's performance, proved popular with critics and the general public alike. He finally won the Academy Award for Best Director with *Out of Africa* (1985), which overcame somewhat mixed reviews to achieve worldwide box-office success. In a *New York Times* interview at the time of the film's release, Redford, who starred in the film opposite Meryl Streep, delivered a thoughtful analysis of his friend, one that perceptively noted how Pollack had mixed artistic and commercial considerations throughout all of his films: "Sydney sees both sides of everything, he really does. If he's committed to anything, it's to a center line. He lives in the gray zone. . . . There's a melancholia that hangs heavy over his stuff, but there's also an eye to the commercial." With a nod back to *The Way We Were*, Redford articulated the through line of his by then six films with Pollack, noting that they "usually involve a very long period of romantic anticipation, the briefest and most stylized of connections, and then a melancholy dissolution." To Redford, the male characters that dominated Pollack's films reflected a key aspect of the director himself: "Sydney identified with the character of an uncommitted man."

After directing thirteen features in seventeen years, Pollack began taking more time between films, dithering over *Rain Man* (1988) until the film was ultimately directed by Barry Levinson. He waited five years before finally signing up to direct Redford for the seventh time in the period romance *Havana* (1990), but the film seemed jinxed for Pollack from the start: producer Richard Roth sued him in 1989 for $1 million in damages, claiming that he had been excluded from the film once Pollack decided to direct and produce it himself.

Pollack's difficulties with Roth, however, paled in comparison to the problems he experienced during shooting with close friend Redford. The film represented the fourth time Pollack had directed Redford in the years after *The Way We Were*, but after a contentious production period in which director and star clashed repeatedly (mending fences only near the end of Pollack's life), the film premiered to scathing reviews and little box office. The lush production values read beautifully on-screen, and the film had moments of clarity and even power. But it never fully ignited, and critics seemed to go out of their way to attack the amiable Pollack, almost as if in retaliation for his successful track record as a director of popular romances. In the words of Pollack himself, "I've never made anything but love stories. No matter if they're thrillers or war films or period pictures or whatever—they're love stories."

For all the box-office popularity of his films, Pollack never had been a critics' darling, and years after *The Way We Were* premiered, he recalled that it "got 65–70% lousy reviews, but everybody speaks very fondly of it now, remembering. . . .It has grown in stature over the years." Like so many others, he could recall derogatory notices with word-for-word accuracy: "On *They Shoot Horses*, *Time* magazine said, 'Oh well, they shoot movies, don't they?' It was a vicious mean, review." His lack of a signature visual style meant that among critics who strongly favored the auteur school of thought, he was relegated to a second- or third-tier ranking. By his own admission, "I was never what I would call a great shooter or visual stylist."

He rebounded from *Havana* with a highly successful 1993 adaptation of John Grisham's best-selling *The Firm*. The film proved so successful at the box office that Paramount Pictures bought new $100,000 Mercedes Benz 500 SL convertible two-seaters for Pollack (who had already received a salary of $5.5 million plus a percentage of the profits), star Tom Cruise (whose fee was a reported $12 million), and producer Scott Rudin.

The Firm represented Pollack's last box-office hit, followed as it was by a wan remake of *Sabrina* (1995), a sparkless romance between Harrison Ford and Kristin Scott Thomas in *Random Hearts* (1999), and the Nicole Kidman–Sean Penn misfire *The Interpreter* (2005). By now, the moviegoing habits of Pollack's natural audience, the vast group of men and women who liked star-driven vehicles with a linear plotline, had with the advent of cable television and DVDs, changed forever, a fact that Pollack himself bluntly acknowledged: "The middle ground is now gone."

When all was said and done, it was Pollack's background as an actor that had served him best in his directing career; he remained sensitive to the drives and insecurities underlying even the biggest of stars, and it was no accident that every movie he made, with the exception of his 2005 documentary *Sketches of Frank Gehry*, featured well-known stars in the lead roles. Said Lois Chiles in later years, "I'm sorry Sydney is no longer here. He was a lovely gentle man. Not a bully. Not a predatory guy. Just a decent, decent person." For a director who remained particularly comfortable with stars, it therefore made a perfect kind of sense that when he died in 2008, three years after he had directed his last feature film, *The Interpreter*, the first movie mentioned in his lengthy *New York Times* obituary was his most star-driven vehicle of all, *The Way We Were*. Said Barbra Streisand, "He knew how to tell a love story. He was a great actor's director because he was a great actor. And he was a very good friend, someone I even shared secrets with." In his relationships with Streisand and Redford lay the proof of Pollack's own words: "Stars are like thoroughbreds. Yes, it's a little more dangerous with them. They are more temperamental. You have to be careful because you can be thrown. But when they do what they do best—whatever it is that's made them a star—it's really exciting."

Ultimately, it was Martin Scorsese, paying tribute in the most fulsome of terms, who best explained the reasons behind Pollack's extraordinary success: "I always viewed Sydney as being part of the great Hollywood tradition. All of his work—as a director, as a producer, as an actor—exudes the best qualities of classical filmmaking. His movies have emotional power often rooted in stellar performances from his actors, whom he clearly loved. And Sydney was a passionate idealist, something to which we can all aspire. He leaves an important legacy, and he will be deeply missed."

As proved to be the case with Barbra Streisand, *The Way We Were* represented the apex of **Robert Redford**'s screen popularity. The role of Hubbell Gardiner had turned Redford into the ultimate romantic object for millions of women, and when paired with his Academy Award–nominated starring role in the same year's *The Sting*, as well as the title role in 1974's *The Great Gatsby*, Redford, for those two years, unquestionably reigned as the most popular male movie star in the world. More than any other film, however, it was *The Way We Were* that had proved a game changer for Redford. Popular as he was before *The Way We Were*, films like *Jeremiah Johnson* and *Downhill Racer* had not turned him into a matinee idol. After playing Hubbell Gardiner, however, he was now looked upon as Hollywood's leading romantic male. In fact, when his less successful 1975 film

The Great Waldo Pepper flopped at the box office, director George Roy Hill apportioned part of the blame to killing off his love interest (played by Susan Sarandon). The decision to kill the character may have been made for sound dramatic purposes, but explained Hill, "in a Redford movie, in the vicarious way women were relating to him after *The Way We Were*, we were doomed because we were effectively killing them off."

In becoming a fantasy object for millions of women, Redford now held an appeal that stretched far beyond the Katie Moroskys in the audience. He may have been more than a bit startled at the change in the public's perception—"I just wasn't prepared for the impact"—but Sydney Pollack was not surprised in the least, having exclaimed to Redford as far back as the daily rushes, "Man, that was some hot stuff. You know what this is going to do to your box office?"

Status as a romantic object did not sit comfortably with Redford, and he continued to work at a feverish pace in films far less overtly romantic than *The Way We Were*. In *The Sting*, his romance really lay in the on-screen reunion with his *Butch Cassidy and the Sundance Kid* costar Paul Newman. Playing Bob Woodward in *All the President's Men*, the sparks were generated by his relentless desire for the story he pursued with Dustin Hoffman's Carl Bernstein. His starring role in the Pollack-directed *Electric Horseman* (1979) opposite his *Barefoot in the Park* costar Jane Fonda proved successful, but with both Fonda and Meryl Streep, his costar in the Oscar-winning *Out of Africa* (1985), the romantic interludes between beautiful WASPy Redford and his equally beautiful and WASPy costars somehow failed to generate the heat or cultural subtext of *The Way We Were*. Similarities, not differences, abounded, and the Redford/Fonda/Streep pairings would not have looked out of place at a tony suburban country club.

Oddly enough, even given their familiarity with one another, both on- and off-screen, Redford and Fonda seem to exhibit a wary respect for each other, rather than any pure passion. That sense of remove could certainly not have been helped when Fonda, then at the peak of her 1970's political activism, declared to the *Village Voice* newspaper that Redford "is, and remains, a bourgeois in the worst sense of the word." Starring opposite Streep in *Out of Africa*, Redford hit box-office gold, but while the film proved a big success, it somehow remains on the same tier as *Crash* and *The Artist* as one of the lesser Oscar-winning Best Pictures. It is nowadays best remembered for John Williams's sweeping score as well as for a scene of Redford washing Streep's hair alongside a hippo watering hole. Just as proved the case with *The Way We Were*, Redford once again felt that his character, the British aristocrat Denys Finch Hatton, was "a symbol, not a character." There really was no role for Redford to act in a screenplay cobbled together by Judith Thurman and Errol Trzebinski (alongside selections from the writings of Karen Blixen), and the decision that he drop the British accent that he had practiced assiduously did not help matters of authenticity.

When it came to matters of romance, even popular films like *Up Close and Personal* (1996), which costarred Michele Pfeiffer, and *The Horse Whisperer* (1998), in which Redford played opposite Kristin Scott Thomas, seemed to succeed in spite of the lack of romantic passion. In the end, both pairings played out as one slightly distant WASP spending time with another, as if the characters somehow longed for a nice gin and tonic to brush away any unpleasantness.

It's a lack that was sorely felt because Redford, whose outer beauty so often warred with an inner sense of genuine star danger, needed an on-screen foil to fully bloom. Said Pollack, "It's a deal with the devil. He will always be thirty, blond, perfection. There will be moments when smart critics will cut through it, but even the best of them want the idealized actor. They want the continuance, because no one wants the death of fantasy, no one can stand too much reality." In the words of producer Walter Kirn at the time of *The Horse Whisperer*,

"While De Niro and Pacino are the sum total of their roles, Redford stands for the industry itself, in all its California dreaminess."

Redford hit a second career peak by winning the Oscar as Best Director for *Ordinary People* in 1980 and through the following four decades, continued to alternate directing (*The Milagro Beanfield War* [1988], *A River Runs Through It* [1992], and *Quiz Show* [1994]) with acting. He turned in a sensational performance in the 2013 feature *All Is Lost*, the only actor in a film that contained exactly fifty-one spoken words of English. He held the screen with a beautifully judged performance, his formidable film-acting skills undiminished, indeed now heightened, but he was inexplicably overlooked at the time of Academy Award nominations. By now, he had won an Honorary Oscar for Lifetime Achievement, founded the Sundance Film Festival, and remained active in numerous environmental causes. After announcing his on-screen retirement with *The Old Man and the Gun* (2018), he nonetheless returned the very next year, at age eighty-three, in *Avengers: Endgame*.

He was, it seemed, nowhere near ready to stop and after sixty years in the industry, still willing to undertake one more roll of the dice, no matter the risks: "Don't be afraid to take a risk, don't be afraid of failure, be bold."

In a career studded by multiple wins of every conceivable major award, **Barbra Streisand** had, with *The Way We Were*, arrived at the top of both the film and the recording industries. She had achieved her goal of being taken seriously as a dramatic actress, with Academy Award and Golden Globe nominations to prove it, and was by now routinely referred to as "La Streisand," a heady reference for a woman who had only recently turned thirty. Part tribute and part reference to her diva-like reputation, the nickname stuck.

Thrilled by the success of *The Way We Were* and deeming the film "a highlight of my career," Barbra seemed almost as happy with the knowledge that her association with Ray Stark was almost at an end. Grateful to Stark for *Funny Girl*, she was nonetheless chafing at what she felt was the servitude of the multipicture deal he had insisted she sign with his Rastar Productions. With the completion of *The Way We Were*, only one film remained, the contractual obligation finally fulfilled by *Funny Lady* (1975). After that successful sequel wrapped, Streisand sent Stark an antique mirror on which she had written in lipstick, "Paid in full." A plaque that came with the mirror then added a final message: "Even though I sometimes forget to say it, thank you, Ray. Love, Barbra." Asked if she would ever work with Stark again, the star's three-word answer carried a world of implications: "Under my terms."

She would, in fact, go on to even greater recording and box-office success with her 1976 remake of *A Star Is Born*, but the film was reviled by critics, a fact partially mitigated by her winning a second Oscar, this time as the composer of the number-one hit "Evergreen." She had a box-office hit with the forgettable comedy *The Main Event* (1979) but stumbled badly with the wildly uneven *All Night Long* (1981). She rebounded with 1983's *Yentl*, the full extent of her talent on display as star, screenwriter, director, and producer. It remains an underrated and beautifully turned out directorial debut, and although it did not achieve the stratospheric popularity of *The Way We Were*, the two films did share one similarity: Oscar controversy continued to follow Streisand. Even after winning a Golden Globe Award as Best Director for *Yentl*, she was snubbed by the Academy Awards, a fact that garnered more press than did the list of actual Best Director nominees. She scored a second directorial triumph with *The Prince of Tides* (1991), and although the film was nominated as Best Picture, when it came to directing, she was overlooked once again. The Academy, it seemed, just did not like Barbra Streisand.

Through the years, she maintained a close friendship with Sydney Pollack, who can be glimpsed cheering her on during her Emmy-winning *Barbra: The Concert* television special. Pollack in fact spoke highly of Streisand the filmmaker, saying of *Yentl*, "Usually when a new director starts directing, you can see the wheels turning, so to speak. . . . Oftentimes you are giving something credit for being well-executed but not particularly polished in its execution. *Yentl* was seamless. It would be polished for a 20th film, but particularly so for a first film. I was terribly impressed with it." Over the years, the bond that Streisand and Pollack had developed during *The Way We Were* grew into a comfortable friendship, and the duo would often talk on the phone, both about directing and Streisand's notorious reluctance to commit herself to a film. Said Pollack, "She'll call and we'll talk for an hour and she'll say 'What am I doing? Why am I not working? What am I saving myself for? This is stupid. I should be out there, Sydney.'"

The same critics who had praised Streisand when she was the kooky young upstart from Brooklyn now often turned on her with a vengeance, and reviews of her films were often strikingly personal. If Woody Allen and Warren Beatty were praised for writing, directing, starring in, and producing their own films in the late 1970s and early 1980s, Streisand was often taken to task for the same actions, the words all but stating, "How dare she? A woman?!" Critics accused her of self-indulgence and egomania in her self-directed efforts, conveniently forgetting the fact that in all three feature films she directed, it was her costars who were nominated for Oscars: Amy Irving in *Yentl*, Nick Nolte in *The Prince of Tides*, and Lauren Bacall in *The Mirror Has Two Faces*.

By this point, she had triumphed as actress, singer, composer, director, writer, and producer, but she remained eager for new mountains to climb, rarely satisfied with anything she had achieved. Her own larger-than-life personality engendered both fierce loyalty—the slings and arrows of the press only strengthened her fans' allegiance to Barbra—and equally strident denunciations. It therefore made a curious kind of sense that in a November 1975 poll by Columbia Pictures and 20th Century Fox, she was voted both the most and least popular movie star.

It was her own essential persona that continued to cause this disparate reaction: those who thrilled to the over-the-rainbow romantic fantasies of the striking-looking, tough but vulnerable girl were matched in number by those who found it all too much and over the top: Barbra Strident. In the aftermath of *The Way We Were*, however, it became clear that Barbra Streisand had changed the rules in Hollywood, ruling the box office as a woman who upended traditional notions of beauty and refused to be silenced. In the words of Isobel Lennart, the screenwriter of *Funny Girl*, "She's made life a lot better for a helluva lot of homely girls." Through sheer force of talent and willpower, she seemed able to now hold her own party, inviting only those she liked. Or as it turned out, she'd invite those she wanted, set the table, cook the dinner, and provide the entertainment. She was, as always, in control.

Outspokenly liberal, in 1986 she gave a full-length concert for the first time in nearly twenty years to raise funds for the Democratic Party. By now she had become a favorite bête noire of the right wing, a fact that seemed to trouble her little. Rubbing people the wrong way was simply chalked up to the cost of doing business. In her own words, "I'm a feminist, Jewish, opinionated, liberal woman. I push a lot of buttons." Just like Katie Morosky.

In her third and to date, last directorial feature, *The Mirror Has Two Faces* (1996), she played Rose Morgan, a woman with more than a passing similarity to Katie: both women are intelligent and plain but possessed of an inner beauty. It all represented another iteration of the Streisand formula that began with Fanny Brice and Nicky Arnstein in *Funny Girl*: the man (in *Mirror*, it is Jeff Bridges) is more attractive than the woman, but she is smarter and more than worthy of his respect and love. In fact, he has to step up his game to be worthy of the chance to love her. In all of her most successful films (*Funny Girl*, *The Way We Were*, and *What's Up, Doc?*), by film's end, Prince Charming all but slaps his own forehead in amazement before declaring, "You ARE beautiful," but in *The Mirror Has Two Faces*, the trope was taken too far. Jeff Bridges, it turns out, loves Rose in spite of, not because of, the fact that she is beautiful. . . . One wondered who Barbra was trying to convince here. She had long since won the battle—no one remains a movie star for thirty years without carrying a sexual charge, no matter how different the packaging—and while her direction remains solid throughout, in her iron-willed determination to prove her point, she did nothing so much as hit the audience over the head with her message. The film, despite several interesting and attention-grabbing scenes between Streisand and her screen mother Lauren Bacall, did not prove particularly successful.

Guilt Trip, however, her 2012 comedy with Seth Rogen that remains her last to date film, found her giving a relaxed and charming performance as a loving, occasionally suffocating mother. If not particularly successful, the film nonetheless demonstrated her undiminished comedic skills, and the lowkey affect of her interactions with screen son Rogen proved winning.

Intellectually, Streisand knew that not every film would prove to be a hit and that a determination to stretch her creative muscles was crucial. She even took to quoting Truffaut on the topic: "You do your work and at the end you have a body of work and some of it is good and some of it is not good, but the stuff that's good will override what isn't good." All of this would seem to speak to a desire to keep working, and yet happy in her marriage to actor James Brolin, she now worked much less often. Although her return to live concerts in 1994 had generated acclaim, awards, and millions of dollars, her on-screen appearances became increasingly rare, and in the forty years after *Yentl* premiered in 1983, she appeared in only six feature films, ranging from *Nuts* (1987) and *The Prince of Tides* (1991) to the popular and juvenile *Meet the Fockers* (2004) and *Little Fockers* (2010).

When it came to working more often, the problem lay in the fact that Streisand's perfectionist instincts made it difficult for her to accept films she didn't control, and each of the three films she directed took years out of her life. Barbra Streisand was a director who worried about every element of the production, right down to whether her blouse would read properly against the background of a couch. There was also, to be sure, a monumental recording career to consider, and she continued to release a new CD nearly every year. In short, a multimedia empire needed to be maintained, and if her demand for perfection bothered some, Barbra was not overly concerned. In her own words, "I just really am blunt. That saves me a lot of time and also loses a lot of friends."

Analyzing the difficulty some had in dealing with Streisand, Sydney Pollack explained: "When you face that kind of talent, all of your own fears come to the surface. You're measuring yourself against her. And that's why people get into trouble with her. As long as you're comfortable with yourself and you know what you know, then she's not a threat to you and you have no problems with her." By now, Streisand had won every award the industry had to offer, but, like Redford, she still wanted to be challenged. And as they acted, sang, directed, wrote, and produced their way from one film to another, one question followed them everywhere: when was there going to be a sequel to *The Way We Were*? Would Hubbell and Katie ever get back together?

The answer to those particular questions depended on who you asked and on what day. Laurents and Stark had one answer, Pollack, Redford, and Streisand another. In fact, each of them had several answers:

There was no script. . . . There were several scripts.

It was a go. . . . It was a no-go. . . . It was a definite maybe.

Hubbell and Katie would never reunite. Hubbell and Katie would live happily ever after.

In the end, one man held the answers, but was Arthur Laurents really ready to leap into battle one more time?

The Sequel

> *"I guess this is the sequel, huh, Babs?"* —Robert Redford accepting the Honorary Oscar for Lifetime Achievement from Barbra Streisand

> *"Dear Bob, it was such fun being married to you for a while. Too bad it didn't work out, but we made something that will last much longer than many real marriages."* —Barbra Streisand presenting Robert Redford with the Lincoln Center Film Society Chaplin Award

Barbra Streisand and Robert Redford certainly carried enormous power when it came to any talk of a sequel to *The Way We Were*, but the path to any such film had to begin with a script both stars deemed acceptable, a state of affairs that meant involving Arthur Laurents. It was therefore all the more surprising that the first meeting about a possible sequel took place between old adversaries Robert Redford and Arthur Laurents.

Some ten years after the film's release, the two men sat down and in Laurents's retelling, figured out that it was Sydney Pollack who had been responsible for poisoning the air between them. Although Redford had gone on record as stating that Sydney Pollack deserved "the lion's share of the credit for *The Way We Were*. It really was his film," director and star had by now grown apart, their long friendship on shaky ground after creative tensions on the sets of *Out of Africa* and *Havana*. For his part, Laurents never had fully forgiven Pollack for his actions on *The Way We Were*, and in *The Rest of the Story*, an autobiography he wrote during the last year of his life, he remained blunt as ever about the director's work: "Totally ignorant of the period, he destroyed its politics. And I had chosen him. I had persuaded Streisand to take him. My enthusiasm was based on his movie *They Shoot Horses, Don't They?* I saw that picture again the other day. I was horrified to see that it wasn't good."

After clearing the air with Laurents, Redford informed the writer that he was in fact open to the possibility of continuing the story of Katie and Hubbell. Just as Barbra retained fond memories of making the film—"Every day was an exciting adventure"—Redford was also making sympathetic noises: "I loved working with Barbra. Everybody warned me, 'Oh, Streisand, she's a pain in the ass.' I said, 'Well, I'm not going to judge her before, but I think she's talented.' I met her and I liked her. She was a joy to work with, and I loved making the film."

Recalling a chemistry with Barbra that he termed "organic," Redford acknowledged that she may have had a crush on him when filming started, but it was "the fun we had" that colored his memories: "It ended up being one of the most enjoyable relationships I've ever had. . . . I remember liking her energy and her spirit; it was wonderful to play off of. I also really enjoyed kidding her." If the laid-back Redford remembered how much he enjoyed teasing the intense, constantly rehearsing Streisand, Streisand now recalled being reduced to bouts of laughter whenever she insisted that Redford attempt to speak Yiddish.

Laurents was intrigued by the idea of writing for the two stars again and sketched out his idea that as the years pass, Katie's marriage to Dr. David X. Cohen notwithstanding, Katie and Hubbell have never stopped loving each other. Perhaps, Laurents theorized,

Katie might have grown jealous of her own daughter, a radical in the mold of Katie herself. In fact, he wondered, what if Katie and Hubbell's daughter came on to Hubbell, not knowing that he was her father? Outtakes from the original film would be interspersed throughout the sequel; when Katie, on the phone in California, and Hubbell, speaking from New York, talked for the first time in fifteen years, they would, courtesy of the outtakes, visualize each other as they had appeared fifteen years previously when parting outside of the Plaza Hotel. The audience, however, would be looking at the present-day fifteen-year-older versions of Katie and Hubbell. That dichotomy appealed greatly to Laurents: "The discrepancy when they finally met up again would be a huge obstacle to renewing a romance in which beauty was so important." Politics would once again prove key, and given the radical politics of Katie and Hubbell's daughter, the ending of the film would take place in 1968 at the Democratic Convention in Chicago, complete with thousands of protestors chanting, "The whole world is watching!"

Laurents wrote a complete draft and decided to first send the script to Redford, even before showing it to either Barbra or Ray Stark. The answer from Redford? Deafening silence. Sydney Pollack then came to New York City to discuss a possible sequel with Laurents, and the ever-blunt screenwriter told Pollack, "You know I don't trust you, Sydney." Wrote Laurents of Pollack's reaction, "'Oh, I know,' he answered as pleasantly as though I had said I did."

Reports of a sequel now began spreading throughout the press, with Marilyn Beck writing in the *New York Daily News* of February 20, 1980, that Pollack had spoken to both Streisand and Redford, each of whom had final script approval. Explained the director, "I have talked to both of them about it and with their encouragement, Ray Stark and I will be assigning a writer to develop the screenplay. . . . We'll take them through the sixties and watch their individual development as they mature and bring them back together when she phones for help with their daughter, who's grown up to be a Berkeley hippie with a drug problem. They'll get back together permanently. And happily. We couldn't do any less for them or for the millions of people who have come to love those characters."

Pollack in fact spent a great deal of time thinking about a sequel, allowing that he imagined beginning the film with a dinner scene, "where Redford had to come to dinner with David X. Cohen and her. I could see Barbra running around the kitchen trying to get this meal ready—a pot roast. And then I figured that Redford would go up to Berkeley to see the daughter he'd never seen. And he'd have an affair with the daughter's roommate." Whether or not all of those plot elements would actually be present in Laurents's draft, Pollack was more than ready to supply story lines for all of the characters: "I knew that at some point the character of J.J., his friend, would have committed suicide, because he was a guy who was dangerously lost in the past, to such an extent he would never have been able to deal with today. And Lois Chiles . . . I would assume would have written a wonderful best-selling book on feminism, would have become a Gloria Steinem kind of lady."

Informed of Pollack's take on her character, Chiles laughed and mused, "That is a very, very interesting idea about Carol Ann. You certainly didn't see that side of Carol Ann in the college years. It would have been interesting to show the growth of every one of the leading characters, to show that we all do hopefully mature, that the things that mattered at one time don't matter further down the road."

What seemed to interest Pollack the most was his belief that the somewhat aimless, writing-for-television Hubbell would have changed by the time of the sequel: "He never was really able to deal with the complexities of growing up. But I think of Hubbell as a guy who'd be a late starter. I think this man will be a helluva man in his late forties and early fifties. . . . I would see the sequel ending with him becoming very active politically."

The public's interest level was ratcheted up several more levels when a four-month-later report in the *New York Post* quoted Pollack as stating that he'd pay both stars $8 million plus a percentage of the profits: "There are just two screen combinations that have built-in box office magic—Redford and Paul Newman and Redford and Barbra Streisand. In the old days it was Katharine Hepburn and Spencer Tracy and Bing Crosby and Bob Hope." The glittering press agentry of the piece stoked interest until the first cold water was thrown on the project by Barbra's own agent, the always tough-minded Sue Mengers: "If Sydney does want Barbra for the movie, he'll have to wait at least a year and a half because when she finishes *All Night Long* with Gene Hackman she goes right into preproduction on *Yentl, the Yeshiva Boy*. I know that Pollack and Stark are developing a sequel, but we haven't seen a word on paper yet. And of course we won't commit to anything until we see a script." (*Yentl* ended up a triumph for Streisand, but *All Night Long*, directed by Mengers's husband, Jean-Claude Tramont, was to prove a disaster for Barbra, a monumental flop at the box office that halted her reign as queen of the box office.)

Four months later, Liz Smith reported in the *New York Daily News* that Redford had put a halt to any sequel speculation, quoting the star as saying that rumors of his participation in a sequel were "ridiculous." Redford, she further disclosed, "never said he'd take $10 million for the fee. . . . Redford is so fed up with this kind of speculation that he is considering taking legal action."

In June of the following year, Marilyn Beck filed a second report, this time stating that Redford knew one thing for certain: "he won't be starring in a sequel to *The Way We Were*. . . . Redford's camp insists there are no such plans." By now, Pollack was also singing a very different tune, suddenly explaining to Beck that he, Redford, and Barbra had "investigated the thought of a sequel—and dropped it a long time ago. Bob and Barbra don't want to do it. Neither do I. And neither does producer Ray Stark."

Laurents, however, continued researching the tumultuous events of 1968 at both Berkeley and Chicago, hiring a research assistant, Sheila Possner, who supplied him with a thick folder full of photocopied political articles from that turmoil-racked year. Contrary to Pollack's assertion, Ray Stark still remained interested, and given Laurents's desire to utilize footage left out of the original film, in a letter of October 21, 1981, his assistant Sherry Worn wrote the screenwriter to enclose *The Way We Were*'s final shooting script; so continuous had been the changes and so numerous the writers that Laurents himself did not even possess a final, complete shooting script. In closing, and seemingly just to make sure that Laurents knew who remained in control, Stark asked the screenwriter to indicate exactly which scenes from the original film he was interested in viewing, and explained that the possibility of a sequel could be discussed when Stark returned from his travels.

Undaunted, Laurents had Sheila Possner reach out to Don Koué, who had been a student at Berkeley in the 1960s, to obtain additional background information about campus politics. In a letter dated November 19, 1981, Possner informed Laurents that she would also contact Jim Devor, a participant in the Chicago riots of 1968, for his firsthand recollections. All of this background research culminated in a March 1982 letter from Possner to Laurents in which she enclosed a detailed timeline stretching from 1967 through 1968; Katie and Hubbell's daughter would now willingly participate in student uprisings stretching from Berkeley to Chicago. Like mother, like daughter.

As Laurents continued to research and write, public talk of a reunion for Katie and Hubbell remained constant. *New York Post* columnist Stephen M. Silverman discussed the possibility in a lengthy December 13, 1982, piece prophetically headlined, "The Way They Were—and Will Be ($$$ Permitting)," with Pollack himself reversing course once again. Speaking in decidedly more positive terms, albeit still remaining hesitant about the obstacles attached to such a high-profile project, Pollack admitted to liking Laurents's script, now titled *The Way We Changed*, and approved of the story line's focus on the daughter Hubbell has never seen. There remained no doubt about the public's interest in a sequel, but as Silverman's headline pointed out, money problems remained paramount. Asked Pollack rhetorically, "How'd you like to pick up the bill for Barbra and Bob today?" It wasn't just a question of two very busy schedules; Streisand and Redford, he explained, were now each receiving $5 million per picture.

Still, he remained enthusiastic, particularly about including unused footage from the first film as flashbacks. Calling the new film "more of a continuation than a rehash," Pollack felt energized by the possibilities: "I'm excited every time I think of the new scenes, because the two of them will have got rid of all the difficult stuff between them in the first part. . . . I think they both would have changed. He'd have become more political and she less."

All then remained silent until society columnist Suzy reported in November 1983 that the Laurents-penned screenplay was now projected to start filming in mid-1984. The more noteworthy news, however, came in a *New York Post* article for which Stephen Silverman once again spoke at length to Pollack. In rather true-to-form fashion, the director equivocated throughout: two separate scripts, he reported, had now been written, but neither one had fully solved the problems inherent in a continuation of the story: "There have been a few thoughts—Katie has married again, but she and Hubbell become adulterers, for instance. Both Bob and Barbra love these characters but are aware of the problems. A lot of the things that worked the first time, such as Katie being the ugly duckling, couldn't be used again. Now she's married, so what do you do? There is a daughter . . . Katie and Hubbell left each other at the Plaza in 1952. This would give us a way to look at the sixties—through the daughter. It could be interesting."

Through all of the yeses, noes, and maybes, Barbra did not give up hope for the sequel, one she wanted released in 1998 on the twenty-fifth anniversary of the film's premiere: "It's such a good story [told] through their daughter and her political activism at Berkeley in 1968—and a beautiful love story again." By 1996, Streisand allowed as how she wanted to direct and produce the sequel as well as costar with Redford; Redford seemed game to be directed by his costar, and Barbra reported to Laurents that Stark had agreed to sell her the rights to the screenplay. It all sounded promising, but after all of the delays, hesitations, and flat-out misgivings, Laurents felt the film would never actually happen. By the time Ray Stark called him in 1997 about adapting the source material into a Broadway musical to star Kathie Lee Gifford as Katie, Laurents's prediction seemed prescient, with the idea of Kathie Lee playing Katie Morosky proving a nonstarter.

And yet for all of the pitfalls and missteps, the idea of a sequel has never fully gone away for one simple reason: the public wants to see Barbra Streisand and Robert Redford together on-screen one more time, and Arthur Laurents's papers reveal that even as late as 2004, he was receiving letters from total strangers detailing their ideas for the sequel's plotline.

Queried about his thoughts on the subject of a sequel, lyricist Alan Bergman enthused, "Why not? The characters are interesting and it would be a chance for his character to be more substantial, a doer. Redford is such a skilled actor that it would make the movie all the more interesting. There's such history from the first film—such rich emotion." It's a view echoed by Lois Chiles: "Yes, there's the risk that the sequel would not have the same impact as the original, and maybe even dilute the story, but it makes sense that over time Hubbell would have grown more political and Katie less so. The story of two people who have loved and lost—that's universal and relatable. The differences between Katie and Hubbell really resonate with audiences, and there's also that beautiful score—poignant and bittersweet. It's a very potent mix."

Bergman's and Childs's enthusiasm was shared by both Redford (on occasion) and Streisand (wholeheartedly), and through all of the rumors, stumbles, and might-have-beens, their bond remained as strong as ever. When Streisand was honored with the American Film Institute's Lifetime Achievement Award in 2001, Redford gave a heartfelt tribute to his costar:

> Working with Barbra I hold as one of the highpoints of my film experience. I knew her before, particularly as a performer. On that level I thought she was talented, innovative, and sure. Sure of her ability, her craft, but also sure what she wanted from it. Her power as a performer created an inner beauty that made the prospect of working with her attractive. For someone so determined and in such control of herself, there are certain to be stories about how difficult she was, but such stories abound in our business and are probably best ignored. Well, guess what? She was a pain in the ass. . . . Just kidding. She was a delight and our connection was a delight. She was simply very alive—a critic, tough on herself, questioning, doubting, putting forth a huge effort to be the best she could be. So, quite contrary to any foregone notions, she was a joy. I will keep that experience in the sphere of fondest memory."

Returning the favor, it was Streisand who was asked—with Redford's approval—to present him with his Honorary Oscar for Lifetime Achievement in 2002. Enthused Streisand at the ceremony, "I adored working with him. . . . Robert Redford's work as director, actor, producer represents the man himself—the artist, the cowboy, the intellectual. . . . I'm very, very proud to bestow the Academy of Motion Picture Arts and Sciences Honorary Oscar for Lifetime Achievement to a man who gave me one of the most exciting and memorable experiences of my career. I was thrilled to be his leading lady and thrilled to present this award to Robert Redford." Exclaimed Redford when Streisand presented him with the award, "I guess this is the sequel, huh, Babs?"

On an hourlong 2010 appearance by Streisand on Oprah Winfrey's television show (itself an unusual event for the interview-shy Streisand), Robert Redford returned the favor by making an unexpected guest appearance. For once, such an appearance really did count as a genuine surprise, and in this, their first-ever joint interview, as Redford entered the stage, Streisand immediately embraced him, calling her good friend "sweetheart." The studio audience and Barbra herself were mutually delighted by the elusive Redford's appearance.

Inevitably, the two stars mused to Oprah about a possible sequel, with Redford at first throwing cold water on the very idea: "I just felt certain things should be left alone, and this was one of them." However, when Streisand detailed that in the sequel, their on-screen daughter would have grown into a radical, just like her mother—"She'd have gone to Berkeley and gotten in trouble, and we'd have to meet again to get her out of jail"—Redford chuckled before musing, "You know, that's not a bad idea."

Even as late as 2012, at the premiere of Streisand's most recent film, *The Guilt Trip*, Barbra discussed the possibility of a sequel. Asked by an interviewer if she'd ever revisit the characters in *The Way We Were*, she responded, "It's an interesting thing you should mention it." Interjected her *Guilt Trip* costar Seth Rogen, "It could be called *The Way We Are*." Barbra's retort, "It *is* called *The Way We Are*." Could it actually happen asked the interviewer? Barbra: "It could be—but I have to convince Bob." And just as had happened in 1972,

Redford remained uncommitted, managing to express interest and disinterest in virtually the same sentence: "It's always a possibility. . . . First of all I love Barbra. I love working with her. I'd work with her again in a flash. Where I put my foot down is I'm not a big fan of sequels. *The Way We Were*—I think it should just be left alone. But doing it again with Barbra is something I would like."

By this point, such was the reach of the film that even reviewers had taken to utilizing *The Way We Were* as a point of reference, with David Edelstein writing in his 2013 review of Redford's acclaimed performance in *All Is Lost*, "in *The Way We Were* that force of Jewish nature Barbra Streisand managed to rock his Waspy reticence like the storm surge does in *All Is Lost*." Redford, ever polite, praised all of his famous female costars: "I loved working with Jane, I loved working with Natalie, I loved working with Barbra. I loved the body language, the mystery, the sexual chemistry," but in a *New York Times* profile written by the reliably caustic Maureen Dowd, she cut to the chase with a blunt assessment that Redford's "most formidable adversary, [was] Barbra Streisand, in *The Way We Were*."

The two stars were reunited once again in 2015 when Streisand delivered a keynote speech at the twenty-fourth annual Women in Entertainment breakfast in Los Angeles, but their most memorable appearance was at another event that year when Streisand was tapped to present Redford with the Lincoln Center Film Society of New York Chaplin Award. By this point, their comfort level with each other was so clear that they seemed to function more than anything else as a well-oiled married couple cum comedy duo.

After words from Redford's three-time costar, Jane Fonda, who described Redford as a "complicated visionary," Streisand appeared in the star spot to present Redford with the actual award, calling him an "intellectual cowboy. . . . You never quite know what he's really thinking, and that makes him fascinating to watch on screen. . . . Bob understands the power of restraint. You're never going to get it all, and that's the secret, I think. That's the mystery. That's what makes you want to keep looking at him."

It was after that rather serious introduction, however, that Streisand delivered a witty, self-deprecating speech: "[On the set the first day], I could hear the crew shouting out my opening lines from *Funny Girl*: 'Hello, gorgeous.' I was thrilled, I was flattered . . . and then I was very upset because they were talking to Bob." Cracking wise, she added, "He kept asking me about Brooklyn, some foreign country over there. . . . I guess he thought I was kind of exotic, but he was the exotic one to me, growing up in sunny California. He'd surfed, fished and swam in the ocean. . . . these were all the things that my mother told me would kill me."

To the vastly entertained audience, it was as if that young Brooklyn dynamo Barbra Streisand had reappeared: "I knew he did daredevil things like skiing . . . coming down a mountain on thin rails, very fast. That's not one of the skills you pick up on the streets of Brooklyn." Plucking a key line from *The Way We Were*, Streisand explained, "Katie says to Hubbell 'people are their principles.' . . . Hubbell may not have believed it, but Robert has lived every day of his life by that creed, so tonight, some 40 years after we first met on that soundstage, I'd like to say, 'Dear Bob, it was such fun being married to you for a while. Too bad it didn't work out, but we made something that will last much longer than many real marriages.'" Walking onstage to a standing ovation, Redford was embraced by Streisand, who then touched his hair in a replay of the movie's signature gesture as the audience roared its approval.

Audiences ate up the still-blazing Streisand–Redford chemistry, so after all of the starts, stops, and might-have-beens, exactly why has the sequel never come to pass? It was actually Sydney Pollack who seemed to most accurately pinpoint one of the problems: the passage of time has changed the very urgency of the characters' romantic dilemma. Analyzed the director,

> I don't know what to say about a sequel. The only sequel I know that's been successful is *The Godfather*. . . . In straight dramas like this—it's hard to do sequels. I didn't know how to do it. There were three screenplays written—Arthur wrote one, David Rayfiel wrote one. The thought was that in the sequel they would end up together. The obvious thought was that the child would be the key to bringing them back together. *The Way We Were* ended in '51 with the era of loyalty oaths so let's say the child was two. The child would be eighteen years old in 1967—you could have a child who was college age at the height of the 60s. We could try to do a bit of the 60s which was a great decade dramatically; perhaps the daughter gets into political trouble that brings them together.
>
> But I don't think any of them really worked. Part of the reason why it's difficult to do a sequel is so much of the appeal of the picture comes from the identification with the kind of yearning you have when those differences matter—who belongs, who doesn't, who's accepted, who isn't. As you get older those things matter less and less—you don't think like that in your forties and fifties. Those values are gone. What would you substitute that would make the longing, yearning, and the ache—you could do a different kind of story—we somehow never got it solved.

When recently asked if she agrees with Pollack's viewpoint, Barbra answered firmly: "No. I don't think there's any age limit on longing, or yearning. After making this movie, I knew Katie and Hubbell so well and felt they had more to say to each other. So I put together a treatment for a sequel that takes place when their daughter is in college. It's her political activism that unexpectedly brings them together and the climax of the film occurs against the backdrop of the 1968 Democratic Convention and the protests in the street. Interestingly, Katie and Hubbell have both changed in ways that make them more in sync, politically, while their love for each other remains the same. So sparks fly, and it's thrilling and passionate and moving."

The desire to make the sequel remained but, mused Barbra, "We tried for twenty years to make the sequel, which is a wonderful story about what happened when their daughter grew up, set fourteen years later—but it's too late to do it now." And yet surprisingly, it was Redford who brought it up as recently as 2011, seeming to muse about the idea without ever mentioning *The Way We Were* by name: "The other movie I want to make is about people who rediscover themselves in older love. . . . They got together out of passion years earlier, but it flamed out and they went their separate ways. They get to be older and somehow come back into each other's lives and regain their relationship with a more mature love. . . . That's an interesting story—and I'm qualified to write it!"

All of which leads to one unexpected but crucial question: has the lack of a sequel actually deepened *The Way We Were*'s enduring appeal? Barbra's own answer to that question is adament: "No, I don't think that factors into the appeal of the film, which is already so strong. It's a classic love story, and it stands on its own. But I always want more, and I think the story I put together really worked on so many levels. I still wish we had made the sequel. The fact that we didn't is one of my biggest regrets."

What can't be denied, however, is that *Godfather Part II* excepted, disappointment invariably seems to accompany audience reaction to every sequel, and might have colored the continuing reaction to the original film. Now, however, absent a sequel, everyone can supply their own continuing story line—steering Katie and Hubbell toward happily ever after or continuing heartbreak, however they see fit. Each passionate fan of *The Way We Were* can now in fact play Arthur Laurents or Sydney Pollack for themselves.

It is the fans' own authenticity of passion that rivets them to those very same qualities in Katie Morosky. Her heartfelt declarations, devoid of irony and defiantly emblematic of the World War II Greatest Generation, defined who we were in a way that the noise of today's endlessly sardonic and snarky discourse can never touch. To James Woods, in fact, the modern age of mean-spirited social media plays out "like a horrible bunch of high school cliques making fun of each other. It's insanity—bereft of any real passion." By way of contrast, the ardor suffusing *The Way We Were*'s mid-twentieth-century America now fills audiences with its own subliminal sense of yearning. Yes, Katie is loud and exhausting, but she is the personification of an authentic spirit. And that is why it makes dramatic and cultural sense to audiences when J.J. muses aloud to Hubbell, "Now losing Katie—that would really be a loss."

Hubbell, of course, is consumed with a rather sad longing for the belief and intensity displayed so naturally by Katie, ultimately realizing that he will likely never acquire it. All of his promise, the seemingly endless string of golden hours lying straight ahead, has come to naught. More realistic than Katie, Hubbell must always have understood Guiderius's song in Shakespeare's *Cymbeline* far better than others: "Golden lads and girls all must, as chimney sweepers come to dust."

Even though suffused with an enormously appealing, bittersweet mixture of love and regret, for all its technicolor romance, at heart *The Way We Were* actually represents a full-bodied, emotional, and defiantly un-ironic outlook on life that no longer exists in twenty-first-century America. And as that vision of an America that believed in its own ability to make the world safe for democracy recedes further into the past, the nostalgic appeal of *The Way We Were* increases all the more, the collective wish for Katie and Hubbell's happy ending, for America's happy ending, now lying permanently, if tantalizingly, just out of reach.

It is in the attempt to grasp such an ending that viewers long for just one more meeting with Hubbell and Katie. A last chance to wallow in a love story set against the swirling panorama of the twentieth century—the American century. A final opportunity for mismatched lovers, one more go-round for everyone who has ever loved with passion if not wisely. A concluding attempt to right wrongs and possibly—just possibly—figure out the happy ending so determinedly ingrained in the American ethos.

One more chance to muse about our singular journeys through that American century as inevitably, onscreen and off, we circle back to our own final meetings outside the Plaza Hotel, private orchestras swelling until just like Katie and Hubbell, we finally and for all time . . .

Acknowledgments

My first thanks go to my agent, Malaga Baldi, and my editor, John Cerullo. Their support proved to be of great help throughout all drafts of this book, and I'm fortunate to be in such good hands. Thanks as well to Mark Erickson, who functioned as a first-class sounding board, and to Christine Pittel for her help in facilitating written interviews. At Rowman & Littlefield/Applause, I owe a true debt to Meaghan Menzel, Jessica Kastner, Della Vache, Barbara Claire, Chris Chappell, and Laurel Myers for their help with myriads of questions and details throughout the process.

I'd also like to extend my thanks to the staff at the music division of the Library of Congress, particularly Caitlin Miller, for her expert help in navigating the Library's collection of the Arthur Laurents papers. Similar thanks to the staff at the New York Public Library's Performing Arts Division; the Library's unparalleled collection of books, articles, and clippings remains one of the many reasons I am glad to live in New York City. A similar debt is owed to Matt Howe's extraordinary Barbra Archives, where Matt's encyclopedic coverage of Barbra's career covers not just *The Way We Were* but all Streisand films and recordings.

A special thanks as well to all those who agreed to interviews and written exchanges about their time on *The Way We Were*: Barbra Streisand, James Woods, Lois Chiles, Hawk Koch, Grover Dale, Art Smith Jr., and Wendy Stark Morrissey. A particular thanks to the talented and always gentlemanly Alan Bergman for our two fascinating conversations, to Dennis Aspland, and as always, to film author/historian/professor Jeanine Basinger, whose knowledge of film history remains without equal.

Finally, thanks to a terrific group of friends and colleagues whose support and encouragement during the past year have been very much appreciated; too numerous to mention, they know who they are, and I hope they understand that I mention only two by name: my sister Sarah and my nephew Parker.

Notes

In the Beginning

"I think that Barbra Streisand is, first and foremost, an actress," https://jamesgrissom.blogspot.com/2012/11/barbra-streisand-ideal-eucharist-part.html?fbclid=IwAR0ZYS97Cp91kWb6mCyzevIYvb3ZenWw0WtUKPCTUbpl6yGnRuGdwmaIV5E.

"By this point he and I had known each other for ten years," Barbra Streisand, written response to author, July 19, 2022.

"a girl I'd known for twenty minutes at Cornell," Kimme Hendrick, "Something Worth Trying," *Christian Science Monitor,* June 1972.

"It's wonderful. I want to do it!" ibid.

"I didn't know Arthur Laurents until this film," Ray Stark in *The Way We Were*: Director's Commentary, 25th Anniversary DVD, Columbia Pictures, 1999.

"I had read somewhere that David Lean," Barbra Streisand, written response to author, July 19, 2022.

"the last of the great old world Hollywood producers," Corey Kilgannon, "Ray Stark, Oscar-Nominated Producer, Is Dead at 88," *The New York Times*, January 18, 2004.

"Ray is adept at throwing people off balance," Myrna Oliver, "Ray Stark, 88; Hollywood Legend, Insider Produced 'Funny Girl,' Other Classic Films," *The Los Angeles Times*, January 18, 2004.

"They are both intuitive women: strong, earthy, intelligent, vital and absolutely honest," Ray Stark, "Come on, Let's Stop a Minute to See Snooks," *The New York Times*, September 15, 1968.

"I was very involved," Ray Stark in *The Way We Were*: Director's Commentary, 25th Anniversary DVD, Columbia Pictures, 1999.

"Always had a kind of fierce passion," Kimme Hendrick, "Something Worth Trying," *Christian Science Monitor* June 1972.

"I believed it wasn't un-American to be a member of the Communist Party," Arthur Laurents, *Original Story By: A Memoir of Broadway and Hollywood* (New York: Knopf 2000), 263.

"Like Barbra, unlike Barbra," ibid., 247.

"the owner of that Sutton Place apartment," ibid., 263.

"with Fanny's outrage and convictions," ibid., 248.

"She was too passionate about too much," ibid., 258.

"A wearer of elegant suspenders," ibid., 259.

"who was blond and Aryan," ibid., 263.

"I took what happened to me in college," Arthur Laurents in *The Way We Were*: *Looking Back*, 25th Anniversary DVD, Columbia Pictures, 1999.

"part me, part a naval lieutenant named Dougal Wyatt," Arthur Laurents, *Original Story By*, 263.

"easier wasn't necessarily better," ibid., 258.

"in a way he was like the country he lived in," ibid., 259.

"The fraud, of course, was me," ibid.

"I reacted somewhat as Robert Redford does in *The Way We Were*," ibid., 12.

"She is a plodder on the page as in life," Neil Gabler, *Barbra Streisand: Rediscovering Beauty, Femininity, and Power* (New Haven: Yale University Press, 2016) 141.

"a person who was everything she wasn't," Laurents, *Original Story By*, 258.

"who *doesn't need* to face the moral issues," Michael Feeney Callan, *Robert Redford: The Biography* (New York: Alfred A. Knopf, 2011), 193.

"I wasn't worried, I knew they would tell me." Laurents, *Original Story By*, 263.

"just as I did in Eve Merriam's," ibid., 260.

"There was both terror and excitement," Arthur Laurents in *The Way We Were*: *Looking Back*, 25th Anniversary DVD, Columbia Pictures, 1999.

"I don't know how Mr. Schary can look at himself in the mirror every morning without vomiting," Laurents, *Original Story By*, 266.

"fellow toads," ibid., 265.

"It was down to her beliefs, his beliefs," ibid., 261.

"Do you think I'm pretty?" *The Owl and The Pussycat*, screenplay by Bill Manhoff and Buck Henry, Columbia Pictures, 1970.

"It's because I'm not pretty," Neal Gabler, *Barbra Streisand*, 115.

"And Laurents admitted to himself that it was true," ibid.

"It's that I'm not attractive—not in the right way, isn't it?" Arthur Laurents, *The Way We Were*, Columbia Pictures 1973.

"She had to be a Jew," Laurents, *Original Story By*, 257.

"She was the essence of every confused, not-very-attractive girl," Neal Gabler, *Barbra Streisand*, 53.

"The connecting tissue is Barbra's passion and her sense of injustice," Arthur Laurents in James Spada, *Streisand: Her Life* (New York: Crown Publishing, 1995), 299.

"She does everything wrong but it comes out right," Kevin Sessums, "Barbra Streisand Queen of Tides," *Vanity Fair*, September 1991.

"One risk I wasn't as fully aware of as I should have been," Laurents, *Original Story By*, 263–64.

"I had doubts that she would accept the part," Rene Jordan, *The Greatest Star: The Barbra Streisand Story* (New York: G.P. Putnam's Sons, 1975), 186–87.

"That's me!" Anne Edwards, *Streisand: A Biography* (New York: Little Brown, 1997), 334.

"I started singing because I couldn't get a job as an actress," Joe Lynch, "Barbra Streisand Reflects on Acting Career, Struggles as a Director during Tribeca Chat with Robert Rodriguez," April 29, 2017, https://www.billboard.com/music/music-news/barbra-streisand-tribeca-robert-rodriguez-7776946/.

"How I came to write a novel," Kimme Hendrick, "Something Worth Trying," *Christian Science Monitor* June 1972.

"The Barbra I first knew was such a bright and alert person," Rene Jordan, *The Greatest Star*, 187.

"Rule Number One," *NYTTheater*, @nyttheater, https://twitter.com/nytimestheater/status/773174682333962240.

Enter Sydney Pollack

"Sydney Pollack was exactly the right director," Jeanine Basinger, interview with author, December 8, 2021.

"He was the only guy on the set as quiet and scared as I was," Tom Buckley, "At the Movies," *The New York Times*, March 2, 1979.

"To him, Sydney did not smell good," Michael Feeney Callan, *Robert Redford*, 191.

"the script had been turned down by other studios," Sydney Pollack in *The Way We Were*: Director's Commentary, 25th Anniversary DVD, Columbia Pictures, 1999.

"Early on when I started to work on it," ibid.

"I realized Sydney was a good director," Ray Stark in ibid.

"Barbra was smart," Michael Feeney Callan, *Robert Redford*, 191.

"She has a tendency to take over a picture," Randall Riese, *Her Name Is Barbra* (New York: Carol Publishing, 1993), 332.

"strong narrative line, craftsmanship, and visual style," Sydney Pollack in *The Way We Were*: Director's Commentary, 25th Anniversary DVD, Columbia Pictures, 1999.

"like Stevens and Wyler and Zinnemann," ibid.

"Laurents is really a playwright and not a novelist," Rocky Lang and Barbara Hall (editors), *Letters from Hollywood: Inside the Private World of Classic American Moviemaking* (New York: Abrams, 2019), 323.

"The problem in the novel," ibid.

"we've seen it all before in fiction and nonfiction," Barbara A. Bannon (Fiction Editor), "The Way We Were," *Publishers Weekly*, February 7, 1972.

"Good reading, a touch of smiles and a trace of tears," Liz Bradley, "Losers and Lovers," *Jacksonville Times-Union*, March 19, 1972.

"The author never grapples with his real issues," Raymond Sokolov, "The Way We Were," *The New York Times*, April 16, 1972.

"I called Arthur right at the start," Michael Feeney Callan, *Robert Redford*, 191.

"really dumped," ibid.

"Ray Stark was the man behind it," ibid., 190.

"Aw, that piece of junk," James Spada, *Streisand: Her Life*, 300.

"I pushed," Michael Feeney Callan, *Robert Redford*, 191.

Robert Redford—or Maybe Not

"No matter how any of us may feel about Redford's skill as an actor," Stephanie Zacherik, "Robert Redford: Mr. Nice Guy," *The New York Times* June 3, 2011.

"but more because he had more sex to begin with than Astaire," Laurents, *Original Story By*, 280.

"When this story began taking shape it occurred to me," Ray Stark in *The Way We Were*: Director's Commentary, 25th Anniversary DVD, Columbia Picutres, 1999.

"If I knew you less well and we weren't friends," Rocky Lang and Barbara Hall (editors), *Letters from Hollywood,* 323.

"Hubbell is NOT a cop-out or a weak guy," ibid.

"We've both talked about doing a love story," ibid., 324.

"And just to show you how dirty I can play," ibid., 325.

"Katie and Hubbell are representatives of people we all have met," Sydney Pollack in *The Way We Were*: Director's Commentary, 25th Anniversary DVD, Columbia Picutres, 1999.

"the glorification of him as a romantic icon made him self-conscious," ibid.

"WASP beige boy," ibid.

"I don't have to say anything about the period," Lang and Hall (editors), *Letters from Hollywood,* 324.

"The whole McCarthy thing can be a great asset," ibid., 323.

"Bob could probably get by on his looks but he doesn't," Tom Buckley, "At the Movies," *The New York Times*, March 2, 1979.

"His not taking part in the same way Katie does," Lang and Hall (editors), *Letters from Hollywood,* 323.

"didn't like the script, he didn't like the character," Christopher Nickens and Karen Swenson. *The Films of Barbra Streisand* (New York: Kensington Publishing Corp., 2000), 105.

"What I was really worried about," Michael Feeney Callan, *Robert Redford*, 191.

"She's unbelievably good in the right thing," Lang and Hall (editors), *Letters from Hollywood,* 324.

"I spent literally eight months beating him to death," Donald Zec and Anthony Fowles. *Barbra: A Biography of Barbra Streisand* (New York: St. Martin's, 1981), 189.

"components of a single person," Randall Riese, *Her Name Is Barbra: An Intimate Portrait of The Real Barbra Streisand* (New York: Carol Publishing Group, 1993), 336.

"In the making of the film I really fell in love with those two characters," Judith Crist, *Take 22: Moviemakers on Moviemaking* (New York: Viking, 1984), 218.

"You don't talk, you lecture," Arthur Laurents, *The Way We Were*, Columbia Pictures, 1973.

"I said there have to be some underpinnings," Neal Gabler, "Redford Talks," *New York* Magazine, December 10, 1990.

"One of the reasons Sydney wanted to do it," Janet L. Meyer, *Sydney Pollack: A Critical Filmography* (Jefferson: McFarland & Company, 2008), 71.

"reducing the clarity, significance and correctness of Katie's character," Zec and Fowles, *Barbra: A Biography of Barbra Streisand,* 190.

"maybe 35 pages of script," Sydney Pollack in *The Way We Were*: Director's Commentary, 25th Anniversary DVD, Columbia Pictures, 1999.

"He liked Redford and wanted Redford," Sydney Pollack in *The Way We Were: Looking Back*, 25th Anniversary DVD, Columbia Pictures, 1999.

"Barbra froze. Next day she told me there was no sex appeal between them," Jordan, *The Greatest Star*, 188.

"I started as an actor in the theater playing a lot of character parts," https://www.oprah.com/own-oprahshow/robert-redford-surprises-barbra-streisand-video, November 16, 2010.

"I did not want to do a Streisand vehicle," Zec and Fowles, *Barbra: A Biography of Barbra Streisand,*190.

"Who is this man?" https://www.closerweekly.com/posts/barbra-streisand-and-robert-redford-reunite-42-years-after-the-way-we-were-plus-see-the-cast-then-and-now-57175/.

"I needed the strength that Redford brings on the screen and Barbra understood that," Zec and Fowles, *Barbra: A Biography of Barbra Streisand,*190.

"They were talking about other people because he had turned it down so many times," https://www.oprah.com/own-oprahshow/robert-redford-surprises-barbra-streisand-video, November 16, 2010.

"I wish he would make up his mind already," Karen Swenson, *Barbra: The Second Decade* (Secaucus, NJ: Citadel Press, 1986), 23.

"What is this picture about, Pollack?" James Spada, *Streisand: Her Life*, 300.

"I would not let him off the hook," Callan, *Robert Redford*, 190.

"Finally I just took the part on faith," Christopher Andersen, *Barbra: The Way She Is* (New York: Harper Collins, 2006), 211.

"The questionable nature of free speech was a provocative notion," Jeanine Basinger, *I Do and I Don't: A History of Marriage in the Movies* (New York: Alfred A. Knopf, 2012), 188.

"The reason I finally decided to do the picture," James Spada, *Streisand: Her Life*, 300–301.

"I was in Africa making a movie," https://www.oprah.com/own-oprahshow/robert-redford-surprises-barbra-streisand-video, November 16, 2010.

"I thought it was a good script," ibid.

"I wanted to work with Barbra," Swenson, *Barbra: The Second Decade,* 23.

"The question was, could you bring a balance into things?" ibid.

"I had turned it down," James Kimbrell, *Barbra: An Actress Who Sings* (Boston: Branden Publishing Company 1989), 344.

"he believes very strongly that the strangeness contributes to the chemistry in a movie," James Spada, *Streisand: Her Life*, 301.

"Barbra was very enamored of Bob," James Woods, interview with author, September 14, 2021.

"Barbra was delighted because she had a crush on him," Michael Feeney Callan, *Robert Redford*, 193.

"He always has something going on behind his eyes," James Spada, *Streisand: Her Life*, 301.

"I saw her [sing] way back in the '60s," https://www.oprah.com/own-oprah show/robert-redford-surprises-barbra-streisand-video, November 16, 2010.

"I didn't want her to sing in the middle of the movie!" *Closer* staff, "Robert Redford Almost Didn't Star as Hubbell in *The Way We Were*," *Closer Magazine*, November 3, 2018.

The Script

"Film's thought of as a director's medium," https://industrialscripts .com/quotes-about-screenwriting/.

"You don't know how everybody in Hollywood is amazed by you," Laurents, *Original Story By*, 270.

"I had this idea of starting with Hubbell on the stand testifying," Sydney Pollack in *The Way We Were*: Director's Commentary, 25th Anniversary DVD, Columbia Pictures, 1999.

"You don't have to alter anything, you tell the same story," Crist, *Take 22*, 220.

"Arthur's position was there was no defense for naming names," Sydney Pollack in *The Way We Were*: Director's Commentary, 25th Anniversary DVD, Columbia Pictures, 1999.

"It was a tough mixture," "Sydney Pollack," *American Film*, April 1978.

"I think then I would have had trouble," Sydney Pollack in *The Way We Were*: Director's Commentary, 25th Anniversary DVD, Columbia Pictures, 1999.

"too unbelievable by half," Callan, *Robert Redford*, 192.

"It's not that he didn't understand HUAC," ibid.

"The combination of old and new was unsightly," Laurents, *Original Story By*, 272

"Oh man, I'm sorry," ibid., 272.

"You're going to build up Redford's part, ibid.

"I got him, alas," ibid., 266.

"Sydney is going to fire you," ibid., 272.

"he, the producer, could do nothing," ibid., 334.

"It's the two of them together and I need Redford," ibid., 272.

"It's hard to talk about Sydney Pollack," Riese, *Her Name Is Barbra*, 336.

"I like to present very strongly both sides of an argument," Sydney Pollack in *The Way We Were*: Director's Commentary, 25th Anniversary DVD, Columbia Pictures, 1999.

"I think what got him angry was he never had a face-to-face confrontation with Redford," Zec and Fowles, *Barbra*, 190.

"It was a beautiful story," ibid.

"Hubbell can see both sides," Arthur Laurents in *The Way We Were: Looking Back*, 25th Anniversary DVD, Columbia Pictures, 1999.

"The problem was that Arthur was so protective of the Katie character," Sydney Pollack in *The Way We Were*: Director's Commentary, 25th Anniversary DVD, Columbia Pictures, 1999.

"I did not alter Laurents's story line 'manipulatively,' as Arthur accused," Callan, *Robert Redford*, 193.

"Sydney and I knew each other," Hawk Koch interview with author, July 23, 2021.

"My original fear when I took the picture," Sydney Pollack in *The Way We Were*: Director's Commentary, 25th Anniversary DVD, Columbia Pictures, 1999.

"I'm going to make a terrible exaggeration here," Crist, *Take 22*, 220.

"I began talking to people like Dalton Trumbo," Sydney Pollack in *The Way We Were*: Director's Commentary, 25th Anniversary DVD, Columbia Pictures, 1999.

"I don't think you have the foggiest notion," Sterling Hayden, *Wanderer* (New York: Knopf, 1963), 66.

"When I read *The Wanderers* and spent time with Hayden," Sydney Pollack in *The Way We Were*: Director's Commentary, 25th Anniversary DVD, Columbia Pictures, 1999.

"The reason I have been so hung up on Hayden's book," Callan, *Robert Redford*, 192.

"I'm telling you people, people are more important," Arthur Laurents, *The Way We Were*, Columbia Pictures, 1973.

"Hubbell, people are their principles," ibid.

"I gave full credit to Sydney," Callan, *Robert Redford*, 193–94.

Casting the Film

"Casting is 65 percent of directing," John Frankenheimer, Brainy Quotes.com.

"I looked for a long time for someone to play Redford's sidekick," Sydney Pollack in *The Way We Were*: Director's Commentary, 25th Anniversary DVD, Columbia Pictures, 1999.

"I met a lot of different girls for that role," ibid.

"I had actually starred opposite Clifton Davis," Lois Chiles interview with author, November 9, 2021.

"Herb Edelman and Redford were pals from *Barefoot in the Park*," Sydney Pollack in *The Way We Were*: Director's Commentary, 25th Anniversary DVD, Columbia Pictures, 1999.

"As a kooky personality, she presented herself in such a charming, loving ballsy way," Nickens and Swenson, *The Films of Barbra Streisand*, 107.

"I think Huston is very easy to play," Barbra Archives, https://www.barbra-archives.info/way_we_were_streisand.

"(She) behaved like most informers," Callan, *Robert Redford*, 192.

"Allyn Ann is a sensational actor as is her husband George Gaynes," Sydney Pollack in *The Way We Were*: Director's Commentary, 25th Anniversary DVD, Columbia Pictures, 1999.

"I was appearing in a bad play in East Hampton," James Woods, interview with author, September 14, 2021.

"I was so unknown," ibid.

"I was chosen as an extra," Barbra Archives, https://www.barbra-archives.info/way_we_were_streisand

Designing *The Way We Were*

"He must have knowledge of architecture of all periods and nationalities," Rose Lagace, "William Cameron Menzies Quote on the Role of the Production Designer," ArtDepartmental.com, July 10, 2013.

"Steven Grimes—I stole him from John Huston!" Sydney Pollack in *The Way We Were*: Director's Commentary, 25th Anniversary DVD, Columbia Pictures, 1999.

"A period film is a gift for the cinematographer," Rachel Morrison, BrainyQuote.com.

"one of the biggest cinematographers in Hollywood, but he had no idea how to operate an instamatic camera!" Hawk Koch, interview with author, July 23, 2021.

"He made [the women] look good," Zec and Fowles, *Barbra*, 193.

"I like the nose," John Hallowell, "Funny Girl on Film; Barbra Streisand's Goofy Ballet," *Life* magazine, September 29, 1967.

"He liked working with her," Zec and Fowles, *Barbra*, 193.

"you can never photograph her outside," ibid., 194.

"Your father never did it like that," Barbra Archives, https://www.barbra-archives.info/way_we_were_streisand.

"That's because I never showed him," Jim Udell, "Footnotes—Harry Stradling Jr.," *Below the Line*, December 7, 2007, https://www.btlnews.com/community/footnotes-harry-stradling-jr/.

"Harry, I saw the film and I thought it was very good," Zec and Fowles, *Barbra*, 194.

"She didn't have to do that at all," ibid.

"[My main goal] was to make Barbra Streisand look good," James Spada, *Streisand* (New York: Abrams, 2014), 166.

"My feeling has always been that Scope is my favorite way to shoot," Sydney Pollack in *The Way We Were*: Director's Commentary, 25th Anniversary DVD, Columbia Pictures, 1999.

"Her special talent," Tom Santopietro, *The Sound of Music Story* (New York: St. Martin's Press, 2015), 70.

"pathologically shy and neurotically modest," ibid., 71.

"an affinity for the past," ibid., 72.

"I'll let my imagination work for me," ibid., 73.

"She very seldom tries to impose her own quirks or ideas on the actors," ibid.

"The canvas is the script," ibid.

"The notion of directing a film," Orson Welles, BrainyQuotes.com.

"They're really paid to execute," Sydney Pollack in *The Way We Were*: Director's Commentary, 25th Anniversary DVD, Columbia Pictures, 1999.

"a legend in Hollywood," ibid.

"When I cut silent films," Claudia Luther, "Margaret Booth, 104; Film Editor Had 70-Year Career," *The Los Angeles Times*, October 31, 2002.

"the final authority of every picture the studio (MGM) made for 30 years," "Margaret Booth," *The Guardian*, November 15, 2002.

"Knowing Barbra like I think I do," Randall Riese, *Her Name Is Barbra*, 335.

"the extras were to be paid," press release, "The Way We Were," September 28, 1972.

"Barbra would say yes to a design, then no, then approve a second version, then change her mind again," Spada, *Streisand*, 302.

"I can't stand all this confusion and indecision," ibid.

"I haven't been this excited," Barbra Archives, https://www.barbra-archives.info/way_we_were_streisand.

"She's got wonderful buns," Spada, *Streisand*, 302.

"Guys, it's fine," Jerry Ziesmer, *Ready When You Are, Mr. Coppola, Mr. Spielberg, Mr. Crowe* (Lanham, Maryland: The Scarecrow Press Inc., 2000), 53.

"What color's the set in the El Morocco?" ibid.

"Barbra is . . . funny, smart, passionate about her work," Hawk Koch, *Magic Time: My Life in Hollywood* (New York: Post Hill Press, 2019), 94.

"Both Al and Barbra stopped only when the director convinced them they had done their best," Ziesmer, *Ready When You Are*, 397.

"Redford could be given direction," ibid., 60.

"We are *with* Barbra," ibid., 62.

"You two are the greatest," ibid., 63.

On the Set and Ready to Roll

"Pollack was very much in control," Art Smith Jr., interview with author, July 23, 2021.

"She would never say it, but Barbra definitely had a crush on Redford," Andersen, *Barbra: The Way She Is*, 212.

"I said, 'It feels like that's appropriate,'" https://www.oprah.com/own-oprahshow/robert-redford-surprises-barbra-streisand-video, November 16, 2010.

"There was almost a mystery about Streisand and Redford in the way they were together," Nickens and Swenson, *The Films of Barbra Streisand*, 106.

"Robert Redford, as I remember, was very friendly," Barbra Archives https://www.barbra-archives.info/way_we_were_streisand.

"Extras and bystanders were repeatedly warned," Kimbrell, *Barbra: An Actress Who Sings*, 346.

"At the time I was just out of the army and in college," Art Smith Jr., interview with author, July 23, 2021.

"The extras loved Barbra," Ziesmer, *Ready When You Are*, 68.

"If I had extras for a classroom," ibid., 67.

"Jerry, let me know," ibid., 69.

"Would arrive barely ten minutes before," ibid., 68

"Redford was a lot of fun," ibid.

"The way Redford and I work," Sydney Pollack in *The Way We Were: Looking Back*, 25th Anniversary DVD, Columbia Pictures, 1999.

"I suppose I have a small anti-intellectual bias," Martha Weinman Lear, "Anatomy of a Sex Symbol," *The New York Times*, July 7, 1974.

"Barbra would talk and talk and talk and drive me nuts," James Spada, *Streisand*, 304.

"Blah-Blah—'So how's Blah-Blah today?'" Andersen, *Barbra: The Way She Is*, 212.

"Even though he had some harmless fun," ibid., 214.

"create an inner life of enjoyment between the two characters," James Spada, *Streisand*, 304.

"She was simply mesmerized because she found him so beautiful," Edwards, *Streisand*, 338.

"The coffee shop is a wonderful sequence," James Woods, interview with author, September 14, 2021.

"elliptically, so that it comes out organically," William Grimes, "David Rayfiel, Screenwriter with Sydney Pollack, Dies," *The New York Times*, June 23, 2011.

"You think not getting caught," ibid.

"She wasn't much. I just liked her, having her around," *The Way We Were*, screenplay by Arthur Laurents, Columbia Pictures, 1973.

"It's not like losing Katie," ibid.

"It would have made my life easier," Lois Chiles, interview with author, November 9, 2021.

"I'm celebrating," *The Way We Were*, screenplay by Arthur Laurents, Columbia Pictures, 1973.

"Go get 'em Katie," ibid.

"See you Hubbell," ibid.

"It was that little pat," Barbra Streisand in *The Way We Were: Looking Back*, 25th Anniversary DVD, Columbia Pictures, 1999.

"That's a certain style of writing," Sydney Pollack in ibid.

"Barbra began to worry," Koch, *Magic Time*, 99.

"Are you sure this place is safe," ibid.

"Of course, it is," I lied." ibid.

"These Schenectady teamsters were tough," Hawk Koch, interview with author, July 23, 2021.

"Needless to say," Koch, *Magic Time*, 100.

"I like Hollywood," *The Way We Were*, Columbia Pictures, 1973.

"Barbra and I were walking down a street, quite near Central Park West," Craig Hall, "BarbraNews Talks to Sally Kirkland," June 26, 2002, http://www.barbranews.com/sallykirkland.htm.

"I'll never forget it," Nickens and Swenson, *The Films of Barbra Streisand*, 107–8.

"has one of the most insatiable curiosities," Swenson, *Barbra: The Second Decade*, 27.

"She had to be convinced that Katie was in the right place for the scene," Ziesmer, *Ready When You Are*, 86.

"Don't act. Just try the words," ibid., 87.

"Sydney as director was the general of this collaboration," Lois Chiles, interview with author, November 9, 2021.

"extreme intensity like a dial turned all the way up," Sydney Pollack in *The Way We Were*: Director's Commentary, 25th Anniversary DVD, Columbia Pictures, 1999.

How to Direct Superstars? Carefully

"There's a creative way to talk to actors," Janet Maslin, "That Pollack Touch," *The New York Times*, December 15, 1985.

"discuss what this picture was about, where we might have trouble," Nickens and Swenson, *The Films of Barbra Streisand*, 105.

"When I hear an actress talking to me with an understanding of a role that's so close to my own understanding," ibid.

"I was knocked out by Barbra's performance in the film of *Funny Girl*," Sydney Pollack in *The Way We Were: Looking Back*, 25th Anniversary DVD, Columbia Pictures, 1999.

"I really wanted to get her back to a kind of simple truth in her performance," Zec and Fowles, *Barbra*, 192.

"want to go straight with this movie and not rely on what we normally expect of her," Nickens and Swenson, *The Films of Barbra Streisand*, 106.

"She has a passion that you can hear in her singing," Zec and Fowles, *Barbra*, 198.

"Of course a dynamo hooked up wrongly is dangerous." ibid.

"like any other enormously talented person," Spada, *Streisand*, 302.

"he knew, like any genius knows," Zec and Fowles, *Barbra*, 199.

"I'm blunt. It saves me a lot of time but also costs me friends," Tom Santopietro, *The Importance of Being Barbra* (New York: St. Martin's Press, 2006), 161.

"The only thing I could go by," Zec and Fowles, *Barbra,* 190.

"She'd call at 11 p.m. "Oh! My God! Every night!" ibid., 193.

"A lot of directors don't know what they want," Maslin, "That Pollack Touch," *The New York Times*, December 15, 1985.

"were healthy arguments. They were never ego arguments," Zec and Fowles, *Barbra*, 192.

"Sydney was a very quiet person," Ziesmer, *Ready When You Are*, 58.

"Streisand and Redford both cited Pollack's self-effacing side," Maslin, "That Pollack Touch," *The New York Times*, December 15, 1985.

"She's inquisitive, extraordinarily curious," Riese, *Her Name Is Barbra*, 337.

"Redford preferred fewer takes but Barbra liked to keep going," Hawk Koch, interview with author, July 23, 2021.

"spontaneous and improvisatory," ibid.

"made hell for me and it made hell for the editor to match continuity," Callan, *Robert Redford*, 195 .

"The terrible tragedy for every director," Maslin, "That Pollack Touch," *The New York Times*, December 15, 1985.

"There's no one more interested in control than Sydney," ibid.

"Each of them was a pain in the ass from time to time," Callan, *Robert Redford*, 195.

"A discomfort about her nose from one or the other angle," ibid.

"In Bob's case he has moles on the right side of his face," Andersen, *Barbra: The Way She Is*, 213.

"some sort of soft light behind them," ibid.

In the Heat of Battle

"It's what always happens," Joyce Haber, "With the Stars," *Los Angeles Times*, November 7, 1972.

"Truthfully, nobody had any faith in the picture," Spada, *Streisand*, 303.

"Bob didn't get along with Ray Stark, and neither did I," ibid., 302.

"Ray was a strong producer, very involved," Sydney Pollack in *The Way We Were*: Director's Commentary, 25th Anniversary DVD, Columbia Pictures, 1999.

"Bob was worried he would end up as a lump of a sex symbol," ibid.

"doing overtime at Dachau," Spada, *Streisand*, 303.

"It's what always happens," Joyce Haber, "With the Stars," *Los Angeles Times*, November 7, 1972.

"You win, pal!" Laurents, *Original Story By*, 273.

"Ray was eating crow with enthusiasm." ibid.

"They wanted me to repair the damage," ibid., 273.

"nervous, not even very confident," ibid., 274.

"I wasn't so focused on looking at this as," Lois Chiles, interview with author, November 9, 2021.

"had been a wonderful pest," Laurents, *Original Story By*, 274.

"a stare of ice that could sink a Titanic," ibid.

"Redford glared at me the first day I walked on the set," ibid., 267.

"As it was written," Spada, *Streisand*, 300–301.

"Redford does not want to be an actor, he wants to be a 'movie star.'" Zec and Fowles, *Barbra*, 189.

"Redford glared at me the whole time," Edwards, *Streisand*, 335.

"a good bit, nothing more," ibid., 340.

"Streisand never came over to speak to me," ibid.

"And again, it was 'Sally, how are you? What have you been doing?'" Nickens and Swenson, *The Films of Barbra Streisand*, 108.

"easiest to deal with because she was very happy with her part," Sydney Pollack in *The Way We Were*: Director's Commentary, 25th Anniversary DVD, Columbia Pictures, 1999.

"There are all those stories in magazines about how Barbra demands this and that," Rene Jordan, *The Greatest Star*, 188.

"When I worked with Barbra on *Sandbox*," Hawk Koch, interview with author, July 23, 2021.

"Jer, keep the bar area filled with a bit older folks, you know?" Ziesmer, *Ready When You Are*, 58.

"The sounds were pure tones," ibid., 83.

"Shhh! Maybe she's going to sing!" ibid.

"What? What are you looking at?" ibid.

"I'll never forget Barbra's playing," ibid.

"When he offered me a ride on his motorcycle," "Chaplin Award," *New York Post*, April 29, 2015.

"He knew I wasn't your motorcycle kind of gal," K.C. Baker and Kate Hogan, "Robert Redford and Barbra Streisand Reunite. We Get Nostalgic with *The Way We Were* Photos," People.com April 28, 2015. https://people.com/celebrity/barbra-streisand-robert-redford-the-way-we-were-photos/.

"I wasn't scared at all," ibid.

"Sorry, Jer—what are you mad at?" Ziesmer, *Ready When You Are*, 91.

"vow he'd never get to me again," ibid.

"Jer, how are you?" ibid.

"You know what the wind and salt air and all does to my hair," ibid.

"Out of Barbra's motor home," ibid, 94.

"He could be the most unique, creative producer," ibid., 96.

"Shooting on a college campus was easy compared to trying to film in New York City," Hawk Koch, interview with author, July 23, 2021.

"I remember those dates very well," ibid.

"it's the only Dr. David X. Cohen in the book," Arthur Laurents, *The Way We Were*, Columbia Pictures 1973.

"You never give up, do you?" ibid.

"How is she?" ibid.

"See you, Katie," ibid.

"The scenes we shot today involved a quiet and intimate farewell," Barbra Archives, https://www.barbra-archives.info/way_we_were_streisand.

"wonderful as always," Ziesmer, *Ready When You Are*, 99.

"What exactly do you do, anyway?" ibid.

Editing the Film

"Margaret Booth turned out to be a magnificent lady," Sydney Pollack in *The Way We Were*: Director's Commentary, 25th Anniversary DVD, Columbia Pictures, 1999.

"my folks were always easier," Arthur Laurents, *The Way We Were*, screenplay draft of May 15, 1972. Arthur Laurents Papers, Library of Congress.

"It gave people too much, put them ahead of the characters," Sydney Pollack in *The Way We Were*: Director's Commentary, 25th Anniversary DVD, Columbia Pictures, 1999.

"big payoff scene," ibid.

"It'll be years before I know," Arthur Laurents, *The Way We Were*, screenplay draft of May 15, 1972. Arthur Laurents Papers, Library of Congress.

"how am I for you?" Arthur Laurents, *The Way We Were*, screenplay draft of May 15, 1972. Arthur Laurents Papers, Library of Congress.

"Was the Pacific awful?" ibid.

"We've been cooped up here for two days," *The Way We Were*, 25th Anniversary DVD, Deleted Scenes, Columbia Pictures, 1999.

"Margaret Booth was a legend in Hollywood," Sydney Pollack in *The Way We Were*: Director's Commentary, 25th Anniversary DVD, Columbia Pictures, 1999.

"He'd say—I don't know what he'd say," *The Way We Were*, 25th Anniversary DVD, Deleted Scenes. Columbia Pictures 1999.

"It's a quiet house," ibid.

"I love you, Hubbell," ibid.

"We were aware of the chemistry between Redford and Barbra," Ray Stark in *The Way We Were*: Director's Commentary, 25th Anniversary DVD, Columbia Pictures, 1999.

"'How does Bob *do* it? I stink, don't I?'" Andersen, *Barbra: The Way She Is*, 212.

"How does she do it?" ibid.

"I thought he was great in *The Way We Were*," Barbra Streisand in *The Way We Were*: *Looking Back*, 25th Anniversary DVD, Columbia Pictures, 1999.

What about a Title Song?

"Most of the time a title is all I need," Sharon Rosenthal, "A Day in the Life of Marvin Hamlisch," *The New York Daily News*, March 27, 1981.

"I think this is up your alley," Marvin Hamlisch, *The Way I Was* (New York: Scribner's, 1992), 120.

"no harm, no foul," ibid.

"I must confess that I sensed from the beginning," ibid.

"We met when I was twenty-one," Barbra Streisand in *The Way We Were*: *Looking Back*, 25th Anniversary DVD, Columbia Pictures, 1999.

"We used to go to the automat all the time," Sharon Rosenthal, "A Day in the Life of Marvin Hamlisch," *The New York Daily News*, March 27, 1981.

"to give a sense of hope to this tragic story," Hamlisch, *The Way I Was*, 121.

"if it were in the minor mode," Thomas Maremaa, "The Sound of Movie Music," *New York Times*, March 28, 1976.

"determined not to write something drippingly sentimental," Hamlisch, *The Way I Was*, 121.

"one day I wrote a melody that just got to me," ibid.

"A tall, gangly, awkward, and visibly nervous young guy," Koch, *Magic Time*, 98.

"I'll play the horns with my mouth," ibid.

"pressed his lips together," ibid.

"Alan and Marilyn Bergman are *unique*," Sydney Pollack in *Program for Lyrics and Lyricists: An Evening with Marilyn and Alan Bergman*, 1982.

"He was a great director," Alan Bergman, interview with author, July 30, 2021.

"the spine," "Lyricists Extraordinaire: Alan and Marilyn Bergman," *Backstage*, January 27, 1995.

"in the case of a ballad—unless you have Richard Rodgers," ibid.

"in film if the lyric writer or the screenwriter or the composer," ibid.

"go deeper," ibid.

"anxiety and circular emotions," ibid.

"the kinds of things you feel just before you go to sleep." ibid.

"If we are writing for her only, we can't help being nourished," ibid.

"The challenge was to write the song," Marilyn Bergman in *The Way We Were: Looking Back*, 25th Anniversary DVD, Columbia Pictures, 1999.

"The song is a corridor back in time," Alan Bergman, interview with author, July 30, 2021.

"Daydreams light the corners of my mind," Marvin Hamlisch, Alan and Marilyn Bergman, "The Way We Were."

"Misty watercolor mem'ries," ibid.

"In the documentary on the 1999 DVD," Barbra Streisand, written response to author, July 19, 2022.

"a long A section," Marvin Hamlisch in *The Way We Were: Looking Back*, 25th Anniversary DVD, Columbia Pictures, 1999.

"The third line of the melody I had written," Hamlisch, *The Way I Was*, 122.

"luscious," Marvin Hamlisch in *The Way We Were: Looking Back*, 25th Anniversary DVD, Columbia Pictures, 1999.

"As I was looking more closely at the lyric," Barbra Streisand, written response to author, July 19, 2022.

"just didn't feel right," Barbra Streisand in *The Way We Were: Looking Back*, 25th Anniversary DVD, Columbia Pictures, 1999.

"I don't know why I suggested," ibid.

"It was an excellent suggestion," Alan Bergman, interview with author, July 30, 2021.

"maybe we could do even better," Hamlisch, *The Way I Was*, 122–23.

"I can't beat this melody," Marvin Hamlisch in *The Way We Were: Looking Back*, 25th Anniversary DVD, Columbia Pictures, 1999.

"We said to Marvin," Alan Bergman, interview with author, July 30, 2021.

"They loved it. Why do that?" ibid.

"After all we don't always write just for them," ibid.

"It was such a wonderful title," Marilyn Bergman in *The Way We Were: Looking Back*, 25th Anniversary DVD, Columbia Pictures, 1999.

"came about only because they had finished," Barbra Streisand, written response to author, July 19, 2022.

"When I wander," Marvin Hamlisch, Alan and Marilyn Bergman, "The Way We Were."

"very French," Barbra Streisand in *The Way We Were: Looking Back*, 25th Anniversary DVD, Columbia Pictures, 1999.

"I was concerned that maybe the song was not complex enough," Sydney Pollack in ibid.

"This was not a difficult decision," Barbra Streisand, written response to author, July 19, 2022.

"The only way to test a song is to see how it feels with the images," Alan Bergman, interview with author, July 30, 2021.

"I liked that song," Sydney Pollack in *The Way We Were*: Director's Commentary, 25th Anniversary DVD, Columbia Pictures, 1999.

"Marty named the day it would be the number one song in the country!" Alan Bergman, interview with author, July 30, 2021.

"I called these versions A, B, and C," Hamlisch, *The Way I Was*, 123.

"I suddenly heard that incredible voice in my earphones," ibid., 124.

"just give me ten seconds, Barbra," ibid.

"Plan B, boys," ibid.

"You can actually manipulate people's emotions with theme music," ibid.

"It's the only way I can tell if a scene is going to work," Sydney Pollack in *The Way We Were*: Director's Commentary, 25th Anniversary DVD, Columbia Pictures, 1999.

"If you score exactly what is up there on screen, you're putting white paint on white paint," Earl Wilson, "It Happened Last Night—Marvin, Oscar, and Grammy," *The New York Post*, March 5, 1975.

"It's such an intricate balance," Marvin Hamlisch in *The Way We Were: Looking Back*, 25th Anniversary DVD, Columbia Pictures, 1999.

"We spent 14 hours just on the rally," Barbra Archives, https://www.barbra-archives.info/way_we_were_streisand.

"overplayed my hand," Marvin Hamlisch in *The Way We Were: Looking Back*, 25th Anniversary DVD, Columbia Pictures, 1999.

Forget the Critics: What Did Arthur Laurents Think?

"I was always surprised that people liked the picture," Arthur Laurents in *The Way We Were: Looking Back*, 25th Anniversary DVD, Columbia Pictures, 1999.

"He was Bob Redford playing Redford playing Hubbell Gardiner," Laurents, *Original Story By*, 280.

"grand," ibid.

"It damaged Barbra's performance," ibid.

"a decathlon man," ibid., 275.

"making her a shrill, insensitive harridan," ibid.

"Hubbell—you are telling me," Arthur Laurents, *The Way We Were*, Columbia Pictures, 1973.

"Hubbell, people are their principles," ibid.

"I knew why he cut it," ibid.

"She was infatuated with Redford," ibid., 277.

"I pushed her hard," ibid., 278.

"I want us to love each other," Arthur Laurents, *The Way We Were*, Columbia Pictures, 1973.

"The studio says they are going to fire me," ibid.

"despite, not because," Laurents, *Original Story By*, 279.

"So if we get a divorce and you don't have a subversive wife," ibid.

"That's where the two stories came together," Edwards, *Streisand*, 339.

"The chemistry between Streisand and Redford," Laurents, *Original Story By*, 280.

Sneak Previews

"To say a movie is in trouble because of a bad screening," Patrick Goldstein, "Movies: Previews—How Early Is Too Early," *Los Angeles Times*, February 6, 1994.

"no one else is noticing that," Alan Bergman, interview with author, July 30, 2021.

"The love story and political scenes strengthened each other," Ray Stark in *The Way We Were*: Director's Commentary, 25th Anniversary DVD, Columbia Pictures, 1999.

"We didn't have a movieola," Sydney Pollack in *The Way We Were: Looking Back*, 25th Anniversary DVD, Columbia Pictures, 1999.

"It's a scene about what has happened to me as Katie," Barbra Streisand in ibid.

"Everything about the scene is wonderful," Sydney Pollack, *The Way We Were*: Director's Commentary, 25th Anniversary DVD, Columbia Pictures, 1999.

"Barbra and I have had a 30-year discussion," Sydney Pollack in *The Way We Were*: *Looking Back*, 25th Anniversary DVD, Columbia Pictures, 1999.

"By itself it was a very moving scene," Sydney Pollack, *The Way We Were*: Director's Commentary, 25th Anniversary DVD, Columbia Pictures, 1999.

"That scene was the very definition of the title," Barbra Streisand, written response to author, July 19, 2022.

"She fought for certain scenes," Arthur Laurents in *The Way We Were: Looking Back*, 25th Anniversary DVD, Columbia Pictures, 1999.

"horrified," Rachel Montpelier, "Barbra Streisand Started Directing Because She Couldn't Be Heard," https://womenandhollywood.com/barbra-streisand-started-directing-because-she-couldnt-be-heard-bf642241b1bc/, May 1, 2017.

"scenes that [she] felt illustrated," ibid.

"The political background of this beautiful love story," Barbra Streisand in *The Way We Were: Looking Back*, 25th Anniversary DVD, Columbia Pictures, 1999.

Rachel Montpelier, "I directed because I couldn't be heard," Rachel Montpelier, "Barbra Streisand Started Directing Because She Couldn't Be Heard," https://womenandhollywood.com/barbra-streisand-started-directing-because-she-couldnt-be-heard-bf642241b1bc/, May 1, 2017.

"The government—my government, is now threatening to imprison a writer," Arthur Laurents, *The Way We Were*, Columbia Pictures, 1973.

"Goddamit, Katie, you are not in college!" Arthur Laurents, *The Way We Were*, Columbia Pictures, 1973.

"The implication was the politics caused the breakup," Sydney Pollack, *The Way We Were*: Director's Commentary, 25th Anniversary DVD, Columbia Pictures, 1999.

"He what? That's crazy," Arthur Laurents, *The Way We Were*, Columbia Pictures, 1973.

"If we got a divorce you wouldn't have a subversive wife," ibid.

"There was a void at the center of the story," Barbra Streisand, written response to author, July 19, 2022.

"The problem was that the breakup was inherent in the picture right from the beginning," Sydney Pollack, *The Way We Were*: Director's Commentary, 25th Anniversary DVD, Columbia Pictures, 1999.

"The political and social areas should only be background," Lang and Hall (editors), *Letters from Hollywood*, 323.

"I didn't want to lose sight of the fact," Sydney Pollack, *The Way We Were*: Director's Commentary, 25th Anniversary DVD, Columbia Pictures, 1999.

"I could feel that the problem wasn't the politics," ibid.

"Why her?" Arthur Laurents, *The Way We Were*, Columbia Pictures, 1973.

"we had to emasculate the picture," Zec and Fowles, *Barbra, 198.*

"From the end of the screening room scene," Sydney Pollack, *The Way We Were*: Director's Commentary, 25th Anniversary DVD, Columbia Pictures, 1999.

"It was the first time the movie worked," Sydney Pollack in *The Way We Were*: Looking Back, 25th Anniversary DVD, Columbia Pictures, 1999.

"I think it dealt very well with politics," ibid.

"Hubbell really belonged in Hollywood," Barbra Streisand interview in ibid.

"I had to look at the reviews while I was writing my own book," Barbra Streisand, written response to author, July 19, 2022.

"The climax wasn't there—and no one cared. No one knew and no one cared," Arthur Laurents in *The Way We Were: Looking Back*, 25th Anniversary DVD, Columbia Pictures, 1999.

"fifteen minutes," Ray Stark in *The Way We Were*: Director's Commentary, 25th Anniversary DVD, Columbia Pictures, 1999.

"When we previewed it the next night," Nickens and Swenson, *The Films of Barbra Streisand*, 109.

"Actually what we cut helped the politics that remained in the film," Ray Stark in *The Way We Were*: Director's Commentary, 25th Anniversary DVD, Columbia Pictures, 1999.

"Rationally that made perfect sense. . . . Emotionally . . . big mistake," Marvin Hamlisch in *The Way We Were*: *Looking Back*, 25th Anniversary DVD, Columbia Pictures, 1999.

"Marvin, if you play it twenty times," Hamlisch, *The Way I Was*, 125.

"This picture had everything going for it," ibid., 126.

"And knowing it was right made it worth every penny," ibid.

Love Letters, Brickbats, and an Adoring Public

"We lost a lot of innocence in the dark movie palace of our youth," Edwards, *Streisand*, 340.

"made her entrance an hour late," "The Way They Are," *Women's Wear Daily*, October 30, 1973.

"I heard about the premiere," James Woods, interview with author, September 14, 2021.

"a distended, talky, redundant, and moody melodrama," *Variety* staff, "Barbra Streisand and Robert Redford in 'The Way We Were,'" *Variety*, December 31, 1972.

"Robert Redford has too little to work with in the script," ibid.

"The overemphasis on Streisand," ibid.

"Streisand is still too shrill at moments," Vincent Canby, "Screen: Way We Were," *The New York Times*, October 18, 1973.

"It's easy to forgive the movie a lot because of Streisand," Roger Ebert, "The Way We Were," *The Chicago Sun Times*, October 17, 1973.

"inexplicably, the movie suddenly and implausibly has them fall out of love," ibid.

"an ill-written, wretchedly performed and tediously directed film," Richard Schickel, "The Way We Weren't," *Time*, October 29, 1973.

"She seems to know all about it, but it came as a complete shock to me," Molly Haskell, "Would Nicholson Make A Better Gatsby," *The Village Voice*, December 9, 1974.

"the decisive change in the characters' lives which the story hinges on," Pauline Kael, *Reeling* (Boston: Little Brown and Company, 1976), 176.

"ugly," ibid., 175.

"whining title tune ballad," ibid.

"excruciating," ibid.

"The damn thing," ibid., 178.

"hit entertainment," ibid.

"glittery trash," Stanley Kaufmann, "The Way We Were," *The New Republic*, November 10, 1973.

"The director, Sidney Pollack," ibid.

"It is hard not to be carried away by the film's lush romanticism," Howard Kissel, "The Way We Were," *Women's Wear Daily*, in Nickens and Swenson, *The Films of Barbra Streisand*, 103.

"What really makes the film such a gripper is two-fold," "The Way We Were," *Christian Science Monitor* in Swenson, *Barbra: The Second Decade*, 30.

"Barbra Streisand acts her head off," Gene Shalit, *The Today Show*—NBC TV, as cited in the liner notes for *The Way We Were* Original Soundtrack Recording, Columbia Records, 1973.

"Barbra Streisand does something quite remarkable in *The Way We Were*," *The New York Daily News*, October 18, 1973.

"They don't live *for* love, they live in *spite* of it, and that's good drama," *Films Illustrated* in Swenson, *Barbra: The Second Decade*, 30.

"I never was. You only imagined it," Arthur Laurents, *The Way We Were*, Columbia Pictures, 1973.

"But if *The Way We Were* is a premeditated tearjerker," Benny Green, "The Way We Were," *PUNCH*, February 20, 1974.

"I would trade many an art film classic," Molly Haskell, "Would Nicholson Make A Better Gatsby," *The Village Voice*, December 9, 1974.

"Critics had trouble with *The Way We Were*," Janet L. *Meyer, Sydney Pollack*, 67.

The Academy Awards

"Most awards, you know, they don't give you unless you go and get them," Barbra Streisand, "103 Fierce and Inspirational Quotes by Barbra Streisand," Quotes.TheFamousPeople.com.

"What can I tell ya? I'd like to thank the makers of Maalox for making all this possible!" Marvin Hamlisch, 1974 Academy Awards Ceremony, April 2, 1974.

"A poll of the public conducted the night before the ceremonies," Rene Jordan, *The Greatest Star*, 192.

"The Oscar has become a political gesture, or a business gesture," Riese, *Her Name Is Barbra*, 340.

"Unlike the year I was up for *Funny Girl*," Nickens and Swenson, *The Films of Barbra Streisand, 112.*

"I thought you said I was going to win the Oscar," Riese, *Her Name Is Barbra*, 350.

The Good, the Great, and the What-Were-They-Thinking: Scene by Scene with Katie and Hubbell

"Like anything that's delicate," Zec and Fowles, *Barbra,* 196.

"I was in another country when the film came out," https://www.oprah.com/own-oprahshow/robert-redford-surprises-barbra-streisand-video, November 16, 2010.

"Call it a Jewish *Love Story* or a WASP dilemma," Swenson, *Barbra: The Second Decade*, 28.

"We are naturally opposites," Barbra Streisand in *The Way We Were*: *Looking Back*, 25th Anniversary DVD, Columbia Pictures, 1999.

"No question—I identified with Barbra's character," Lois Chiles, Interview with Author, November 9, 2021.

"tension between morality and aesthetics," Gabler, *Barbra Streisand: Redefining Beauty, Femininity, and Power* (New Haven, CT: Yale University Press, 2016), 140.

"There is a sense of innocence to that love," *Closer* staff, "Robert Redford Almost Didn't Star as Hubbell in The Way We Were," *Closer Magazine*, November 3, 2018.

"When you have the top level of craft in every department," Jeanine Basinger, interview with author, December 8, 2021.

"You can play around with time," Sydney Pollack, *The Way We Were*: Director's Commentary, 25th Anniversary DVD, Columbia Pictures, 1999.

"So we beat on," F. Scott Fitzgerald, *The Great Gatsby* (New York: Scribner 1925), 189.

"Was it all so simple then," "The Way We Were" by Marvin Hamlisch, Alan Bergman, Marilyn Bergman.

"drippy co-ed humor," Arthur Laurents, *The Way We Were*, Columbia Pictures, 1973.

"disturbed when she is humiliated," Sydney Pollack in *The Way We Were*: *Looking Back*, 25th Anniversary DVD, Columbia Pictures, 1999.

"I liked that scene," Paul Busa, *The Barbra Streisand Film Guide* (Middletown, DE: CreateSpace Independent Publishing Platform 2016), 104.

"Look who's here," Arthur Laurents, *The Way We Were*, Columbia Pictures 1973.

"Onions? In the Coke," ibid.

"You couldn't do much improvisation here," Sydney Pollack, *The Way We Were*: Director's Commentary, 25th Anniversary DVD, Columbia Pictures, 1999.

"He's such a great film actor," James Woods, interview with author, September 14, 2021.

"I was thinking about how I could be a part of the scene," ibid.

"He was open to this last minute improvisation and change," ibid.

"I loved working with both of them," ibid.

"complex major Hollywood film," ibid.

"bridge," Sydney Pollack, *The Way We Were*: Director's Commentary, 25th Anniversary DVD, Columbia Pictures, 1999.

"In a way he was like the country he lived in," Arthur Laurents, *The Way We Were*, Columbia Pictures, 1973.

"But of course by then they were too lost, or too lazy," ibid.

"Unfortunately, neither commitment nor a first class mind," ibid.

"Howard Koch came up to me and said I just have to warn you," Sydney Pollack in *The Way We Were*: *Looking Back*, 25th Anniversary DVD, Columbia Pictures, 1999.

"No one can sing the way she can," ibid.

"She needs relaxing," ibid.

"Sydney could articulate," Barbra Streisand in ibid.

"He was a master at casting the right actors for his films," Hawk Koch, interview with author, July 23, 2021.

"Sydney was 100% an actor's director," James Woods, interview with author, September 14, 2021.

"When we started on *The Way We Were* she wanted me *to be* Hubbell," Callan, *Robert Redford: The Biography*, 195.

"I just loved working with him," ibid.

"something soulful," Sydney Pollack, *The Way We Were*: Director's Commentary, 25th Anniversary DVD, Columbia Pictures, 1999.

"There's a part of me in every part I play," Charles Michener, "The Great Redford," *Newsweek*, February 4, 1974.

"I felt he was really happy when he saw her," Sydney Pollack, *The Way We Were*: Director's Commentary, 25th Anniversary DVD, Columbia Pictures, 1999.

"You never quit, do you?" Arthur Laurents, *The Way We Were*, Columbia Pictures, 1973.

"Commencement, what a funny word for the end," ibid.

"Go get 'em Katie," ibid.

"Welcome to the age of un-innocence," Darren Star and Candace Bushnell, *Sex and the City*, Season 1, Episode 1, air date: June 6, 1998.

"James Woods danced. Brad Dillman danced," Ziesmer, *Ready When You Are*, 77.

"One brave tuxedoed extra," ibid.

"I went to public school in Rhode Island," James Woods, interview with author, September 14, 2021.

"ended up following Barbra Streisand around," Grover Dale, interview with author, July 28, 2021.

"Let me see what you've got," ibid.

"I remembered that when I was on Broadway," ibid.

"They danced—everyone applauded," Grover Dale, interview with author, July 28, 2021.

"With her musicianship, Barbra learned the dance right away," James Woods, interview with author, September 14, 2021.

"they brought over the camera and lights," Grover Dale, interview with author, July 28, 2021.

"These were the last shots in Schenectady," James Woods, interview with author, September 14, 2021.

"The cameraman was in his socks trying to dance with them," Sydney Pollack, *The Way We Were*: Director's Commentary, 25th Anniversary DVD, Columbia Pictures, 1999.

"Hubbell—it's Katie," Arthur Laurents, *The Way We Were*, Columbia Pictures, 1973.

"heartbreaking—heartbreaking because she doesn't know," Sydney Pollack, *The Way We Were*: Director's Commentary, 25th Anniversary DVD, Columbia Pictures, 1999.

"Hey, what do you know," Arthur Laurents, *The Way We Were*, Columbia Pictures, 1973.

"The scene has comedy in it but it has a sweet touching comedy," Sydney Pollack, *The Way We Were*: Director's Commentary, 25th Anniversary DVD, Columbia Pictures, 1999.

"Like anything that's delicate," Zec and Fowles, *Barbra*, 196.

"I actually had a zoom lens on the camera," ibid.

"You looked stark-raving naked in that bed," Charles Michener, "The Great Redford," *Newsweek*, February 4, 1974.

"How do you know what the party says?" Arthur Laurents, *The Way We Were*, Columbia Pictures, 1973.

"Your style is gorgeous," Arthur Laurents, *The Way We Were*, Columbia Pictures, 1973.

"What doesn't come easy now?" ibid.

"The first time they really are consciously together," Sydney Pollack, *The Way We Were*: Director's Commentary, 25th Anniversary DVD, Columbia Pictures, 1999.

"You haven't changed at all," Arthur Laurents, *The Way We Were*, Columbia Pictures, 1973.

"I think the talk of their very different styles," Lois Chiles, interview with author, November 9, 2021.

"Her husband is dead!" Arthur Laurents, *The Way We Were*, Columbia Pictures, 1973.

"Everything in the world does not happen to you personally!" ibid.

"You're too good for Hollywood," ibid.

"The first rule of any love story," Sydney Pollack, *The Way We Were*: Director's Commentary, 25th Anniversary DVD, Columbia Pictures, 1999.

"I'm a pain in the ass," Arthur Laurents, *The Way We Were*, Columbia Pictures, 1973.

"I was too easy for you," ibid.

"(Bob and Barbra) were really right for these roles," Sydney Pollack, *The Way We Were*: Director's Commentary, 25th Anniversary DVD, Columbia Pictures, 1999.

"That speech verbatim was in the treatment," Sydney Pollack in *The Way We Were*: *Looking Back*, 25th Anniversary DVD, Columbia Pictures, 1999.

"I can't sleep, Hubbell," Arthur Laurents, *The Way We Were*, Columbia Pictures, 1973.

"Sydney took Barbra off to the side," Hawk Koch, interview with author, July 23, 2021.

"That scene was done in one take and she was really crying," Spada, *Streisand*, 321.

"I set it up in one shot," Zec and Fowles, *Barbra*, 198.

"Barbra knocked it out of the ballpark," Sydney Pollack, *The Way We Were*: Director's Commentary, 25th Anniversary DVD, Columbia Pictures, 1999.

"I didn't have to prepare for that scene," Barbra Streisand in *The Way We Were*: *Looking Back*, 25th Anniversary DVD, Columbia Pictures, 1999.

"Her concentration seemed to be on producing tears," Laurents, *Original Story By*, 280.

"They would never have denied her the Oscar," Jordan, *The Greatest Star*, 189.

"it looked like she was trying to hide the fact," Spada, *Streisand*, 320–21.

"But I look so beautiful in that scene," ibid., 321.

"I'll change," Arthur Laurents, *The Way We Were*, Columbia Pictures, 1973.

"the audience is anchored," Sydney Pollack, *The Way We Were*: Director's Commentary, 25th Anniversary DVD, Columbia Pictures, 1999.

"The viciousness of the McCarthy period was easier to handle in retrospect," Barbra Archives, https://www.barbra-archives.info/way_we_were_streisand.

"I was looking for a lighter scene in Hollywood," Sydney Pollack, *The Way We Were*: Director's Commentary, 25th Anniversary DVD, Columbia Pictures, 1999.

"for the time that Groucho Marx was on our stage," Ziesmer, *Ready When You Are*, 96.

"Try to show, always," Sydney Pollack, *The Way We Were*: Director's Commentary, 25th Anniversary DVD, Columbia Pictures, 1999.

"Nothing will change," Arthur Laurents, *The Way We Were*, Columbia Pictures, 1973.

"Hubbell, people are their principles," ibid.

"She's wonderful and committed, but it's this cause today, and tomorrow another one," Crist, *Take 22*, 222.

"Go on, turn the world upside down and inside out," *Yentl*, screenplay by Barbra Streisand and Jack Rosenthal, MGM/UA, 1983.

"No one else knows this story the way I do," Arthur Laurents, *The Way We Were*, Columbia Pictures, 1973.

"I know what your concept is," ibid.

"Katie, the day you die," Arthur Laurents, *The Way We Were*, Columbia Pictures, 1973.

"Why did you have to go with her?" ibid.

"Wouldn't it be lovely," ibid.

"Katie, it was never uncomplicated," ibid.

"Isn't it pretty to think so?" Ernest Hemingway, *The Sun Also Rises* (New York: Charles Scribner's Sons, 1926), 250.

"The reason they don't work—his dilemma," James Woods, interview with author, September 14, 2021.

"You don't really want to go to Europe, do you?" Arthur Laurents, *The Way We Were*, Columbia Pictures, 1973.

"I guess I never really thought," ibid.

"there's a disjointed feeling in the third act of the picture," Crist, *Take 22*, 219.

"My strongest feelings in favor of it are the two performances," ibid., 221–22.

"I think there is real value," Sydney Pollack in *The Way We Were*: *Looking Back*, 25th Anniversary DVD, Columbia Pictures, 1999.

"into another interchangeable beige girl," Sydney Pollack, *The Way We Were*: Director's Commentary, 25th Anniversary DVD, Columbia Pictures, 1999.

"The romantic movie of those particular years is a divorce story," Jeanine Basinger, interview with author, December 8, 2021.

"If that feeling is pervasive all throughout the picture," Sydney Pollack, *The Way We Were*: Director's Commentary, 25th Anniversary DVD, Columbia Pictures, 1999.

"You never give up—do you?" Arthur Laurents, *The Way We Were*, Columbia Pictures, 1973.

"I can't come—I can't," ibid.

"See you Katie," ibid.

Katie and Hubbell/Barbra and Bob

"Audiences got this story—the not so attractive girl in love with the campus heartthrob," Jeanine Basinger, interview with author, December 8, 2021.

"Though nothing can bring back the hour/Of splendor in the grass," William Wordsworth, "Ode on Intimations of Immortality from Recollections of Early Childhood," https://victorianweb.org/previctorian/ww/intimationstxt.html.

"Talent is beauty," Pauline Kael as quoted in "Barbra Streisand's 'Encore,'" CBS Sunday Morning with Anthony Mason. https://www.cbsnews.com/news/barbra-streisands-encore/.

"Barbra's femininity brings out the masculinity in a man," Nickens and Swenson, *The Films of Barbra Streisand*, 110.

"stimulating, intellectually, and sexually," Sydney Pollack, *The Way We Were*: Director's Commentary, 25th Anniversary DVD, Columbia Pictures, 1999.

"You never give up," Arthur Laurents, *The Way We Were*, Columbia Pictures, 1973.

"I don't know how you can't," ibid.

"Audiences got this story," Jeanine Basinger, interview with author, December 8, 2021.

"*The Way We Were* has an incredible following," ibid.

"The audience was rooting for Katie and Hubbell," Barbra Streisand, written response to author, July 19, 2022.

"like a lot of women, I suspect, fell in love with her while watching *The Way We Were*," Manohla Dargis, "Barbra Streisand, at a Gala and in Memory," *The New York Times*, April 23, 2013.

"An all-encompassing knowledge and adoration of the New Testament," Andy Tiemann, "The Barbra Streisand Litmus Test," *Diva: Barbra Streisand: The Making of a Superstar*, Ethlie Ann Vare (editor), (New York: Boulevard Books, 1996), 195.

"If they did, she'd eat them alive and not even burp," ibid., 197.

"Streisand was a real woman because Streisand knew how to take care of herself," ibid.

"that was her appeal," ibid.

"any time there's a war, society concentrates on its masculine qualities," Marjorie Rosen "Isn't It about Time to Bring on the Girls," *The New York Times*, December 15, 1974.

"My instinct is to say everyone who worked on this movie," Sydney Pollack, *The Way We Were*: Director's Commentary, 25th Anniversary DVD, Columbia Pictures, 1999.

"David and Alvin made major contributions to the character of Hubbell," ibid.

"Sometime way after that comes me," ibid.

"It all comes together," ibid.

"Sydney Pollack was enormously skilled at casting," Jeanine Basinger, interview with author, December 8, 2021.

"I am always surprised," Arthur Laurents in *The Way We Were*: *Looking Back*, 25th Anniversary DVD, Columbia Pictures, 1999.

"Redford told me rather recently," ibid.

"You had two big stars, a well written script," Alan Bergman, interview with author, July 30, 2021.

"I was either in the dubbing room with Sydney," Hawk Koch, interview with author, July 23, 2021.

"I think that the sheer romance of the story hits the target audience," Art Smith Jr., interview with author, July 23, 2021.

"Everybody loves a good love story," Barbra Streisand, written response to author, July 19, 2022.

"I think we'd both have preferred a more political Dalton Trumbo–type script," Callan, *Robert Redford: The Biography*, 194.

"I was overschedule—I always am," Sydney Pollack, *The Way We Were*: Director's Commentary, 25th Anniversary DVD, Columbia Pictures, 1999.

"estimated in 1976, to be $5.3 million," Riese, *Her Name Is Barbra*, 340.

"Columbia Pictures and Rastar charged off," "Redford, Pollack Sue Columbia, Stark for Cut of "Way We Were,' *Variety*, January 15, 1977.

"substantial amounts of income earned by the film worldwide," ibid.

And on into the Future

"Nothing can explain success," Arthur Laurents in *The Way We Were*: *Looking Back*, 25th Anniversary DVD, Columbia Pictures, 1999.

"I couldn't get anywhere with 'The Way We Were' with disc jockeys," Kay Gardella, "Ma Bell's 100th Really Rings The Bell," *New York Daily News*, July 20, 1975.

"too sophisticated for the character I played," "Barbra Streisand: Newsmakers," *Newsweek* Magazine, December 31, 1973.

"a Jewish woman with a big nose," https://www.last.fm/music/Gilda+Radner/_/Lisa+Loopner+Piano+Recital:+%22The+Way+We+Were%22.

"Hey, Luke, it's me. I know I'm not supposed to be calling," *Gilmore Girls*, Season 5, Episode 14, "Say Something," 2005.

"Your girl is lovely," Arthur Laurents, *The Way We Were*, Columbia Pictures, 1973.

"I don't get it," *Sex and the City*, Season 2, Episode 18, "Ex and the City," October 3, 1999.

"And you never did," ibid.

Life after *The Way We Were*

"I'm a work in progress," Barbra Streisand, "103 Fierce and Inspirational Quotes by Barbra Streisand," Quotes.TheFamousPeople.com.

"Barbra was so hardworking, such a talented artist," James Woods, interview with author, September 14, 2021.

"Someone in the audience asked Sydney," ibid.

"It was very moving to me," ibid.

"Bradford Dillman sounded like a distinguished, phony, theatrical name," Adam Bernstein, "Bradford Dillman, Multifaceted and Prolific Actor of Stage and Screen, Dies at 87," *The Washington Post*, January 19, 2018.

"perfectly capturing the essence," https://www.hollywoodreporter.com/news/bradford-dillman-dead-actor-compulsion-way-we-were-was-87-1075818.

"My first play was *Cat on a Hot Tin Roof*, an absolutely masterpiece," Lois Chiles, interview with author, November 9, 2021.

"put the teaching on pause," ibid.

"Michael Schultz, the director, and I located the film," ibid.

"Ray used to say that the problem with the new Hollywood," Corey Kilgannon, "Ray Stark, Oscar-Nominated Producer, Is Dead at 88," *The New York Times*, January 8, 2004.

"through their success, are creating increased opportunities for the advancement of women working throughout the screen industries: in front of *and* behind the camera," https://womeninfilm.org/updates/wif-awards-retrospective/.

"All the filmmakers had to go through her," "Margaret Booth," *The Guardian*, November 15, 2002.

"film editor," Claudia Luther, "Margaret Booth, 104; Film Editor Had 70-Year Career," *The Los Angeles Times*, October 31, 2002.

"He created people you care about," Robert Diamond, "Barbra Streisand Remembers Arthur Laurents," *Broadway World*, May 7, 2011. https://www.broadwayworld.com/article/Barbra-Streisand-Remembers-Arthur-Laurents-20110507.

"I still need terrific reinforcement," "A Day in the Life: An Interview with Marvin Hamlisch," *Esquire* Magazine, March 1980.

"Now I'm afraid to go near her with a new song," Rex Reed, "The Sweet Sting of Success," *New York Sunday News*, July 20, 1975.

"so far, so terrific." "Chronicle," *The New York Times*, May 25, 1994.

"But that doesn't mean she's a kvetch," ibid.

"I'm devastated," "Tributes Paid to Composer Marvin Hamlisch," https://www.bbc.com/news/entertainment-arts-19177619.

"A question of trust," Richard Denzer, "A Dialogue with Sydney Pollack," *Grand Illusions Magazine*, Spring 1980.

"I think his work in the films we've done together," ibid.

"Sydney sees both sides of everything, he really does," Janet Maslin, "That Pollack Touch," *The New York Times*, December 15, 1985.

"usually involve a very long period of romantic anticipation," ibid.

"Sydney identified with the character of an uncommitted man," "Sydney Pollack," *Current Biography*, September 1986.

"producer Richard Roth sued him in 1989 for one million dollars in damages," *Variety*, September 27, 1989.

"I've never made anything but love stories," "Sydney Pollack," *Millimeter*, December 1985.

"got 65–70% lousy reviews," ibid.

"it has grown in stature," Sydney Pollack in *The Way We Were: Looking Back*, 25th Anniversary DVD, Columbia Pictures, 1999.

"On *They Shoot Horses*, *Time* magazine said," American Cinematheque, Volume II, No. 2, Summer 1985.

"I was never what I would call a great shooter or visual stylist," Michael Cieply, "Sydney Pollack, Director of High-Profile Hollywood Movies, Is Dead at 73," *The New York Times*, May 26, 2008.

"The middle ground is now gone," ibid.

"I'm sorry Sydney is no longer here," Lois Chiles, interview with author, November 9, 2021.

"He knew how to tell a love story," Liz Smith, "Pollack Was Loved," *The New York Post*, May 29, 2008.

"Stars are like thoroughbreds," Dennis McLellan, "Actor, Director Pollack Dies," *Los Angeles Times*, May 27, 2008.

"I always viewed Sydney as being part of the great Hollywood tradition," Tatiana Siegel, "Sydney Pollack: Many-Faceted Master," *Variety*, June 2, 2008.

"in a Redford movie," Callan, *Robert Redford: The Biography*, 217.

"I just wasn't prepared for the impact," https://www.oprah.com/own-oprahshow/robert-redford-surprises-barbra-streisand-video, November 16, 2010.

"Man that was some hot stuff." Callan, *Robert Redford: The Biography*, 196.

"is, and remains, a bourgeois in the worst sense of the word," ibid., 260.

"a symbol, not a character," ibid., 301.

"It's a deal with the devil," ibid., 388.

"While De Niro and Pacino are the sum total of their roles," ibid.

"Don't be afraid to take a risk," "Robert Redford Tells Maine College Students: The World is 'Rough' and 'Chaotic,'" *The Hollywood Reporter*, May 24, 2015.

"La Streisand," Paul Hoffman, "Rome: Voice of La Streisand Heard in Land of Verdi," *The New York Times*, April 22, 1973.

"highlight of my career," Barbra Streisand in *The Way We Were: Looking Back*, 25th Anniversary DVD, Columbia Pictures, 1999.

"Streisand sent Stark an antique mirror," Army Archerd, "Barbra Farewells Ray Stark; Future as She Dictates" *Variety*, July 17, 1974.

"Even though I sometimes forgot to say it," ibid.

"Under my terms," ibid.

"Usually when a new director starts directing," Swenson, *Barbra: The Second Decade*, 253.

"She'll call and we'll talk for an hour," Zec and Fowles, *Barbra*, 199.

"She's made life a lot better for a helluva lot of homely girls," Santopietro, *The Importance of Being Barbra*, 3.

"I'm a feminist, Jewish, opinionated, liberal woman. I push a lot of buttons," ibid., 161.

"You do your work and at the end," Zec and Fowles, *Barbra*, 200.

"I just really am blunt. That saves me a lot of time and also loses a lot of friends," "Who Am I Anyway," *Life* magazine, January 9, 1970.

"when you face that kind of talent," Donald Zec and Fowles, *Barbra*, 200.

The Sequel

"I guess this is the sequel, huh, Babs?" "Robert Redford Receives an Honorary Award: 2002 Oscars," https://www.youtube.com/watch?v=hr-v9cGG_vA.

"Dear Bob, it was such fun being married to you for a while," Scott Feinberg, "Robert Redford Feted by Film Society of Lincoln Center, Barbra Streisand and Other Friends," *Hollywood Reporter*, April 28, 2015.

"the lion's share of the credit for *The Way We Were*," "Robert Redford Discusses Barbra Streisand and *The Way We Were*," https://www.youtube.com/watch?v=lvQ1KiUGLPQ.

"Totally ignorant of the period, he destroyed its politics," Arthur Laurents, *The Rest of the Story* (Milwaukee: Applause, 2011), 11.

"every day was an exciting adventure," "Robert Redford Almost Didn't Star As Hubbell in 'The Way We Were' plus More On-Set Secrets Revealed (EXCLUSIVE)," *Closer Weekly*, https://www.closerweekly.com/posts/the-way-we-were-secrets/, November 3, 2018.

"I loved working with Barbra," "Robert Redford Discusses Barbra Streisand and *The Way We Were*," https://www.youtube.com/watch?v=lvQ1KiUGLPQ.

"organic," "Robert Redford Almost Didn't Star As Hubbell in 'The Way We Were' plus More On-Set Secrets Revealed (EXCLUSIVE)," *Closer Weekly*, https://www.closerweekly.com/posts/the-way-we-were-secrets/, November 3, 2018.

"the fun we had," https://www.oprah.com/own-oprahshow/robert-redford-surprises-barbra-streisand-video, November 16, 2010.

"It ended up being one of the most enjoyable relationships I've ever had," ibid.

"The discrepancy when they finally met up," Arthur Laurents, *The Rest of The Story*, 148.

"You know I don't trust you, Sydney," Laurents, *Original Story By*, 284.

"Oh, I know," ibid.

"I have talked to both of them about it," Marilyn Beck, "Streisand and Redford to Carry On," *New York Daily News*, February 20, 1980.

"where Redford had to come to dinner with David X. Cohen and her," Crist, *Take 22*, 219.

"I knew that at some point the character of J.J., his friend," ibid.

"That is a very, very interesting idea about Carol Ann," Lois Chiles, interview with author, November 9, 2021.

"He never was really able to deal with the complexities of growing up," Crist, *Take 22*, 221.

"There are just two screen combinations that have built-in box office magic," Jack Martin, "Bob and Barbra May Rake in $8 M Each on Film Sequel," *The New York Post*, June 3, 1980.

"If Sydney does want Barbra for the movie," ibid.

"ridiculous," Liz Smith, *The New York Daily News*, October 8, 1980

"never said he'd take $10 million for the fee," ibid.

"he won't be starring in a sequel," Marilyn Beck, "Redford Accentuates the Negative," The *New York Daily News*, June 1, 1981.

"investigated the thought of a sequel," ibid.

"How'd you like to pick up the bill for Barbra and Bob today?" Stephen M. Silverman, "The Way They Were—and Will Be ($$$ Permitting)," *The New York Post*, December 13, 1982.

"more of a continuation than a rehash," ibid.

"I'm excited every time I think of the new scenes," ibid.

"There have been a few thoughts," Stephen M. Silverman, "Pickin' Up The Pieces," *The New York Post* March 20, 1986.

"It's such a good story [told] through their daughter," "Robert Redford Almost Didn't Star As Hubbell in 'The Way We Were' plus More On-Set Secrets Revealed (EXCLUSIVE)," *Closer Weekly*, https://www.closerweekly.com/posts/the-way-we-were-secrets/, November 3, 2018.

"Why not? The characters are interesting," Alan Bergman, interview with author, July 30, 2021.

"Yes, there's the risk that the sequel would not have the same impact," Lois Chiles, interview with author, November 9, 2021.

"Working with Barbra I hold as one of the highlights," Barbra Archives, https://www.barbra-archives.info/way_we_were_streisand.

"I adored working with him," "Robert Redford Receives an Honorary Award: 2002 Oscars," https://www.youtube.com/watch?v=hr-v9cGG_vA.

"I guess this is the sequel, huh, Babs?" ibid.

"sweetheart," https://www.oprah.com/oprahshow/barbra-streisand-and-robert-redfords-first-interview-together/all.

"I just felt certain things should be left alone," ibid.

"She'd have gone to Berkeley and gotten in trouble," ibid.

"You know that's not a bad idea," Meg Grant, "Robert Redford Unedited," *AARP The Magazine*, March/April 2011.

"It's an interesting thing you should mention it," "Barbra Streisand Hints at Possible Reunion with Robert Redford," https://www.youtube.com/watch?v=iI0snq0mNuE.

"It could be called *The Way We Are*," ibid.

"It *is* called *The Way We Are*," ibid.

"It could be—but I have to convince Bob," ibid.

"It's always a possibility," https://www.oprah.com/own-oprahshow/robert-redford-surprises-barbra-streisand-video, November 16, 2010.

"in *The Way We Were* that force of Jewish nature Barbra Streisand," David Edelstein, "Found at Sea," *New York Magazine*, October 10, 2013.

"I loved working with Jane," Maureen Dowd, "The Sun-Dried Kid," *The New York Times*, October 13, 2013.

"most formidable adversary," ibid.

"complicated visionary," Scott Feinberg, "Robert Redford Feted by Film Society of Lincoln Center, Barbra Streisand and Other Friends," *Hollywood Reporter*, April 28, 2015.

"intellectual cowboy," ibid.

"I could hear the crew shouting out," Jeff Labrecque, "Barbra Streisand Reunites with Robert Redford at Lincoln Center," https://ew.com/article/2015/04/28/robert-redford-receives-chaplin-award/.

"He kept asking me about Brooklyn," K.C. Baker and Kate Hogan, "Robert Redford and Barbra Streisand Reunite. We Get Nostalgic with *The Way We Were* Photos." April 28, 2015. https://people.com/celebrity/barbra-streisand-robert-redford-the-way-we-were-photos/.

"I knew he did daredevil things like skiing," "Chaplin Award," *New York Post*, April 29, 2015.

"Katie says to Hubbell," Scott Feinberg, "Robert Redford Feted by Film Society of Lincoln Center, Barbra Streisand and Other Friends," *Hollywood Reporter*, April 28, 2015.

"I don't know what to say about a sequel," Sydney Pollack in *The Way We Were*: Director's Commentary, 25th Anniversary DVD, Columbia Pictures, 1999.

"No. I don't think there's any age limit," Barbra Streisand, written response to author, July 19,2022.

"We tried for twenty years to make the sequel," "Barbra Streisand Chats about Her New Album, and What She Thought of Beyonce's Cover," https://www.youtube.com/watch?v=R3_-rWWzqCU.

"The other movie I want to make is about people who rediscover themselves in older love," Meg Grant, "Robert Redford Unedited," *AARP The Magazine*, March/April 2011.

"No, I don't think that factors into the appeal of the film," Barbra Streisand, written response to author, July 19, 2022.

"It's like a horrible bunch of high school cliques making fun of each other. It's insanity—bereft of any real passion," James Woods, interview with author, September 14, 2021.

"Now losing Katie," Arthur Laurents, *The Way We Were*, Columbia Pictures, 1973.

"Golden lads and girls all must," William Shakespeare, *Cymbeline*, Act IV, Scene II.

Bibliography

Books

Andersen, Christopher. *Barbra: The Way She Is*. New York: HarperCollins, 2006.

Basinger, Jeanine. *I Do and I Don't: A History of Marriage in the Movies*. New York: Alfred A. Knopf, 2012.

Busa, Paul. *The Barbra Streisand Film Guide*. Middletown, DE: CreateSpace, 2016.

Callan, Michael Feeney. *Robert Redford: The Biography*. New York: Alfred A. Knopf, 2011.

Crist, Judith. *Take 22: Moviemakers on Moviemaking*. New York: Viking, 1984.

Edwards, Anne. *Streisand: A Biography*. New York: Little Brown, 1997.

Fitzgerald, F. Scott. *The Great Gatsby*. New York: Scribner, 1925.

Gabler, Neal. *Barbra Streisand: Redefining Beauty, Femininity, and Power*. New Haven, CT: Yale University Press, 2016.

Hamlisch, Marvin. *The Way I Was*. New York: Scribner, 1992.

Hayden, Sterling. *Wanderer*. New York: Alfred A. Knopf, 1963.

Hemingway, Ernest. *The Sun Also Rises*. New York: Scribner, 1926.

Jordan, Rene. *The Greatest Star: The Barbra Streisand Story*. New York: G. P. Putnam's Sons, 1975.

Kael, Pauline. *Reeling*. Boston: Little Brown, 1976.

Kimbrell, James. *Barbra: An Actress Who Sings*. Boston: Branden Publishing, 1989.

Koch, Hawk. *Magic Time: My Life in Hollywood*. New York: Post Hill Press, 2019.

Lang, Rocky, and Barbara Hall, eds. *Letters from Hollywood: Inside the Private World of Classic American Moviemaking*. New York: Abrams, 2019.

Laurents, Arthur. *Original Story By: A Memoir of Broadway and Hollywood*. New York: Alfred A. Knopf, 2000.

Laurents, Arthur. *The Rest of the Story*. Milwaukee, WI: Applause, 2011.

Laurents, Arthur. *The Way We Were*. New York: Harper & Row, 1972.

Meyer, Janet L. *Sydney Pollack: A Critical Filmography*. Jefferson, NC: McFarland & Company, 2008.

Mordden, Ethan. *On Streisand: An Opinionated Guide*. New York: Oxford University Press, 2019.

Nickens, Christopher, and Karen Swenson. *The Films of Barbra Streisand*. New York: Kensington Publishing, 2000.

Riese, Randall. *Her Name Is Barbra*. New York: Carol Publishing, 1993.

Santopietro, Tom. *The Importance of Being Barbra*. New York: St. Martin's Press, 2006.

Santopietro, Tom. *The Sound of Music Story*. New York: St. Martin's Press, 2015.

Spada, James. *Streisand*. New York: Abrams, 2014.

Spada, James. *Streisand: Her Life*. New York: Crown Publishing, 1995.

Swenson, Karen. *Barbra: The Second Decade*. Secaucus, NJ: Citadel Press, 1986.

Taylor, William R. *Sydney Pollack*. Boston: Twayne Publishers, 1981.

Vare, Ethlie Ann, ed. *Diva: Barbra Streisand and the Making of a Superstar*. New York: Boulevard Books, 1996.

Zec, Donald, and Anthony Fowles. *Barbra: A Biography of Barbra Streisand*. New York: St. Martin's Press, 1981.

Ziesmer, Jerry. *Ready When You Are, Mr. Coppola, Mr. Spielberg, Mr. Crowe*. Lanham, MD: Scarecrow Press, 2000.

DVDs

The Owl and The Pussycat. Screenplay by Bill Manhoff and Buck Henry. Columbia Pictures. 1970.

The Way We Were. Screenplay by Arthur Laurents. Columbia Pictures. 25th Anniversary Special Edition. 1999.

Yentl. Screenplay by Barbra Streisand and Jack Rosenthal. MGM/UA. 1983.

Soundtrack

The Way We Were. Original Soundtrack Recording. Columbia Records. 1973.

Periodicals

American Cinematheque II, no. 2 (Summer 1985).

Archerd, Army. "Barbra Farewells Ray Stark; Future as She Dictates." *Variety*, July 17, 1974.

Bannon, Barbara A. (Fiction Editor). "The Way We Were." *Publishers Weekly*, February 7, 1972.

"Barbra Streisand," Newsmakers. *Newsweek*, December 31, 1973.

Beck, Marilyn. "Redford Accentuates the Negative." *The New York Daily News*, June 1, 1981.

Beck, Marilyn. "Streisand and Redford to Carry On." *New York Daily News*, February 20, 1980.

Berlind, William. "The Sweet Smell of Hamlisch." *New York Observer*, March 18, 2002.

Bernstein, Adam. "Bradford Dillman, Multifaceted and Prolific Actor of Stage and Screen, Dies at 87." *Washington Post*, January 19, 2018.

Bradley, Liz. "Losers and Lovers." *Florida Times—Union*, March 19, 1972.

Buckley, Tom. "At the Movies." *New York Times*, March 2, 1979.

Canby, Vincent. "Screen: Way We Were." *New York Times*, October 18, 1973.

"Chaplin Award." *New York Post*, April 29, 2015.

"Chronicle." *New York Times*, May 25, 1994.
Cieply, Michael. "Sydney Pollack, Director of High-Profile Hollywood Movies, Is Dead at 73." *New York Times*, May 26, 2008.
Dagan, Carmel. "Biz Maestro Knew the Score." *Daily Variety*, August 8, 2012.
Dargis, Manohla. "Barbra Streisand, at a Gala and in Memory." *New York Times*, April 23, 2013.
"A Day in the Life: An Interview with Marvin Hamlisch." *Esquire*, March 1980.
Denzer, Richard. "A Dialogue with Sydney Pollack." *Grand Illusions*, Spring 1980.
Dowd, Maureen. "The Sun-Dried Kid." *New York Times*, October 13, 2013.
Ebert, Roger. "The Way We Were." *Chicago Sun Times*, October 17, 1973.
Edelstein, David. "Found at Sea." *New York*, October 10, 2013.
Feinberg, Scott. "Robert Redford Feted by Film Society of Lincoln Center, Barbra Streisand and Other Friends." *Hollywood Reporter*, April 28, 2015.
Gabler, Neal. "Redford Talks." *New York*, December 10, 1990.
Gardella, Kay. "Ma Bell's 100th Really Rings the Bell." *New York Daily News*, July 20, 1975.
Goldstein, Patrick. "Movies: Previews—How Early Is Too Early." *Los Angeles Times*, February 6, 1994.
Green, Benny. "The Way We Were," *PUNCH*, February 20, 1974.
Grimes, William. "David Rayfiel, Screenwriter with Sydney Pollack, Dies." *New York Times*, June 23, 2011.
Guarino, Ann. "Lyrical Living." *New York Daily News*, April 27, 1976.
Guerrero, Dan. "Screen Scene." *Drama-Logue*, March 10, 1983.
Hendrick, Kimme. "Something Worth Trying." *Christian Science Monitor*, June 1972.
Haber, Joyce. "With the Stars." *Los Angeles Times*, November 7, 1972.
Hallowell, John. "Funny Girl on Film; Barbra Streisand's Goofy Ballet." *Life*, September 29, 1967.
Haskell, Molly. "Would Nicholson Make a Better Gatsby?" *The Village Voice*, December 9, 1974.

Hochman, David. "Robert Redford: A Rare Interview." *Playboy*, November 2007.

Hoffman, Paul. "Rome: Voice of La Streisand Heard in Land of Verdi." *New York Times*, April 22, 1973.

Holden, Stephen. "Bergman Team Finds Just the Right Words." *New York Times*, December 24, 1982.

Holden, Stephen. "Retro Retrospective of Movie Songs." *New York Times*, January 24, 1995.

Itzkoff, Dave. "Memories of the Way He Was." *New York Times*, September 20, 2012.

Kael, Pauline. "The Way We Were." *New Yorker*, November 2, 1973.

Kaufmann, Stanley, "The Way We Were." *The New Republic*, November 10, 1973.

Kilgannon, Corey. "Ray Stark, Oscar-Nominated Producer, Is Dead at 88." *New York Times*, January 8, 2004.

King, Susan. "Alan and Marilyn Bergman Give Streisand More to Sing About." *Los Angeles Times*, August 31, 2011.

Kissel, Howard. "Alan and Marilyn Bergman: A Marriage of Words." *Women's Wear Daily*, February 28, 1979.

Lang, Brent. "Barbra Streisand: Sexism Cost Me Multiple Oscar Nominations." *Variety*, April 29, 2017.

Lardine, Bob. "He Got Stung on 'The Sting,'" *New York Sunday News*, October 20, 1974.

Lear, Martha Weinman. "Anatomy of a Sex Symbol," *The New York Times*, July 7, 1974.

Lee, John. "The Way We Were: Premiere." Columbia Pictures Press Release, September 15, 1973.

Lemon, Brendan, "Making Room for Remembering." *New York Times*, February 20, 2000.

Luther, Claudia. "Margaret Booth, 104; Film Editor Had 70-Year Career." *Los Angeles Times*, October 31, 2002.

"Lyricists Extraordinaire: Alan and Marilyn Bergman." *Backstage*, January 27, 1995.

Maremaa, Thomas. "The Sound of Movie Music." *New York Times*, March 28, 1976.

"Margaret Booth." *The Guardian*, November 15, 2002.

Martin, Jack. "Bob and Barbra May Rake in $8 M Each on Film Sequel." *New York Post*, June 3, 1980.

"Marvelous Marv." *Time*, June 3, 1974.

Maslin, Janet. "That Pollack Touch." *New York Times*, December 15, 1985.

McLellan, Dennis. "Actor, Director Pollack Dies." *Los Angeles Times*, May 27, 2008.

Michener, Charles. "The Great Redford." *Newsweek*, February 4, 1974.

Natale, Richard. "Director Pollack Tells of The Way We Were." *Women's Wear Daily*, October 22, 1973.

Oliver, Myrna. "Ray Stark, 88; Hollywood Legend, Insider Produced 'Funny Girl,' Other Classic Films." *The Los Angeles Times*, January 18, 2004.

"Pressure Gets to Marvin Hamlisch." *New York Post*, June 11, 1977.

Rayner, Richard. "Existential Cowboy." *New Yorker*, May 18, 1998.

"Redford Is Voted Top Money Maker." *New York Times*, December 28, 1974.

"Redford, Pollack Sue Columbia, Stark for Cut of 'Way We Were.'" *Variety*, January 15, 1977.

Reed, Rex. "The Sweet Sting of Success." *New York Daily News*, July 20, 1975.

"Robert Redford Tells Maine College Students: The World Is 'Rough' and 'Chaotic.'" *Hollywood Reporter*, May 24, 2015.

Robinson, Ken. "The Way We Were." *Movietone News*, #29 January/February, 1974.

Rosen, Marjorie. "Isn't It about Time to Bring on the Girls?" *New York Times*, December 15, 1974.

Rosenthal, Sharon. "A Day in the Life of Marvin Hamlisch." *New York Daily News*, March 27, 1981.

"Roth Sues Pollack." *Variety*, September 27, 1989.

Schickel, Richard. "The Way We Weren't." *Time*, October 29, 1973.

Sessums, Kevin. "Barbra Streisand Queen of Tides." *Vanity Fair*, September 1991.

Shattuck, Kathryn. "Robert Redford Isn't Going Anywhere, for Now." *New York Times*, September 30, 2018.

Siegel, Tatiana. "Sydney Pollack: Many-Faceted Master." *Variety*, June 2, 2008.

Silverman, Stephen M. "Pickin' Up The Pieces." *New York Post*, March 20, 1986.

Silverman, Stephen M. "The Way They Were—and Will Be ($$$ Permitting)." *New York Post*, December 13, 1982.

Simon, John. "Films." *Esquire*, January 1974.

Smith, Liz. *New York Daily News*, October 8, 1980.

Smith, Liz. "Pollack was Loved." *New York Post*, May 29, 2008.

Smith, Liz. "Those Who Lunch." *New York Post*, October 1, 2002.

Sokolov, Raymond. "The Way We Were." *New York Times*, April 16, 1972.

Stark, Ray. "Come On, Let's Stop a Minute to See Snooks." *New York Times*, September 15, 1968.

Suzy. "Streisand and Redford: The Way They'll Be." *New York Daily News*, November 20, 1983.

"Sydney Pollack." *American Film*, April 1978.

"Sydney Pollack." *International Herald Tribune*, Saturday-Sunday, May 27–28, 1972.

"Sydney Pollack." *Millimeter*, December 1985.

"Sydney Pollack." *Women's Wear Daily*, October 30, 1973.

"The Triumph of Barbra Streisand." *Cosmopolitan*, October 1991.

"The Way We Were." Columbia Pictures Press Release, September 28, 1972.

Variety Staff. "Barbra Streisand and Robert Redford in 'The Way We Were.'" *Variety*, December 31, 1972.

Weinraub, Bernard. "Good Job! Here's Your Mercedes." *New York Times*, July 12, 1993.

"Who Am I Anyway?" *Life*, January 9, 1970.

Wilson, Earl. "It Happened Last Night—Marvin, Oscar, and Grammy." *New York Post*, March 5, 1975.

Zacherik, Stephanie. "Robert Redford: Mr. Nice Guy." *New York Times*, June 3, 2011.

Videos and Websites

Baker, K. C., and Kate Hogan. "Robert Redford and Barbra Streisand Reunite. We Get Nostalgic with The Way We Were Photos." April 28, 2015. https://people.com/celebrity/barbra-streisand-robert-redford-the-way-we-were-photos/.

Barlow, Helen. "Robert Redford Talks His Career, Sundance, and How Paul Newman Backed His 'Butch Cassidy' Casting." Collider.com. Published December 16, 2019. https://collider.com/robert-redford-interview-marrakech-film-festival/.

Barbra Archives. *The Way We Were*. October 16, 1973. https://www.barbra-archives.info/way_we_were_streisand.

Barbra Streisand and Robert Redford. "Recreating a Memory." ("The Way We Were" featurette.) Posted December 28, 2019. https://www.youtube.com/watch?v=uhPoiCCQqsY-.

"Barbra Streisand Chats about Her New Album, and What She Thought of Beyonce's Cover." The Project. August 15, 2021. https://www.youtube.com/watch?v=R3_-rWWzqCU.

"Barbra Streisand Hints at Possible Reunion with Robert Redford." Extra TV. December 12, 2012. https://www.youtube.com/watch?v=iI0snq0mNuE.

"Barbra Streisand on Her Friendship with Prince Charles, Memoirs and Preparing to Turn 80." August 12, 2021. https://www.youtube.com/watch?v=8XGjPbWhhY0.

"Barbra Streisand's 'Encore.'" *CBS Sunday Morning*. August 28, 2016. https://www.cbsnews.com/news/barbra-streisands-encore/.

Barnes, Mike. "Bradford Dillman, Actor in 'Compulsion' and 'The Way We Were,' Dies at 87." *Hollywood Reporter*, January 18, 2018. https://www.hollywoodreporter.com/news/general-news/bradford-dillman-dead-actor-compulsion-way-we-were-was-87-1075818/.

Birkinbine, Julia. "Your Girl Is Lovely Hubbell": Barbra Streisand and Robert Redford Reunite 42 Years after 'The Way We Were'—Plus See the Cast Then and Now!" April 28, 2015. Updated December 10, 2015. https://www.closerweekly.com/posts/barbra-streisand-and-robert-red

ford-reunite-42-years-after-the-way-we-were-plus-see-the-cast-then-and-now-57175/.

Closer Staff. "Robert Redford Almost Didn't Star as Hubbell in 'The Way We Were.'" *Closer*, November 3, 2018. https://www.closerweekly.com/posts/the-way-we-were-secrets/.

Diamond, Robert. "Barbra Streisand Remembers Arthur Laurents." *Broadway World*, May 7, 2011. https://www.broadwayworld.com/article/Barbra-Streisand-Remembers-Arthur-Laurents-20110507.

Extra TV. "Barbra Streisand Hints at Possible Reunion with Robert Redford." December 12, 2012. https://www.youtube.com/watch?v=iI0snq0mNuE.

Gilmore Girls, Season 5, Episode 14, "Say Something." February 15, 2005.

Grant, Meg. "Robert Redford Unedited." *AARP The Magazine*, March/April 2011. https://www.aarp.org/entertainment/movies-for-grownups/info-01-2011/robert-redford-unedited.html.

Hall, Craig. "Barbra News Talks to Sally Kirkland." Barbra News, June 26, 2002. http://www.barbranews.com/sallykirkland.htm.

Labrecque, Jeff. "Barbra Streisand Reunites with Robert Redford at Lincoln Center." April 28, 2015. https://ew.com/article/2015/04/28/robert-redford-receives-chaplin-award/.

Lagace, Rose. "William Cameron Menzies Quote on the Role of the Production Designer." ArtDepartmental.com, July 10, 2013.

Lisa Loopner: "Piano Recital—The Way We Were." Posted January 23, 2017. https://www.youtube.com/watch?v=OUnyEkV7E-Y.

Lynch, Joe. "Barbra Streisand Reflects on Acting Career, Struggles as a Director during Tribeca, Chat with Robert Rodriguez." April 29, 2017. https://www.billboard.com/music/music-news/barbra-streisand-tribeca-robert-rodriguez-7776946/.

Matelski, Marilyn J. "The Way We Were . . . and Wish We Weren't: A Hollywood Memoir of Blacklisting in America." *Studies in Popular Culture* 24, no. 2 (October 2001): 79–98. https://www.jstor.org/stable/41970383.

Montpelier, Rachel. "Barbra Streisand Started Directing Because She 'Couldn't Be Heard.'" May 1, 2017. https://womenandhollywood.com/barbra-streisand-started-directing-because-she-couldnt-be-heard-bf642241b1bc/.

NYTTheater (@nyttheater). "Never Bet against Babs. Barbra Streisand Has a Number One Album Yet Again." Twitter, September 6, 2016. https://twitter.com/nytimestheater/status/773174682333962240.

"103 Fierce and Inspirational Quotes by Barbra Streisand." Quotes.TheFamousPeople.com.

Oprah.com. "Hollywood Legends Barbra Streisand and Robert Redford." November 16, 2010. https://www.oprah.com/oprahshow/barbra-streisand-and-robert-redfords-first-interview-together/all#ixzz6rSWNxOhV.

Oprah Winfrey Show. "Robert Redford Surprises Barbra Streisand." November 16, 2010. https://www.oprah.com/own-oprahshow/robert-redford-surprises-barbra-streisand-video.

Rick's Reel/Real Life. "Redford and Streisand: Memorable in 'The Way We Were.'" August 14, 2016. https://ricksrealreel.blogspot.com/2016/08/robert-redford-and-barbra-streisand.html.

"Robert Redford Discusses Barbra Streisand and The Way We Were." February 8, 2014. http://www.youtube.com/watch?v=lvQ1KiUGLPQ 2014 SBIFF.

"Robert Redford Receives an Honorary Award: 2002 Oscars." January 30, 2013. https://www.youtube.com/watch?v=hr-v9cGG_vA.

Schwartz, Paula. "Barbra Streisand Presents Robert Redford with Chaplin Award." April 29, 2015. https://www.reellifewithjane.com/2015/04/barbra-streisand-robert-redford-chaplin-award/.

Sex and the City, Season 1, Episode 1, "Sex and the City," June 6, 1998.

Sex and the City, Season 2, Episode 18, "Ex and the City," October 3, 1999.

The Victorian Web. "Wordsworth's 'Ode: Intimations of Immortality from Recollections of Early Childhood.'" https://victorianweb.org/previctorian/ww/intimationstxt.html.

"The Way We Were—Deleted Scenes." Posted July 13, 2008. https://www.youtube.com/watch?v=XDfdzcLD1s4.

"Tributes Paid to Composer Marvin Hamlisch." BBC News. August 8, 2012. https://www.bbc.com/news/entertainment-arts-19177619.

Udel, Jim. "Footnotes—Harry Stradling Jr." *Below the Line*. December 7, 2007. https://www.btlnews.com/community/footnotes-harry-stradling-jr/.

Libraries

Library of Congress, Washington, DC, Arthur Laurents Papers
New York Public Library—Library of the Performing Arts

Interviews

Interview with Jeanine Basinger, December 8, 2021
Interview with Alan Bergman, July 30, 2021
Interview with Lois Chiles, November 9, 2021
Interview with Grover Dale, July 28, 2021
Interview with Hawk Koch, July 23, 2021
Interview with Wendy Stark Morrissey, September 14, 2021
Interview with Art Smith Jr., July 23, 2021
Interview with James Woods, September 14, 2021
Written interview with Barbra Streisand, July 19, 2022

Index